OUR
COUNTRY,
OUR
CULTURE

The Politics of Political Correctness

•••

Edited by Edith Kurzweil
and William Phillips

A Partisan Review Press Book

ISBN 0-9644377-3-2

CONTENTS

Introduction

This volume includes a number of comments on the subject of what has become known as "political correctness." The term refers to an ensemble that takes in various beliefs and causes, and often includes a rejection of the traditions of the West. Some aspects of these phenomena are individually acceptable, but as a whole and especially in its extreme forms, this "movement" has created a dogmatic and intolerant atmosphere in the universities and elsewhere in the culture that is hostile to the exchange of ideas and harmful to the education of the students. It has spread a certain amount of confusion: for example, the fact of multiculturalism has been transposed into a rejection of the past as the product of "dead white males." It also has floated the notion that the so-called "canon," which is supported by opponents of the "politically correct," is frozen and has not been subject to change and variation, as it always in fact has been. In an age of mass education, the rejection of the past and the substitution of fashionable but destructive trends leaves students without the standards, values, and knowledge to judge the politically correct curriculum.

Even though you have expressed yourself on some of these issues before, we'd like to know what you think the future holds. You may, of course, approach the subject any way you wish. But you might want to consider some of the following questions:

1. How strong is this movement?

2. What can – or should – be done to oppose it?

3. Do you see multiculturalism as politically or intellectually motivated?

4. How do you think standards may be raised in our system of mass education?

5. How important are traditions, and how would you suggest teaching them?

ROBERT ALTER

The Persistence of Reading

The degree to which American campuses have become captive to the movement of political correctness is hard to assess. The wave of articles in the popular press a year and a half ago about the new "thought police" at the universities was no doubt exaggerated, a tactic of sensationalist journalism, as many of those criticized in the articles justifiably protested. To be sure, the political correctniks are out there in clamorous numbers, and some of them are prepared to be ruthlessly coercive in relation to curriculum, appointments, promotions, and the evaluation of scholarship. Nevertheless, the evidence about the extent of their activity is anecdotal, not statistical, something that can be readily seen in the book-length exposés by Roger Kimball and Dinesh D'Souza, which are strong on monitory tales and deficient in their vision of the larger variegated picture of American higher education at the end of the twentieth century. All of us who teach at the university level have our own scare stories, and so I would assume that most of the specific instances Kimball, D'Souza, and other critics have reported are reasonably accurate. There is also, however, anecdotal evidence to be offered on the other side of the balance sheet, and I will presently invoke some from my own observation. If the powers that be in some departments of English, impelled by the desire to exhibit the appearance of political virtue at any cost, have made Toni Morrison more important than Shakespeare – required reading for all sections of freshman English, the subject of special faculty workshops, an inevitable item on graduate reading lists – there is evidence that many students of literature still find more material for passionate admiration in Shakespeare than in Morrison, despite Shakespeare's undeniable whiteness and deadness and maleness and his reputed implication in the corrupting discourse of imperialism.

The ideologically driven trend in teaching and scholarship is an odd phenomenon – a would-be revolutionary movement operating within the circumscribed sphere of the academy, in the context of a society that offers not the slightest prospect of radical political change. In sentiment it is certainly intensely political, though I suspect that what really motivates it is the politics of profession. It is also a revolution neither from below nor from the top down but from the middle, up and down. The revolutionary impulse, by and large, manifests itself in the generation of humanities scholars and social-science scholars now in their thirties and forties. (To see the real proportions of the movement, one must keep in mind that it is limited in its disciplinary scope. It has scarcely touched departments of physics, chemistry, and mathematics; schools of engineering, medicine, and business administration; and even within the humanities, it has made few inroads in some departments, such as Slavic studies and philosophy.) The oldest generation of scholars is usually thought of as the locus of traditionalism, the last bastion of superannuated Western civilization, though it includes influential proponents of one or another radical ideological orientation, like the feminist Carolyn Heilbrun, the neo-Marxist Fredric Jameson, the anti-colonialist Edward Said. Although this generation certainly has its reflexive, proverbially hidebound traditionalists – any healthy tradition lives by being the constant object of critical scrutiny and interpretive revision – its more prevalent trait is conformism, which seems to be endemic to the academic character in every generation, including those who have only recently entered the system. The conformism explains the susceptibility of the senior scholars to the pressures of radicalism from the middle generation below. Departments of literature and of the other affected disciplines, given the great expansion of American universities in the dozen years from 1957 to 1969, are often top-heavy with people in their late fifties or sixties, many of whom are perfectly traditional – indeed, conventional – in their own teaching and scholarship but who are continually anxious to be thought well of by younger people in their profession who are imagined to be "advanced" in their views, at the ever-envied "cutting edge" of critical method. A cutting edge, one might think, should be a razor-thin border between mind and material, but for the generation that has joined academia since the early seventies, it looks more like a crowded social hall where the labor of using precise language is displaced by the recitation of buzzwords, scholarly reflection by conference-hopping, and independent analysis by groupthink. One respect in which Camille Paglia's explosive tirade against the debasement of intellectual life in the academy seems quite justified is in its indignation over academic conformism.

One should not, of course, tar all the members of a generation with the same brush. In a country with thousands of institutions of higher learning, the political demography of the profession has to be considerably more variegated than alarmist accounts would lead us to believe. Over the past dozen or so years, I have lectured on campuses all over the country, presenting a critical view of the current ideological orthodoxies to faculty and student audiences which have usually proved to be surprisingly receptive. Again and again, I have encountered people, including many young people, who resent the expectation that they should march to one or another "theoretical" drummer, and who seem keen on teaching literature because they find abiding interest in the achievements of the literary imagination that have little to do with literature's sup-posed reflection of phallocentrism, colonialism, and the oppression of the working class. It was at Carleton College in Minnesota – a place perhaps off the prestige circuit but one of the better liberal arts colleges in the country – that two assistant professors of English set me on to A. D. Nuttall's vigorous and invigorating polemic against structuralism and poststructuralism, *A New Mimesis,* a book I had not previously heard of. I begin to suspect that some of the really interesting new works of criti-cal thinking may not even be mentioned at Berkeley and Harvard and Yale.

The problem with all such impressionistic judgments about either the prevalence or the limited scope of political correctness is that the quanti-tative dimensions of the phenomenon remain unclear. It must be said that the correctniks may be a distinct minority of the profession – I would guess that in fact they are – and yet exert an influence out of proportion to their numbers. The Slavist scholar Gary Saul Morson, one of the important new critics to have emerged over the last ten years, put it to me this way in conversation not long ago: no more than twenty percent of a department needs to be made up of ideological activists in order to ensure the takeover of the department. Morson's Law works because, within the other eighty percent, at least twenty percent are likely to be indifferent to issues of departmental policy, even to the point of rarely attending meetings, and half of the remaining forty percent can be counted on to fall in line with the activists out of sheer conformist fear of being deemed retrograde. This schematic approximation suggests that those who would impose some rigid political measure on all aca-demic matters do constitute a real threat to the variety and freedom and complex pleasures of intellectual life on the campuses. This is a threat that is likely to continue in the near future, though my guess is that its scope and gravity have been exaggerated by most conservative reactions and in the popular media.

The group I have not yet accounted for in my schema of revolution from the middle is the most crucial one – the bottom stratum, the stu-dents. The received wisdom is that the young are unformed, uninformed, and naively idealistic, and thus on all three grounds are highly manipula-ble from above, especially when the manipulation is adorned with the banners of supposedly progressive causes. Admittedly, there is a good deal of truth in this sad analysis. One can scarcely avoid running into twenty-year-olds on the campuses who after one semester with a single insistent professor have become party-liners of one sort or another, spouting the predictable formulas, having replaced the challenging stuff of literature and history with a set of deadening abstractions that lull the young mind with a false sense of profundity. But not every late adolescent is inclined to succumb to these seductions, and my own experience is that there is more of a saving remnant among the young than is allowed for in the standard apocalyptic accounts.

Last year at Berkeley, after a hiatus of seventeen years, I offered an undergraduate lecture course on modernist fiction – Biely's *Petersburg, Ulysses, Mrs. Dalloway,* the first volume of Proust, *The Castle,* and *The Sound and the Fury.* (I had given up on this course in the mid-seventies, after a paltry student turnout led me to conclude that these works, which had been riveting for my own generation, were simply of no interest to the young.) To my surprise, about sixty students showed up for the course, a relatively large group for any offering in comparative literature on our campus. What was more surprising was how keenly engaged in the readings the students proved to be. Most of them, as far as I could tell from class discussion and papers, were making their way through these long and challenging works with scrupulous attentiveness and a sense of intellectual excitement over what they were discovering in the books. We spent a good deal of time on issues of historical context as well as on the formally innovative aspects of the novels, but none of the students tried to make the case that gender, or imperialism, or the evils of Eurocentrism, was the crucial consideration for any of these texts. In an open-ended discussion of Virginia Woolf, whom we read immediately after Joyce, no one in the class was impelled to argue that Woolf had suffered in reputation because of the prejudices of "masculinist" criticism; and, in fact, though students were quite responsive to the magical qualities of her prose, several volunteered the opinion that her range and resonance looked a little limited alongside Joyce's.

In moments of discouragement, to which anyone in college teaching these days is prone, I had begun to worry that students like these no longer existed. On reflection, I realized that this was after all a self-se-lected group: only someone with a passion for literature and an appetite for arduous works would be inclined to sign up for a course with a reading list like this one. It would be foolish, then, to imagine that my sixty eager readers were an image of the academic future. Serious reading is no doubt a skill exercised by dwindling numbers in our culture, and on the campuses reading for motives that are not ideologically tendentious is surely less common than it ought to be. It is nevertheless heartening, and also instructive, that one can find a whole group of students like these on a politically superheated American campus in the 1990s. The construction of imaginative realities – narrative, lyric, and dramatic – through the evocative power of language remains a central activity of human culture, even in an age of high technology and electronic distraction. There will continue to be people who respond to these complex verbal constructs both as aesthetic objects and as representations of experience that may be morally, psychologically, and socially illuminating. This is not in the least to deny that literature, as we have been reminded perhaps too often, is deeply implicated in class, race, gender, economics and politics, but it is not reducible to any of those categories, as many campus ideologues have tended to argue.

There are still some students who come to our universities with a strong sense of this irreducibility of literature because at the age of fifteen they have actually read Jane Austen or Dickens or Conrad and have found a great deal to engage the mind and excite the imagination which is not exhausted by the political contexts of the books, implicit or explicit. One should of course not discount the possibility that some of these young people will be persuaded to see the "naiveté" of their early reading by a sufficiently magnetic instructor promulgating a particular ideology. Can anything be done to counter such influences? On the level of university politics, my impulse would be to urge people who still care about literature and humanistic inquiry not to be pusillanimous in speaking and voting on curriculum and appointments, but given the academic subspecies of human nature, any such exhortation would clearly be futile. It is the classroom that seems to me the crucial arena for the future of the humanities. The teaching of literature has to do above all with the reading of literary texts, not merely with reading through them to a supposed network of discourses of power. The activity of reading remains urgently involving, and the willingness to abandon it is the real treason of the intellectuals – a betrayal of their vocation as teachers – in our time.

But what, after all, is reading? Many will hasten to object that after deconstruction, hermeneutic theory, the new historicism, reader response theory, de Man and Foucault, reading has been irrevocably "problematized": the myth of the authoritative reading – did it ever really exist? – has been exploded, and a reading, say, of Jane Austen that makes masturbation or British imperialism the crucial issue is at least as legitimate as one that traces the subtle play of her ironies. I would be the first to concede that there are wheels within wheels in any act of literary interpretation; in fact, what I would consider to be the high fun of reading really good literature is intimately associated with the formidable capacity of densely imagined literary artifacts to generate multiple readings, some complementary, others mutually contradictory. Fun of any sort, however, is little in evidence in the earnest homiletic and hortatory stances typically assumed by the ideological critics. Though one must grant the justice of their repeated contention that everyone who teaches literature has at least an implicit "agenda," there is a world of difference between possessing an explicit, fervently nourished agenda, for which all literary works become mere proof-texts and hence are made to sound numbingly similar, and a commitment to values – no doubt, bourgeois – like individual experience, reflectiveness, and aesthetic achievement, which encourages one to attend to the nuanced articulations of the given text with loving patience, an openness to surprise, and a capacity for delight. At its worst, the current fashion of insistently reading for the agenda has led to classes in literature that are little more than ideological indoctrination sessions, or what may be even more ominous because of the way it impinges on the freedom of privacy, sexual encounter groups. This is precisely what I mean by a treason of the intellectuals.

Much of this reading for the political agenda can be sold to the young through the sheer weight of authority exerted by their teachers, but it also appeals strongly to one of the most venal instincts: the desire not exactly to be virtuous but to feel virtuously superior to society at large. The great intrinsic limitation of such moral self-confirmation is that, like all elevating rituals, in the end it becomes boring. It is far more interesting to discover in *The Sentimental Education* Flaubert's endlessly inventive narrative deviousness, his elegant descriptive precision, his delicate lubricity, the seamless transitions he creates between "solid" nineteenth-century reality and the phantasmagoric, than to see the novel as still another confirmation of commodification under high capitalism or the objectification of the female body. I have a stubborn faith that new generations of readers do not have an infinite tolerance for ideological tedium and are susceptible to the deep interest of great books, especially if they get a modicum of encouragement from their teachers.

Marjorie Perloff, in a recent essay on modernist literary studies, attests that her undergraduate students, most of them reading Joyce's *Ulysses* for the first time, are completely captivated by it. "Captivating" is not a word that has any status in current critical usage. Indeed, there are many who would no doubt hasten to say that to be captivated by a work of literature is precisely to succumb to the false consciousness that writers, in unwitting and more or less helpless complicity with regnant ideologies, foist on their audiences. As with all forms of fundamentalism, it is not really possible to argue with adherents of this sort of dour ideological puritanism. For students as yet not born again to political correctness, and perhaps even for some already baptized in the new redeeming truths, the best argument is the work itself. Captivation strikes me as an entirely worthy aim of literary studies, and, to mention just a few novels in English, books like *Tom Jones, Tristram Shandy, Emma, Bleak House, Lolita,* and, of course, *Ulysses* deploy a dazzling array of resources to captivate the open-minded and discriminating reader. What a teacher can do is to try to keep the students' minds open and to offer certain practical help in the process of discrimination. There is obviously no single recommended procedure for doing this, and I would guess that Marjorie Perloff's way is different from mine. When students are encountering for the first time a work as technically innovative as *Ulysses,* special guidance, from the elucidation of formal structures to the glossing of allusions, is called for. Beyond providing such textual road maps, my own preference is to remind students through manifold illustration that *Ulysses* is one of the funniest novels in the English language and that the stream of consciousness, whatever else it may represent, is an extraordinarily athletic and amusing verbal game in which the agile reader is invited to participate by tracing the half-hidden chains of associations, spotting the puns, and enjoying the sheer exuberant play of the mind.

We are clearly not so literate a culture as we once were, and the ideological intransigents in literary studies, some of them openly avowing their distaste for literature, are themselves a high-level manifestation of the erosion of literary cultivation. Nevertheless, there are still twenty-year-olds capable of keenly appreciating Bloom in the butcher shop, as his mind skids from hanging skirts of beef to female buttocks swinging in skirts to plump melons in the Promised Land, and who can respond with excitement to the gorgeous poetry of Molly's soliloquy. If there are some people in the teaching profession, as I believe there must be, who continue to serve such readers, the brave new world of academically instituted barbarism is by no means inevitable.

BRIGITTE BERGER

Multiculturalism and the Modern University

Every so often I ask myself why I am so deeply skeptical about the multi-cultural paradigm on the rise in the American university today. By every measure of biography, education, and intellectual curiosity, not to mention professional avocation, I should be favorably predisposed toward an ordering principle that promises to enrich and enhance our knowledge, if not our lives. Like multiculturalists, I am convinced that culture is an evolving process, never complete, always open to new additions and perspectives, and I take it as a given that each generation is compelled to review the "cultural canon" that holds the academic curriculum to-gether, to decide which parts have lost their power to inform and en-lighten and which new works to incorporate. And it goes without say-ing that with a task as precarious and essential as this, debate is to be ex-pected, and rhetoric and tempers are likely to fly high.

I, too, am convinced that decent men and women, whoever they are and wherever they may be, are obliged to make determined efforts to transcend the narrow confines of their personal lives which have been determined by accidents of birth, ethnicity, gender, nationality, religion, and social class. To be introduced to new worlds of knowledge and to acquire the analytical skills needed to this end is one of the most exhila-rating experiences the academy has to offer students during long and of-ten tedious educational careers. Vice versa, to show students how diverse and complex bodies of knowledge can be approached and mastered re-mains one of those rare gratifying moments in the life of an otherwise harassed professoriate. Efforts to deepen and refine this quintessential ped-agogical task abound today, as they did in the past, and while some aca-demics may be faulted for having failed to pay sufficient attention to par-ticular dimensions of discrete bodies of knowledge, even for having abused their authority, hardly anyone would deny the singular impor-tance of this educational mission of the university. During the last decades America's much-lamented parochialism has become a thing of the past. Today there are hardly any institutions of higher education where courses on a great variety of cultures have not become a part of the standard fare.

Nor, I must confess, am I overly distraught by the misuse of the term "multiculturalism" currently bandied about in the public arena. To be sure, the term itself is a misnomer, and it is not difficult to agree with critics who argue that a good portion of the multiculturalist menu does not amount to much more than a celebration of the politically correct sensibilities of a new class of intellectuals, whose muddled pronounce-ments swamp the campus today. At the same time, it is useful to bear in mind that the academy has always had its share of fads and fools, and on more than a few occasions knowledge of dubious quality and value has ruled the day.

When, however, on occasion I force myself to overcome an inclina-tion to intellectual sloth – natural for most, to be sure, but indefensible in an academic – the reasons for my continued skepticism about the nascent multicultural movement are not difficult to explain: To put it simply, at its hard, ultimate kernel the multiculturalist agenda is over-whelmingly a political agenda and has very little to do with the essential tasks and mission of a modern university. This is not to say that academic pursuits may not receive their inspiration from politics – or, for that matter, from religion, aesthetics, the market, personal experiences, or what have you – but if the university is to stay true to its mission, if it is to continue to carry out its vital functions for individuals and modern society, it is essential to understand that politics cannot be made into the touchstone of *any* academic work.

The inability of the rank and file of academics to comprehend the implications of a politicized agenda for the future of the academy reveals the university's fundamental failure to provide clear intellectual criteria that would allow academics to sort out the legitimacy of multiculturalist claims in an intellectually responsible manner. The political nature of the agenda of such claims also provides a sorry testimony to the intellectual shallowness of the multiculturalist movement itself. The combination of unrelenting agitation by feisty though wrongheaded multiculturalists on the one hand, and the quiescence of a woefully underprepared and intel-lectually slothful professoriate on the other, have brought the university today to the point of self-destruction.

Future social historians are likely to decide that the most powerful instrument in bringing about the erosion of the modern university and, I would argue, of our civilization as well, was none other than a multi-culturalism left unexamined by a soft-thinking, though well-meaning, professoriate which seriously believed that by giving in to the demands of multiculturalists, academic harmony and enduring human felicity could be achieved. It is one of the sad facts of the academy that its denizens tend to view disputes over the value of the Western world as quixotic, if not mad, and to enter the fray in defense of the unique achievements of Western thought and civilization would appear to border on the suicidal for most. Rather, they prefer to get on with their careers, bask in feelings of good fellowship, and display "good" sentiments toward the pursuit of political agendas of which they have little or no knowledge.

While the record shows that a few courageous scholars have taken the lead in drawing attention to gross inaccuracies in particular multiculturalist claims, and even more appear to be willing to admit, at least in private, that many of the new paradigm's stated premises are counterfactual and logically flawed, we have yet to address the basic, almost existential questions at issue in the current debate. The paradox of our current situation is that unless we do so, we stand little chance of channeling the mindless onslaught against the essence of the modern university in intellectually productive directions. And yet, if we are to understand the seriousness of multiculturalism's challenge, a review of the distinctive intellectual achievements of Western thought is precisely in order.

dangers. The first relates to its disregard, if not disavowal, of a distinctive organization of knowledge (*what* is to be studied) and a distinctive cognitive style (*how* it is to be studied), both of which not only hold different academic disciplines together but also are important to the entire fabric of the modern university. The second danger relates to the multiculturalist paradigm's denial of the importance of the "radical individualism" that serves as an essential underpinning to the modern academic enterprise. And the third danger relates to a fundamental relativization, if not rejection, of the unique civilatory achievements of the Western university itself. If these dangers are left unchallenged and the multicultural paradigm should become the new reality of academic life, the first will lead to the final undermining of the autonomy of the modern university; the second to a retribalization of American society and thereby to a repeal of the principles on which this nation is founded; and finally, as the first two combine and take on a dynamics of their own, a massive delegitimation of the modern university – and by extension of Western civilization itself – is sure to follow. All three dimensions are closely interconnected historically and functionally in a complex set of ways, and it may well be argued that the fate of the modern university and the fate of Western civilization are inextricably intertwined. Let me spell out in some detail why this is so.

As generations of historians have shown, the modern university is a unique institution. It is a distinctly Western and, at the same time, a distinctly modern creation which did not simply fall from heaven, nor did it rise out of hell. It most certainly is not merely a concoction of power-hungry dead white males who sought to secure their privileges and to lord it over the ignorant masses. Rather, it is the consequence of very long processes which led individuals to think in new ways about their relationship to God, nature, their communities, and, ultimately, themselves. As Eric Voegelin has shown, we can locate these processes as far back as in the prophetic writings of the Hebrew Bible, the philosophical and literary texts of Greek antiquity, and the religious scriptures of a triumphant Christianity. Central to this slowly emerging and often contested way of thinking has been the idea of an autonomous individual who, not inherently embedded in religion, nature, and community, is capable of overcoming the constraints flowing from them and even of turning against them. These cognitive predispositions have provided fundamental commonalities to the civilizations of the West, in spite of vast differences in history and culture and the many bloody wars fought among them.

It is precisely these cognitive predispositions, it can be argued, that have provided the West with its "creative potential," allowing it to outdistance other older civilizations which remained embedded for much longer periods of time in religion, nature, and immutable community structures. Further enriched by the tenets of the Enlightenment, the French Revolution and the Industrial Revolution, representative democracy, the rule of law, and the market economy, as well as an ever more finely honed morality based on individual responsibility, these shared principles have served to promote and solidify the cultural, economic, and political achievements of the West.

Hence, it is not accidental that the "texts" reflecting these fundamental shifts in cognition have come to play an important role in the academic curriculum down to our own time. In that such texts reflect the emergence and subsequent institutionalization of the *organization of knowledge* and the *cognitive style* peculiar to the West, they synonymously provide us with an illuminating record of the evolution of modern thought and Western culture alike. In other words, far from engaging in a simplistic glorification of the West, the texts that have come to constitute "the canon" allow us to glean a sense of the civilatory process that revolutionized the world. At the same time, I think it of some importance to understand that while distinctly modern forms of cognition and knowledge have undoubtedly been a product of the West — and, perhaps more precisely, of particular geographical regions and social groupings — they are not the exclusive property of the West. They are available to anyone or any group caring to cultivate them, just as they can be disregarded, even dispensed with, by groups who once were distinguished by this distinctive cognitive mode.

In the forefront of this revolution in thought stood philosophers and men of learning who, at one and the same time, became the carriers, the advocates, and the guardians of the revolutionizing approaches to knowledge. These tiny platoons of men of letters, originally located in niches of Western society – the monastic orders and the courts of the powerful – only slowly found a home in a separate institutional order. The firm institutionalization of the pursuit of human knowledge in the university was accomplished only with the rise of the Enlightenment. This, again, did not occur overnight. It took considerable time and ingenuity on the part of scholars to create an autonomous space free from external interferences, be they of theological, political, economic, or vernacular provenance. It was a hard-won autonomy, and the challenges were many. Then as now, as the history of Nazism and Communism in our own century shows, scholars cannot always be relied upon to defend this precious intellectual freedom.

Let me repeat my main argument: the modern university must be seen as a product as well as a carrier of the forces of modernity. As an institution, it is charged with the special task of acting as a trustee of the cognitive culture distinctive of modernity. In that the modern university is a "fiduciary system," in the terminology of Talcott Parsons, its functions go far beyond the educational and professional preparation of future elites. The university must be seen as the intellectual guardian of an entire civilization. By definition, it favors the development of cognitive rationality in individuals on the one hand, and on the other the rational organization of knowledge (by means of the collection, testing, verification, and systematized ordering of knowledge in a cumulative way) by individual scholars or teams of scholars. While the university provides an "open space" for all sorts of disagreements and challenges, and indeed encourages skepticism and quests into new territories of thought and knowledge as essential for the life of the mind, it is intrinsically bound to standards of scholarship based on cognitive rationality. This cognitive style compels scholars to carefully define the concepts used; to differentiate sharply and argue cogently; to constantly examine and reexamine for adequacy and completeness the data used and measure its plausibility by the hand of empirical reality; to critically assess whether and to what degree data can be "falsified"; and above all, to know that this knowledge is always open to challenge and modification, or in more technical terms, is "true until further notice."

All this multiculturalists are eager to dismiss as rules established by dead white males and as therefore tainted, biased, and to be done away with. In its place they want to put vague and impossible-to-define ap-

proaches to the study of materials selected on the basis of their class–specific political convictions that, by and large, reflect an almost total reliance on criteria of intuition and emotion. "Compassion," an identification with the lot of "the poor," "the oppressed," "the outsider," and
other such groups (however self-contradictorily defined) now is advocated as the desired mode of inquiry and the only moral one as well.

What we are dealing with here, then, is something quite beyond the
long-overdue correction of the academic curriculum advocated by multiculturalists, which sounds so eminently reasonable at first blush. Rather
than being a reasoned case to provide room in the curriculum for writers
like James Baldwin or Zora Heale Hurston, to pay respect to "non-
traditional" lifestyles of whatever kind, or to advance the cause of
"oppressed" minorites however defined, the multiculturalist agenda is in
fact far more radical and perhaps even revolutionary.

It is one of the ironies of intellectual life that in advocating to students a particular, empathic approach as the only true and moral one,
multiculturalists themselves fall prey to new forms of cultural imperialism.
Rather than pursuing their much-propagated agenda of inclusion, they
become guilty of exclusion to the point of setting before us a monocul-
tural program, peculiar to a small group of intellectually homeless discontents. The folly that has led multiculturalists to abandon cognitively
binding standards of scholarship as irrelevant, if not immoral, will undoubtedly come to haunt them one day, perhaps sooner than later.
Multiculturalists who feel inspired to proclaim a better university of the
future promote their own extinction. For if one form of intuitive
thought can be declared as supreme, then why cannot another, totally
different form be equally valid?

The end result of all this turbulence will be the elevation of a smorgasbord of contradictory claims, all unable to unite their propagators in
the search for truth which has given shape and legitimacy to the modern
university. The lines that used to sharply distinguish the political, economic, religious, and personal pursuits of wider society from those carried out in the autonomous sphere of the academy will be removed and,
to paraphrase the slogan of the sixties counterculture in which the personal became the political, the political will become the academic. Thus,
in caving in to the destructive demands of multiculturalism, the university
will be deprived of its essential moral and pedagogical function.
Forgotten is the fundamental lesson of the past that united scholars regardless of their disciplines or perspectives: to be a moral community in
its own right, the university must maintain a primary commitment to its
own moral values rather than attempt to be a microcosm of the moral-

ity of society as a whole.

Along with this politicization an astounding "primitivization" of thought makes its entrance in the academy. As argued earlier, multiculturalism's reliance on intuition, in place of exegesis and analysis based on the premises of cognitive rationality, brings with it an inability to clearly define, sharply differentiate, and cogently explicate. Everything must be expressed unequivocally and starkly. Lost is the ability to convey sophisticated meanings, to comprehend shadings in communication, subtle distinctions, and with it the belief in the necessity of precise and abstract conceptualization. In its dominant impulse to derationalize and simplify, multiculturalism imperils the essential worth and validity of any knowledge.

Such impulses, the German philosopher of culture Arnold Gehlen argued some time ago, "undermine the proud self-sufficiency of conceptual mastery and condemn it to irrelevance." In today's atmosphere, it may be argued, individuals are compelled to form opinions and feelings concerning aspects of reality which are far beyond their actual intellectual and emotional reach. Instead of patiently and systematically acquiring the habits and tools for rational analysis, students are pressured to form this or that "good" sentiment. In the multicultural university of the future, students and faculty alike will be condemned to live and function in the "haze of sentiment" the philosopher Arnold Ruge warned against more than a century ago.

These reflections take us to the highly problematic question of how to integrate the cognitive mission of the university with our modern historical situation, in which the value commitments of academics and students have their origin outside of the university. This is a long-standing problem, and multiculturalists cannot be held responsible for it. The dangers of modern knowledge becoming simultaneously over-rationalized, over-aestheticized, and over-moralized have occupied scholars working in the tradition of Max Weber for some time and cannot be dealt with here. Within the context of our argument, we may merely observe that the tensions deriving from the gap between academic knowledge and the different order of knowledge individuals gain in the course of their ordinary lives have made the university vulnerable to accusations both of irrelevance and of cultural imperialism. Irrelevant, because the inner dynamics of cognitive rationality propel academic conceptualizations and efforts to work on ever higher levels of abstraction and aridness, thereby becoming increasingly unable to bind academic knowledge back to experienced reality. Imperialistic, because the rational mode of thought is increasingly diffused from the academy into wider society, reaching deeper into ever more parts of the lifeworld of individuals, frequently with disastrous effects.

Philosophers like Jürgen Habermas write about "the colonization of the lifeworld by rationality" to describe this trend. A general discontent with the progressive rationalization of the lifeworld has served to unite students and intellectuals of the 1960s generation into a counterculture movement aimed at bringing vernacular sentiments, at least as envisioned by themselves, back into the academy. To be sure, the counterculture in its pure form is dead today, but multiculturalism and other movements, such as feminism and environmentalism, based on similar cognitive predis- positions have taken its place. Common to all, however, is the premium paid to sentiments and passions and the neglect of cool, dispassionate thought fostered by the modern university.

It may well be, as the ethiologist Lionel Tiger has argued, that pas- sion and sentiment are expressions of youth and closer to human nature, while cognitive rationality is a game of older people, one which requires elaborate, ingenious, and even expensive pedagogical devices to hone and foster cognitive habits, in order that people may function in a modern world driven by technology and the alienating systems of bureaucracy. Perhaps, as Tiger is inclined to argue, there even may be dimensions of gender involved in fundamentally different approaches to life and knowl- edge.

Be this as it may, within the context of the present argument, I think it legitimate to argue as follows: Regardless of the fallout that the transfer of distinctively modern forms of organization of knowledge and its corresponding cognitive style may have created in the private sphere of everyday life, today, with multiculturalism triumphant in the univer- sity, we are compelled to arrive at conclusions which defy those observa- tions made in the countercultural mode. Rather than witnessing a colo- nization of the lifeworld by rationality *á la* Habermas, we appear to be in the midst of a *colonization of rationality by the lifeworld*. Following in Marx's footsteps — and if a pun is permitted — the present situation war- rants the observation that what must be done is to turn Habermasean- type analyses on their head and explore the implications that the multi- cultural conquest of the academy have for the future of the modern uni- versity and, by extension, for modern Western society as well.

We appear to be caught in a process that is fundamentally altering the essence of the modern university. Rather than providing an au- tonomous space for the cultivation of rational thought and analysis, the university today is in the process of becoming yet another sphere of the general culture. I think it of some importance to realize that this reversal spells the end of the modern university in the Enlightenment mode. What will take its place is unclear as of yet, and much will depend on the outcome of the current battle over the mind of the university.

The implications of this reversal also spell grave dangers for the future of American society. For what is at issue here is a renunciation of
the very premises that have provided the American experience with its
unifying principle. As historians and sociologists have shown, almost *ad
nauseam* by now, everyday reality in our culturally and socially diverse society is variegated and precarious. Distinct worlds stratified by ethnicity,
religion, and socioeconomic class coexist side by side and are separated
by gulfs of experience and lifestyles. The best chance for succeeding as a
multicultural nation, a vast majority of observers would agree, has been
provided by the principles on which this nation was founded and which
are best embodied in the Declaration of Independence. At their essential
level, these principles rest on a rugged, even radical, some would say, individualism which allows men and women to pursue their goals regardless of the constraints their origins may place in their way. The premium
on individual achievement has always been the hallmark of the American
experience and has provided an anchor to a nation of immigrants and
cohesion to American culture. This emphasis on individualism has served
as the ideological basis for a truly democratic and multicultural America
and made this nation the envy of others.

Nowhere is this type of individualism more pronounced than it has
been in the academy. In America's pluralistic situation and with university
credentials becoming increasingly important for entrance into the positions of high income and status, education based on the achievements of
the individual has served a vital integrative function. Regardless of so cial
origin – as defined by ethnicity, religion, or social class in the American
experience – social status and economic success has been an individual
achievement. In the jargon of sociologists: status in the American experience is not ascribed but achieved. While our reality has frequently fallen
short of the ideal, as any social scientist is prepared to demonstrate, this
ideal has served as the lodestar of American politics, to the same degree
as it came to be an article of faith to successive waves of immigrants and
aspiring individuals, wherever they were located.

Again, it is all these singular achievements multiculturalists are sport-
ing to dispense with. In advocating for group preferences in lieu of criteria for individual achievement; in insisting on the celebration of group
experiences instead of providing a record, as texts from "the canon" aim
to do, of how individuals can rise above their groups; and in seeking to
replace the systematic application of a cognitive rational mode of analysis, along with the carefully cultivated distance from the object of analysis, multiculturalism opens the academy's gates to distortion, to a displacement of academic standards, and, ultimately, to a misappropriation

of the American creed. It also signals the end of the modern university as we know it.

Let me come to an end of these reflections with a question: What are the chances that an academy deconstructed by multiculturalists will be able not only to develop a new basis for an adequate view of the history of Western civilization and the American experience, but also to establish intellectual and ethical principles powerful enough to guarantee cohesion to our progressively multicultural nation? The thinkers of the Enlightenment – philosophers, scientists, and politicians standing on the shoulders of a long line of giants – were able to offer such principles, which found their embodiment in the modern university. They were the beginning; we are the end. My question is, what has multiculturalism to offer us in this age of transition? Of course, I cannot answer it. But I would recommend it to my colleagues and to all men and women of intelligence and good will. Experience shows us that those who ask little tend to be accorded nothing – an observation which may well become the epitaph of the twentieth-century university.

With culture moving at an ever faster pace these days, the fissioning and fragmenting of our cultural heritage appears to many to have become inevitable. People tend to read fewer and fewer of the same books and listen to fewer of the same authorities. A media hailed by many as the new unifier is out of bounds, contentless though technologically dazzling, singularly unequipped to take over any integrative functions other than those based on the lowest denominators of sex, violence, and excitement. A university wavering between the mindless visions of multi-culturalist propagandists and the complacency of an intellectually slothful professoriate is about to abandon its *raison d'etre* and civilatory mission. Rather than witnessing "the end of history" as Francis Fukuyama argued a few years ago, today we must face up to the prospect of the end of a civilization.

ROBERT BRUSTEIN

Dumbocracy in America

The letter of invitation to contribute to this symposium describes an unarguable condition. The only debate is over how to interpret and manage the situation. Few will dispute that American cultural and university life have become subject to a whole new set of regulations – speech codes, revised canons, new departments, lowered standards, increased pressure for faculty and student diversity, excessive vigilance regarding the sensitivity of minorities – in an atmosphere of intellectual constraint. The dispute centers on whether these are the best ways to advance the interests of the disadvantaged, and if so, whether it's worth jettisoning traditional artistic and intellectual values in order to accomplish this end. The conservative position is clear and unequivocal – a return to things as they were, regardless of the social and political consequences. Liberals are more divided over whether the current method of increasing the rights of minorities, a cause they approve, can achieve its goals without affronts to truth, history, art, reason, and civility.

Ironically, the popular phrase associated with this method – "political correctness" – has recently lost most of its currency, having been bombarded with ridicule from all sides of the political spectrum. Beginning with the conservative Dinesh D'Souza's *Illiberal Education,* a comprehensive look at the collapse of universities under pressure from radical demands; proceeding through Arthur Schlesinger, Jr.'s *The Disuniting of America,* deploring the fragmentation of the national identity by racial and ethnic entities; to Nat Hentoff's *Free Speech for Me – But Not for Thee,* recounting the liberal intolerance expressed towards that impeccably liberal author for opposing abortion; to Robert Hughes's *Culture of Complaint,* describing the fraying of American culture under assaults from right and left; and to Jonathan Rauch's *Kindly Inquisitors,* cataloguing restraints on free thought through academic monitoring, "political correctness" has been subject to remorseless scrutiny in a variety of books and articles, with little intelligible response other than to deny the nomenclature. But how can anyone defend an expression that sounds so prim, narrow, and inquisitorial?

These broadsides may have succeeded in destroying political correctness as a phrase, but not as a sentiment. It has resurfaced, more powerful than ever, under the rubrics of "cultural diversity" and "multiculturalism" or, to use the prevailing White House slogan, "representing the true face of America." Whatever you call it, PC has crypto-Maoist roots, and, in extreme form, is dedicated to a program not unlike that of the unlamented cultural revolution by the People's Republic of China – replacing an "elite" system with a "populist" agenda through egalitarian leveling. Chairman Mao's little red books now take the form of little black books by a variety of authors – including dictionaries of euphemisms advising us how to identify various members of minority groups without hurting their feelings (pale penis people, namely white males living or dead, are not assumed to have feelings). Such glossaries may seem ludicrous, but their impact on uninhibited expression can be menacing. Even more threatening is the related effort to proscribe offensive ideas, censor improper books and syllabi, and cleanse the culture of independent thought. In the movie *Invasion of the Body Snatchers,* people possessed by alien forces identify all those still left human by bugging their eyes, pointing their fingers, and issuing horrible guttural sounds from their throats. This strikes me as a good description of the way those dissenting from political correctness are now being treated in the arts and humanities.

This crypto-Maoist process is a heritage of the 1960s. Many, if not most, of today's PC leaders were active members of the New Left twenty-five years ago. The radical students who once occupied university buildings over the Vietnam War and the "harassment" of the Black Panthers are now officially occupying university offices as professors, administrators, deans, and even presidents. Having helped to promote increased enrollment by minority students, a desirable goal, they are now responding to the inevitable consequence: increased demands for new departments, beginning with black and women's studies, and now extending to virtually every "oppressed" minority in the land. Meanwhile, today's students assume the old roles of the newly tenured radicals, using sixties methods to achieve their ends – protests, sit-ins, occupations, shouting down speakers, shutting down universities. At the University of Pennsylvania, for example, a group of black students expropriated an entire run of a student newspaper to protest a "racist" article, while at the University of California, Berkeley, Chicano students went on a hunger strike until officials granted their demand for a department of Chicano studies.

Some of these new departments have proved extremely useful additions, opening up whole new areas of research. Others have been created less to increase knowledge than to increase power and presence. This exposes the most serious consequence of PC in the university, which is the growing politicization of academic life, usually at the cost of scholarship and learning. On the pretext that everything is political and always was, courses are created for no other purpose than to redress past injustice and validate minority claims. It is not surprising that hitherto ignored people should desire more information about their history and culture, not only in order to inform themselves but to educate others. Yet the need to increase self-esteem has developed malignant side effects, leading, for example, to conditions of self-segregation where hard-won advances in civil rights have been vitiated by separate classrooms, exclusive dormitories, and sequestered dining facilities.

In this politicized atmosphere, some members of the PC professoriate will not hesitate to use fabricated or skewed research in order to consolidate feelings of racial or gender superiority (the "sun people-ice people" theory and the current myths about the intellectual influence of "black" Egypt on Periclean Athens are only two examples). Just as historical fact is manipulated for racial purposes, so the issue of free speech becomes selective. PC professors and students can protest such speakers as Colin Powell for his position on gays in the military and, in the same breath, cite the privileges of free expression to defend the presence of notorious anti-Semites like Leonard Jeffries. (Some fellow-traveling academics – notably Stanley Fish of Duke University – have even begun questioning the First Amendment when it doesn't promote social equality or conform to PC thinking.)

As demoralizing as the insults to truth, history, and civil liberties are PC restrictions in the field of knowledge. The multiplication of special studies and special departments has made it possible for minority students not just to be better informed about their culture but to go through college without learning about anything else. What Christopher Lasch called "the culture of narcissism" has now found its politically-approved form. Students learn by looking in a mirror and studying themselves. And what they see have got to be "positive images" – no example of non-Caucasian brutality, or instance of female misbehavior, is allowed to upset the historical melodrama of minority victims and white male oppressors. It goes without saying that the university exists not to confirm what you desire to believe or believe already, but to extend the reach of your mind into areas of ignorance. Yet gays want to learn the virtues of being gay, blacks study their own role models, and women search for instances of gender discrimination throughout the history and literature of the West (replacing the witch-hunts of the seventeenth century with twentieth-century warlock hunts).

PC's narcissistic agenda begins early, particularly in the schools. In a number of states, most notably New York, the basic subjects required for advancement in society are being replaced by a "Rainbow" curriculum more preoccupied with inspiring self-esteem and promoting tolerance than with teaching reading or writing. The time is nigh when eight-year-olds will have more knowledge about Native American totem rituals than about the multiplication tables and will be better instructed in how to use a condom than in how to apply the rules of grammar. In a recent newspaper cartoon, two little girls are walking down the street. One of them says, "My friend has two mommies," and the other replies, "How much is two?" The skills with which young people advance are being smothered in a wash of feel-good civics lessons, as if achievement was produced by self-esteem and not the other way around.

In culture, the problem is, if anything, more acute. If there was a time when intellectuals could fight for social justice and high art simultaneously, when it was possible to study both Leon Trotsky and James Joyce (or, like Shaw in the British Museum, both Marx and Wagner), that time is no more. Today we are being asked to choose, in the belief that "elite" culture (the dismissive phrase for the entire Western tradition) is simply another instance of white male oppression. "Multiculturalism" – in its true sense the fertilization of one culture by another – has become a process for promoting exclusive "life styles" and endorsing struggles for artistic supremacy. Instead of integrating a variety of cultures and peoples, it has led to isolated enclaves and polarized constituencies.

Culture wars are nothing new. What is novel about "multiculturalism" is the effort of its practitioners and publicists to demolish what little remains of high culture in this country. Just as rock and hip-hop stations on FM radio often drown out the weaker signals of National Public Radio's classical programming, so the multiculturalists, using a variety of political means and aesthetic arguments, try to drown out the weaker signals of high art. Although this is represented as another form of equal opportunity, popular or mass culture has never wanted for audiences or acclaim – or money for that matter (popular recording artists are now among the highest paid in the land) – in America. The branding of serious art as "elitist" is simply another power ploy to promote supremacy, by hoisting popular culture into the lofty niche formerly reserved for more complicated, profound, and discriminating work.

This is being done in a variety of ways, but primarily by trying to demolish our traditional standards and values. Just as all objective academic research is now labeled as "political," as being a secret means of exalting Western civilization over that of the third world, so the very idea of "quality" is assumed to be racist, a conspiratorial method of excluding popular and folk artists from serious consideration. In the multicultural aesthetic, all values are relative — only high art is subject to absolute judgment, as a pernicious form of "Eurocentrism."

The Clinton administration revealed "the true face of America" by orchestrating a Hollywood-inspired inaugural entertainment (even Kathleen Battle was obliged to sing a popular song), commissioning an inaugural poem by a writer of modest talents, obviously chosen because she was an African-American woman, and otherwise behaving less like an appointments agency examining qualifications than a casting agency looking for types ("Get me a black female lawyer for the part of Assistant Attorney General!"). The "true face of America," apparently, has features primarily determined by color and gender, and those who fail to observe these new requirements are stigmatized for racism and sexism, even when their works have popular appeal. In July of this year, an assistant dean at Harvard's School of Public Health wrote an op-ed piece in *The Boston Globe* attacking *Jurassic Park* because the survivors were blonde and the victims were dark. She had no comment about the color (or sex) of the all-female dinosaurs.

Many of the same quota systems and populist demands are being imposed on the serious arts by the cultural bureaucrats who control their fate. Whether in arts councils or private foundations, in the editorial offices of newspapers or from critics' desks, audiences are being scanned to determine the proportion of non-Caucasian faces, while art exhibitions, repertory theaters, opera and dance companies, symphony orchestras, and smaller musical groups (not to mention their boards) are continually evaluated according to racial, sexual, and other background considerations. In the past, such inquiries into the origins of any employee were usually considered evidence of discrimination, if not invasion of privacy. Today, through the reverse discrimination called "cultural diversity," this procedure is being used as a basis for evaluating most grant applications.

Funding blackmail is, in fact, the means by which political correctness, masquerading as multiculturalism, has proceeded to harass the world of serious art. In the past, public and private foundations, as well as individuals, usually gave their money to not-for-profit artistic institutions for general operating support. Today, it is a rare foundation indeed that doesn't reserve the lion's share of its revenue for incremental multicultural projects. Artistic support, in short, is posited not on quality (most foundation officers admit that excellence is an obsolete standard) but on evidence of affirmative action. *The Hudson Review* and *The Paris Review* both lost their federal subsidies recently because they failed to contract enough minority contributors.

Whereas in the past artistic institutions were considered autonomous, today artistic directors are being forced to share their decisions with foundation program directors, panel groups, and service organizations. Edward Rothstein, music critic for *The New York Times,* recently wrote about a report from the American Symphony Orchestra League which decreed that orchestras "should reflect more closely the cultural mix, needs, and interests of their communities." Orchestras were ordered to overhaul themselves from the repertory to the boardroom and to hire consultants to begin "diversity sensitivity training." Otherwise, funding sources would be urged to reserve their grants for "the inclusion of certain kinds of repertoire," meaning popular, folk, and racial-ethnic expressions. As Rothstein concludes: "This is not artistic leadership; the league is actually threatening its constituency: We know what is best for orchestras, and if you orchestras don't listen, our views will be imposed; your financing depends on your compliance. . . . This report is a disgrace."

Indeed, it is a disgrace, but it is not an isolated disgrace. In their humanitarian effort to increase the number of minorities in companies, audiences, boardrooms, and repertoires, the minions of political correctness have succeeded in imposing personnel restrictions on not-for-profit arts groups, very similar to the content restrictions being sanctioned by Jesse Helms and his moral myrmidons. Both have totalitarian implications. Those who refuse to conform to the required aesthetic cleansing are not sent to labor camps, as in Stalinist Russia, but rather to an economic gulag where they are starved of resources. But the result is similar, and so is the disgusting Orwellian technique known as "sensitivity training," where people are asked to confess to unconscious racism and brainwashed of any thought diverging from current ideological conformity. It is a pitiful development indeed when some of the very same agencies responsible for the great resurgence of high art in this country between the sixties and the nineties are now preparing the way for its extinction.

Are these politically correct methods improving the lot of minorities? Yes, I suppose they are to some extent. While the dropout rate among black college students remains inordinately high, the number of African-Americans entering the middle class through law, business, education, and medicine has increased dramatically. The number of black, female, and Latino artists has also been multiplying exponentially, and while many insist their work can be judged only by black, female, and Latino critics (more evidence of narcissism), some are impressive by any standards. One hopes, as their number and standing increase, that minority artists will come to be regarded as belonging to a fraternity of creative people rather than to any special class, gender, race, or group.

A similar hope is that the more superfluous of the new university departments will eventually wither away when their social work is done – as Marx foresaw the withering away of the state after the fulfillment of the revolution. But even this hope is daunted by the fact that Marx's utopian prophecy was never fulfilled. All that withered away was the Soviet Union, leaving a swarm of balkanized nations menacing each other over bristling borders.

This resembles our present condition under political correctness – a series of hostile self-absorbed enclaves in a disunited America. I first wrote about this in 1978, while observing the balkanization of theater audiences, and things have gotten much worse in the intervening years. Few Americans share or pursue a common good, and Martin Luther King's majestic vision of an integrated nation is still far from realization. Although our treatment of minorities, though far from perfect, is as good or better than that of any nation in the world, there is more protest and complaint here than in any nation in the world. You cannot clear your throat without hurting people's feelings or cough without wounding their self-esteem. This accounts for the spread of vigilante organizations, not just monitoring hateful actions, but vetting speech for evidence of anti-Semitism, sexism, racism, ageism, lookism, or homophobia. Are our skins so paper-thin that words and names have power to inflict such lasting damage? Yes, judging from campus speech restrictions and farcical episodes like the "water buffalo" incident at the University of Pennsylvania. Friedrich Nietzsche's advice is still relevant today: "Life is hard to bear, but do not affect to be so sensitive."

One of the worst side effects of political correctness is the way it chokes the aesthetic atmosphere. Simply put, it's boring. The politically correct are invariably humor-impaired, finding racist or sexist insults even in the most innocuous jokes. The phrases they use to describe these imagined slights eventually have a numbing effect on everybody's senses, but they are so contagious that they become a substitute for thinking. Left-wing scholars and journalists, quick enough to charge other people with racial stereotyping, riddle their own prose with PC stereotypes and clichés. Language is used as a form of incantation by people who respond to any original idea as a dangerous form of deviance.

In one important sense, political correctness is even proving to be counterproductive. When words like "racism," "sexism," or "homophobic" are thrown around so promiscuously, they cease to have any function except as epithets. If you are continually accusing well-meaning people of prejudice, you may cease to recognize the genuine article when you stumble upon it. How many have noticed, while the

media is preoccupied with earthquakes like the hurt feelings of black co-
eds or the incidence of "date rape," that the skinhead population of the
country is growing at an alarming rate? The noisy majority in the arts
and the universities may be successfully pushing guilt buttons, but the
much larger silent majority in the factories and on the farms is either suffering compassion fatigue or preparing a violent backlash. (The white
supremacist plot for a race war in Los Angeles may be 'a harbinger.) That
is why liberals, who support the ends of social justice, must expose the
stupid means promoted by the politically correct before conservatives and
reactionaries abolish ends and means altogether.

I confess I have no easy solutions or ready suggestions to stem the
tide of this movement. At the moment, it is powerfully entrenched in
the present generation and the next. Anyone who works with young
people knows how indoctrinated most of them are in the ABCs of political correctness, how guilty some of them are about their white skins
and middle-class privileges. For PC spreads its tentacles not only into
culture and education, but also into television, radio, journalism, child-
rearing, even the Academy Awards. A Hollywood actor can't even open
an envelope anymore without mentioning the plight of the homeless or
deploring the situation in Tibet.

In his preface to *The Liberal Imagination*, Lionel Trilling quoted
Goethe's remark that liberals have no ideas, they have only sentiments.
Obviously, little has changed in the intervening years. What has changed
is the virtual monopoly on ideas by the conservative camp. Trilling had
cautioned liberals to take as their motto, "Lord, enlighten thou my enemies," because intelligent opposition was the only way he saw to develop a sensible body of liberal thought. He did not foresee a time when
the opposition would dominate thinking, while liberals sat impotent,
mired in sentiment or paralyzed with guilt.

The growing library of books on PC, and this symposium, suggest
that liberals may at last be awakening from their long slumber. It is in-
cumbent on us now to spur the liberal imagination further before the
darker forces in our society initiate a reaction that none of us wants. An
important way to start is by recognizing that equality of opportunity is
not the same as equality of achievement. The democratization of art and
culture for political purposes will only make us dumber than we are, and
dumbocracy in America is presently at its height. We must support and
facilitate the entry of minority groups into the mainstream, but not by
tolerating lies and debased standards. It is neither racist nor sexist to believe that some people are more beautiful than others, some more intelligent, some braver, and some more talented. It is only racist and sexist if

we believe these qualities exist *because* of (rather than *regardless* of) race, sex, class, or religion. Both the politically correct and their reactionary opponents share that position, the one by denying the past, the other by denying the future. Chekhov once wrote: "Great writers and thinkers must occupy themselves with politics only to put up a defense against politics." Lest the mindless form of politics called political correctness roll over us like a juggernaut, obliterating all serious art and original thought, we had better find that protective line of defense, and find it soon.

ANDREW DELBANCO

The Politics of Separatism

I think I first fully realized what was happening to my profession when, a year or so ago, I was participating in a seminar far from New York with a group of high school teachers. We were discussing a poem by Emily Dickinson. It is a poem that may be profitably read as a woman's account of what it means (and how it feels) to be directed by a man, confined to the status of an instrument of his will, and allowed only enough independence to serve as a facilitator of his pleasure. At first the teachers seemed convinced by such a reading, as I was, and added to the discussion many particular insights that tended to support it. Then, toward the end of the session, one usually voluble member of the seminar (who had been strikingly silent) spoke up. What she said was roughly this: This poem moves me as an expression of erotic power. It reads like a transcript of my own marriage. It celebrates the completion of one human life by its cleaving to another. It is about the mystery of how the surrender of will can enlarge the self. It is a love poem.

As she made these points — which she delivered with a precision and passion that my bald summary does not begin to convey — I realized I was hearing something I almost never hear in my university classes. Her remarks were neither mawkish nor narcissistic, but they had great personal conviction. They manifested an independence from (though not a dismissal of) prevailing ideologies and a fidelity to the text that are among the qualities literary study is supposed to sustain and encourage, but which are sorely missing in the current atmosphere on campus.

During the weeks I spent with these teachers, I was exhilarated by how different they were in spirit from what I usually encounter in the academy. They were not scholars or theorists, but exemplars of what used to be called intelligence. They disagreed violently with each other, but with no sense of righteousness or lingering ill-will. They maintained an attitude that a friend of mine (a distinguished poet who teaches in a major university) recently told me was no longer present in discussions of prospective appointments or curricular questions in his department. He called this attitude *disinterestedness*. By invoking this much-discredited Arnoldian ideal, he did not, I think, mean to lament the passing of some naive conception of uncontested truth, but rather the spirit of truth-

seeking – the ability and will, in evaluating the work of a writer or another critic, to assess fairly the human value of some point of view different from one's own. He was talking about the ability to make not
merely applications of an ideological test, but good-faith efforts to enter
the imaginative world of another consciousness, however different it may
be from one's own. The ability to do this seems an uncontroversial
value. But in many humanities departments it is getting little more than
lip service. This is true, I fear, on both sides of the "political correctness"
divide – a term I don't much like, since it implies a relation, if not an
equivalence, between a mood in American academic life and a political
orthodoxy that has been enormously costly to the world in blood and
hope. There is a tactless disproportion in the term. Yet it does refer to a
real phenomenon; and like any member of a lively English department, I
have witnessed its effects: fragmentation into ideological blocs; rising
anxiety among graduate students about which camp is best to join; a
rush to bring into the curriculum works of marginal intellectual significance for the sake of their representativeness; timidity in evaluating the
work of minority candidates for degrees and appointments; and most of
all, an atmosphere of mutual suspicion and intolerance.

Unfortunately, much of the polemical literature on this situation
tends to attribute it to the work of a cabal (either the young "PC"
crowd or the "old boys," depending on the sympathies of the observer).
The problem gets talked about through military metaphors that suggest
an executed strategy – a raid or offensive conducted by one generation,
or gender, or ethnic minority, or sexually dissident interest group, under
orders from its headquarters in Durham or Berkeley or some other capital from which subversive agents are dispatched.

This is, I believe, a wrong way to think. In fact, bad effects in many
humanities departments often flow from good causes: the desire to reexamine prescribed curricula, to think historically about texts, and to work
toward human diversity in the composition of student bodies and faculties. I have found myself, therefore, trying to take a retrospective view of
the problem in an effort to explain things to myself – an effort in which
I was recently encouraged by reading a posthumously published essay of
Lionel Trilling's which he had delivered as a lecture in 1974, the year
before he died.

Trilling's piece bears a somewhat portentous title, "The Uncertain
Future of the Humanistic Educational Ideal," and it has the forgivable
nostalgia of the reminiscing veteran. But it is fundamentally modest and
almost bewildered in making its report of what turned out to be the
onset of one of the worst features of our current mess: a "growing indifference to the ideals of general education." As early as 1964, when
Daniel Bell presented a report on the core curriculum to the Columbia

College faculty, Trilling noticed in his colleagues a slackening of what had, for more than three decades, been their "zeal" for thinking collectively about the effects of a liberal education upon the "shape and disposition" of the minds of their students. He proposed no historical explanation for this change, but spoke only, with a poignant sense of helplessness, of "some persuasion of the Zeitgeist" that was sweeping away the old consensus of what education had been all about.

This was, I think, the moment in which the seeds of the "PC" movement of thirty years later were sown. Trilling noticed in his younger colleagues an eagerness for "pressing upon [their students] the solid substance and the multitudinous precisions of [their] . . . particular discipline," as opposed to a disinterested commitment to cultivate their students' gifts for thinking critically about *all* ideas, including those held dear by the teacher. When I read Trilling's essay, it was with something like a shock of recognition, since in the nearly ten years I have taught at Columbia, the conspicuous professionalism of literary study has enormously increased (the preposterous self-importance that now infects academic criticism, along with its panoply of conventions and journals, is best documented in the novels of David Lodge), while I can recall exactly two sparsely attended department meetings in which the agenda included discussion of the undergraduate curriculum. This does not mean that my colleagues do not care about college students; in fact, many of them are passionately committed teachers, and care about them more than ever. What it does mean is that we no longer have a commonly acknowledged pedagogic purpose to discuss.

It may be helpful to look for a moment at how this happened. The breakup of common purpose had its origins, as Trilling sensed, in the early 1960s – before the outbursts of visible anger that marked the end of that decade. This was the moment at which the consensus that had governed American education for roughly three decades began to disintegrate. In the 1930s, the war years, and then, with augmented urgency, during the Cold War, American colleges and universities had been broadly conceived (by those within them, and by those who supported them from without) as instruments of education toward citizenship in a culture based on Enlightenment principles. Columbia's core curriculum, and later, Harvard's General Education program, were devised, and subsequently modified, as self-conscious responses to the disasters that had ravaged Europe and that were threatening to do so again. Under the GI Bill, American colleges were opened to a new kind of student whose intellectual appetite had been quickened by service in a war in which ultimate moral issues had seemed at stake.

The idea of liberal education was understood in these years – certainly in the mind of a teacher like Trilling – as a kind of inoculation against barbarism. And to this end, the Anglo–American college plan (expensive to conduct, fundamentally elitist, and basically a product of the British imperial mentality) was to educate the ruling class of the world's ruling nation in such a way that would nurture its ambition, self-discipline, and a peculiar strain of democratic *noblesse oblige*. Critics of "canonical" undergraduate education who situate it historically in this way seem to me (even if I do not share their hostility toward it) to be perfectly right.

Around 1960, the consensus that this sort of education was a good and sufficient thing began to fall apart. At the time that Trilling was shocked by his colleagues' indifference to Daniel Bell's report, there was an incipient animosity stirring toward all forms of "retrograde and depriving authority" in American life. Why this happened is a complicated historical question that I can't broach here, but I think it can be fairly characterized in its early stages as a good-humored antagonism – a kind of mild adolescent rebellion on a national scale. It had a tone of cajoling irony that had begun to take form already in the fifties – in, for instance, Norman Mailer's celebration of the hipster as "The White Negro"; or, a little later, in Gore Vidal's affection for President Kennedy as a man "watching with amusement his own performance . . . an ironist in a profession where the prize usually goes to the apparent cornball."

These writers set the tone for the new phase of our culture that would come to be known simply as "The Sixties." As usual, the academy was a little slow in picking up the new tune. It begins to be heard, I think, with the rise of anthropology, which attained new prestige among the humanistic disciplines – as the best way of apprehending the contingency of all cultural arrangements, and therefore of appreciating how absurd it is to take any of them too seriously. The essays of Clifford Geertz, for instance, which came to exert considerable influence on literary studies in the 1970s and 1980s (but for which Geertz did the fieldwork in the late 1950s), can be howlingly funny – as in his famous account of the Balinese cockfight (published in 1972) as social ritual.

It is not, I think, too much to call this shift toward playfulness and the deliberately outrageous (*Dr. Strangelove, Catch-22*) a revolution in sensibility. It marked a very considerable change from the moral urgencies of the thirties and forties, when intellectuals like Trilling (along with spiritual counterparts like Reinhold Niebuhr and the young Arthur Miller) had been permanently chastened by the political obscenities of Nazism on the right and Stalinism on the left – and a phrase like Arthur Schlesinger, Jr.'s title *The Vital Center* could be issued as a fervent battle

cry of liberal democracy. By contrast, the writers and young teachers of
the 1960s were offended by moderation. They had had enough of liberal
centrism. They were drawn to books like Herbert Marcuse's *Eros and
Civilization* and Norman O. Brown's *Life Against Death* — books that
dreamt of a universal end to repression.

What they got instead were the disasters of Vietnam, Watts, and a
series of soul-killing assassinations. There is no need to rehearse here the
impact of these years upon my generation, except to say that I think the
spiritual devastation of that war has been deeper and more abiding than
even its closest students tend to think. To academic historians, the heroes
of Beard and Parrington (Jefferson, Jackson, Lincoln) were now revealed
as dissembling villains; and all of American history was rewritten in the
light of a national penchant for violence and racist brutality.

For intellectuals in general, the war provided an occasion for the
convergence and crystallization of ideas that had previously been inchoate: a sense that the middle-class myth of American life hid the reality
of class antagonisms; that we had accepted the mantle of exhausted
European empires and were acting out the imperial script Marxist theory
had prophesied for us; that the whole morality play of the Cold War
had to be rewritten — not the way Schlesinger had proposed it, but with
our part made much more sinister and disingenuous. It was not too far
from these indictments to the propositions that the Enlightenment
premises upon which our culture is based were a sham: that individualism
did not mean rights, but was merely a pretty name for greed; that the
endemic racism of our society meant that its founding principle of
equality was an expression of base hypocrisy. The sixties generation, in
short, became permanently estranged from the political traditions of the
American republic — and this is the generation that is now moving into
the intellectual and administrative leadership of our universities.

We took our B.A.'s roughly between 1968 and 1975. While we
were in college and graduate school, we witnessed the return of Richard
Nixon and his not-quite-complete disgrace; the failed interregnum of
Jimmy Carter; and finally the rise to power of the ultimate American
political caricature, Ronald Reagan. In the meantime, however, universities continued to pursue the liberal agenda that had been initiated in
the fifties and accelerated in the sixties, and the result was an enormous
change in the social mix of students who entered our best institutions.
Instead of being finishing schools for families which essentially owned
them, universities found themselves on the frontlines of the struggle for
what was to be called "assimilation" into the normative American identity. Yet in the wake of Vietnam and Reaganism, many young academics

no longer believed there *was* a legitimate American identity. For this reason, the function of education has become fundamentally unclear. The unqualified word "American" is in some quarters no longer an acceptable term, as the culture at large has all but lost its legitimacy – even as the market and consumer energies that make it an object of contempt to many academics have invaded and been welcomed into the universities.

Amid this sort of moral confusion, the natural resort is to pure ideological clarities. In the 1930s, when real economic deprivation was known by many students as a fact of life rather than as an academic topic, Marxism was the ideology of choice. It had a genuinely consolatory and prophetic force. Its techniques of dialectical analysis seemed capable of disclosing the source of evil. In the 1960s, when students were personally endangered by the draft, Marxism still provided a conceptual framework for understanding the "imperialist" war that was the immediate reason for the danger. But in the 1980s, this singular, omni-explanatory theory of evil was lost; although American academics still employ its vocabulary, and some of its key ideas remain salient, Marxism in its dogmatic form is over.

In this post–Cold War era, our students feel more dispirited than menaced, and they are without a sense of common cause even with one another. They find themselves having either to choose among or to resist an array of competing identity politics. These politics – organized according to categories of gender, ethnicity, and sexual orientation ("class," which is still part of the litany of "race, class, gender," is really a grace note) – are in many cases an honest effort to come to terms with the most difficult questions of life-purpose. Although the grand ideological battles – as the Fukuyama "end of history" theory insists – may be over, the pain and desire and confused pride of young people just discovering themselves are no less urgent than they ever have been. But the perennial search for identity and commitment now leads in multiple directions – and one result of this scattering has been the balkanization of the university.

Students and faculty are being pulled into separate enclaves where one may lay claim, with the approval of one's peers, to a respectable, quasi-private history and practice a kind of corporate politics of resentment. What my generation does not seem to have learned is that the psychic satisfactions of anger are fleeting. Some even seem to believe that a faculty must be a kind of representative assembly, mirroring the segregated identity-groups of the students of the moment.

These impulses have been strengthened in proportion to the weakening of the common civic culture. It now seems clear that what died in the sixties is what Quentin Anderson once called "the associated life" –

the notion that an individual life can be redeemed by positive commitment to the public world. The new mood of "political correctness" is,
in other words, essentially separatist, not reformist; defensive, not militant. As Andrew Sullivan has recently put it in an eloquent essay arguing
(on grounds of Enlightenment universalism) for "full civil equality" for
homosexuals, the particular identity "politics . . . of gay radicalism" has
become "essentially theatrical" – a politics "in which dialogue with
one's opponent is an admission of defeat." Sullivan argues that the radical politics of "performance, not persuasion," which are also typical of
contemporary academia, can do little to open up human possibilities in
the long run for adult members of society. "Separatism," he says, "is . . .
not a [real] option" for gay soldiers, business persons, construction
workers, indeed for most nonacademic professionals, whose ambitions
and desires for personal happiness remain unfulfilled because of their fear
of contempt and stigma. His point, although specifically about gay radicalism, may serve, I think, as a generalization about what passes for politics in academia – whether based on sexuality, ethnicity, or gender. This
kind of "politics" (one of the most discouraging sights on campus is the
clustering in dining halls and in the back rows of classrooms of black or
Asian or Hispanic students) is built on a "doctrine of separation and difference"; it promotes the satisfactions of feeling victimized; it tends to
avoid discussion of responsibility or civic obligation or human connectedness. Most important, it leads nowhere, except to bitterness and division, in a society based on the idea of individual freedom within a polity
held together by public consent.

What is to be done? My own understanding of the situation has, I
suppose, a certain determinist flavor; academic ideas tend to be more responsive than formative with respect to the larger culture, and for this
reason I feel a hint of optimism in the air. If our political leadership
continues to become less repugnant to academic intellectuals (respectful
of gays, responsible toward and inclusive of women, and less free to exert
power on the international scale), the huddling mood of the university,
under a Democratic president, a Vietnam dissenter born after World War
II, is likely to be at least somewhat dispelled. In some respects, the
fighter for "political correctness" has already begun to resemble a
shadowboxer. There are also signs, especially among undergraduates, of
the natural recoil of the young from any prevailing orthodoxy – which
is what "political correctness" has inevitably become. At the same time,
the equally natural conservatism of parents (combined with the ex-
ploding cost of education) is beginning to exert a healthy accountability
for preparing students to compete in a culture that still rewards people

more for what they can do than for who they are. Liberal education remains the best way I know of pushing the society further toward achieving this latter ideal.

As for our day-to-day obligations, I would say a couple of simple things. Within our departments, we have to match our own willingness to vote for tenure candidates whose work may be at odds with our own, with an insistence that this attitude be mutual – that intelligence be recognized as implying some degree of self-doubt and therefore openness to other points of view. I expect brashness and confidence as natural attributes of brilliance in prospective colleagues, but I also look for the capacity to revise positions, to grow – and, especially, to treat intellectual adversaries with respect.

But the key battleground is, of course, the classroom. There I find myself teaching more and more texts in the American pragmatist tradition – Jonathan Edwards, Emerson, William James, Richard Rorty. The common value of these figures is that they all share the sense of revulsion to justify them as truths anymore. If my students feel a hint of regret about their obsolescence (as I think they do), then we have made a beginning toward regaining some sense of a collective destiny.

MORRIS DICKSTEIN

Correcting PC

This is rather late in the day for a symposium on political correctness. The great public debate peaked in 1991 and its effects can still be felt. I first heard the phrase a year or two earlier as it was still in transition from a stamp of approval to a very effective slogan of opprobrium. My own position has always been somewhat anomalous: I detest political correctness as a form of mindless conformity yet also dislike most of the attacks that brandish the term as a club to batter every liberal initiative. The comically right-thinking mindset of PC, though now on the defensive, remains a nuisance in several fields, yet the phrase became an indiscriminate but highly effective weapon in the culture wars. The term is so inexact, so freighted polemically, that it should be retired forthwith; I use it myself only with reluctance. But as long as we *are* using it, we might as well describe it with some precision.

Perhaps we should begin by agreeing what it is *not*. Political correctness is not a concern for equal treatment of blacks, women, homosexuals, Native Americans, and others who have been subjected to blatant discrimination. Such a concern is shared by virtually every thoughtful American; it has been the aim of our best social movements of the past century. For the same reason, PC is not liberalism, nor can it be closely identified with the values of the 1960s. As a form of orthodoxy and intolerance, PC is the exact opposite of both liberal pluralism and the anarchic individualism dear to the sixties – at least until its last, angry, self-destructive phase. The me-too conformity of PC completely reverses the liberal or radical values in whose name it sometimes pretends to speak. Right now it espouses a cultural nationalism that has deeper roots in the history of the right than in the traditions of the left.

Political correctness is not exclusively a phenomenon of the would-be left. Nothing could be more PC than the rigid ideological test applied during the Reagan and Bush years to all prospective appointments to the Supreme Court, the Justice Department, and dozens of once-autonomous federal agencies. If neoconservatives deserve credit for having pointed up the follies of academe in the 1980s, they did so without shading or discrimination, mixing harmless incidents, serious abuses, and half-understood theories to paint a picture of apocalyptic decline.

Meanwhile, they turned a blind eye on the administration's shameful re-treat on civil rights and its crude manipulation of social symbols – the flag, the fetus, the AIDS epidemic, Willie Horton – to demonize blacks, gays, welfare mothers, and liberals in general. Neoconservative intellectuals, without much power themselves, gave Republicans a new ideological heft, while the religious right hounded candidates who failed to toe the line on social issues. Conformity and intolerance have plagued both sides in the culture wars.

PC is a form of groupthink fueled by paranoia and demonology and imposed by political or social intimidation. During the Reagan–Bush years, Cabinet officers could fall under a cloud if their ideas received favorable notice in *The New York Times,* just as academics could be badgered or ostracized if they audibly departed from the political consensus of their colleagues on race, feminism, the canon, or American imperialism. At academic conferences and even routine department meetings, a certain politics was simply assumed. Alternative views, on the rare occasion they were expressed, would be greeted with embarrassed silence or withering scorn. Similarly, in forums organized by neoconservatives, those who spoke up for liberal positions on affirmative action or on Israel's occupied territories were greeted with savage vituperation, with scarcely a show of civility; the right demonized its adversaries as much as the left.

PC is the opposite of pluralism, which presupposes that your opponent may actually have something worth saying and every right to say it. Hilton Kramer calls PC "liberal McCarthyism," but it conflicts dramatically with any known form of liberalism – by forwarding speech codes on some campuses, for example, and hygienic limitations on speech elsewhere. Ironically, this has allowed some conservatives to emerge as champions of free speech, while others have allied themselves with radical feminists to support local ordinances against pornography. In PC, both ends of the spectrum meet, united against liberal tolerance.

Many conservatives would argue that liberalism itself went through a post-sixties mutation that conflicted sharply with classic liberal positions. This is not even half-true. The real fault-line lies between a liberalism which is open, pragmatic, morally concerned, libertarian – balancing the rights of the individual against the needs of the community – and a complex of skeptical, postmodern, anti-foundationalist positions developed in various forms of critical theory since the 1960s. This later view is anything but liberal. A liberalism grounded in Enlightenment universals has always been its main enemy, as in Stanley Fish's new collection *There's No Such Thing as Free Speech* (where he notes that "the structure of liberal thought . . . is my target in every one of these essays"). Yet critical theory chose to speak in the name of the libertarian movements of the late sixties: black nationalism, anti-colonialism, radical feminism, identity politics.

PC's emphasis on victim groups is a calcification of the political sympathies of the sixties into a repressive orthodoxy. As Todd Gitlin re- cently remarked, "the long overdue opening of political initiative to mi- norities, women, gays, and others of the traditional voiceless has devel- oped its own methods of silencing." The travail of liberals came from seeing admirable political ideals harden into intolerance or flare up into mindless rage. This is why liberals were slower than conservatives to pin- point the abuses of PC: they had more to lose – not simply the solidarity of the left but the elusive goal of improving the condition of society's least fortunate.

What makes PC so paradoxical is that at the core it is an attempt to institutionalize virtue, a way of legislating enlightenment. For the left this ideal of moral perfectibility centered on race and gender, for the right on the sanctity of life, the nuclear family, and traditional sex roles. Liberals opposed to PC have been placed in the position of being against virtue, against two competing forms of righteousness which abridge choice and justify intolerance. Both descend from the moralizing, puri- tanical vein of American culture as well as the bland vision of a world in which no one of any race, gender, or religious persuasion will ever en- counter anything hurtful or offensive. Black students and older profes- sionals have told me they're insulted at this assumption that they're so fragile and vulnerable they need this protection – that they can't handle words they've been dealing with all their lives. Our secular liberal insti- tutions are designed not to make life inoffensive, to sap the young of ego strength, but to prevent the fierce moral will from dictating terms to its neighbors.

The last thing we need from the left or the right is a dictatorship of the pure of heart. The special anguish of liberals is a result of sharing the goals of the well-meaning left without accepting its methods or dog- matic outlook. PC is rooted not in the libertarian thrust of the early sixties, expressed by the SDS in its Port Huron Statement, but in the il- liberal strain articulated by Herbert Marcuse in his famous essay on "Repressive Tolerance" and by Michel Foucault in many versions of his Frankfurt-style argument that all seeming progress is actually an increase of manipulation and control.

Political correctness on the left has been through many phases in the past twenty years – Marxist, anticolonial, poststructuralist, radical femi- nist, now multicultural – but it has been consistent in preferring solidarity over autonomy, the community over the individual, ethnic or racial pride over a broader, more universal view of human rights. Leftist PC has less interest in civil rights than in exposing "hegemony" and delegitimizing authority. It has focused on blacks, gays, and women more as victims than as agents; it is concerned more with exposing ideology than with achieving practical results. PC chooses psychological and cultural critique over politics of any kind, which helps explain its success in the closed-off world of the university. As Gitlin remarks of the theorists of identity politics, "the more their political life is confined to the library, the more aggressive their language."

In this focus on cultural warfare and ideological purity, conservative polemicists have often mirrored their opponents. With his hatred of relativism and love of the classical tradition, Allan Bloom was genuinely committed to his own eccentric vision of Western civilization, anchored in Plato and Rousseau at their least tolerant, the Plato and Rousseau who were our most eloquent spokesmen for a dictatorship of virtue. But Bloom's successors, Hilton Kramer, William Bennett, Roger Kimball, Dinesh D'Souza, merely pay lip service to a complacent, unexamined notion of tradition. Their real aim is trashing the left, satirizing its absurdities and excesses, winning the ideological combat. Writing about the university, they idealize an earlier academic environment in which many issues were simply never discussed, just as they hypostatize the canon into a fixed body of masterpieces, an official set of Western values rather than a constantly shifting series of rhetorical and moral challenges.

Here too both ends meet, for today's ersatz radicals loudly condemn the ossified but factitious tradition that conservatives invent and celebrate. On the other hand, in the liberal view that came to the fore in the sixties, the classics of Western literature and philosophy were unsettling, prismatic, and subversive. Echoing W. H. Auden, Lionel Trilling was fond of saying that great books read us as much as we read them. John Searle describes how his generation

> found the critical tradition that runs from Socrates through *The Federalist Papers,* through the writings of Mill and Marx, down to the twentieth century, to be liberating from the stuffy conventions of traditional American politics and pieties. . . . Ironically, the same tradition is now regarded as oppressive. The texts once served an unmasking function; now we are told that it is the texts themselves which must be unmasked.

It may well be that those of us who began teaching in the sixties were all too ready to extract a subversive outlook from every work we examined, too eager to impose a problematic, modernist viewpoint on the writings of the past. We were quick to discount the politics of authors, the limitations of the times, so that we could find our own politics in all the books we loved. Trained in the New Criticism, we could show how each book escaped its author and subverted its own message. Now, of course, the new historicists and ideology critics have reversed this approach with a vengeance: every author is guilty until proven innocent, every book reflects the ideological currents of its moment, the distributions of power, the circulation of social energy. Nothing is more suspect than the autonomy of the aesthetic, which is seen as little more than an ideology of the bourgeois era.

Conservative critics respond by taking aesthetic values for granted, as if every effort to connect art with history were a leftist plot, a renewal of Stalinism. They are given to sonorous generalities and unquestioned assumptions about Western thought, as when Roger Kimball writes:

> The multiculturalist imperative explicitly denies the intellectual and moral foundations of Western culture – preeminently its commitment to rationality and the ideal of objectivity – and . . . consequently the idea of being "students of Western culture and multiculturalism at the same time" is either an empty rhetorical gesture or a contradiction in terms.

The quoted words are from Catharine Stimpson's MLA presidential address, in which she tried to balance the claims of multiculturalism and the Western tradition. Such a strategy pleases no one, for nothing is more alien to polemicists on both sides than the notion that Western culture has always been porous: an open grid that has continuously integrated and assimilated other cultures.

As John Foster Dulles used to attack the nonaligned bloc in the 1950s, insisting that there was no third way between Communism and the West, conservatives like Kramer are contemptuous of efforts to "occupy some liberal middle ground that . . . simply does not exist"; in other words, to define a liberal multiculturalism, acknowledging – indeed, celebrating – the complex cultural weave of American life. On the left there are many who denigrate pluralism in the same way. In a recent issue of *Critical Inquiry,* Michael Geyer notes with alarm how new hiring practices and a broader undergraduate curriculum are transforming the "notion of *différance* . . . into an administrative concept of 'diversity' and the scholarly praise for a new pluralism":

This is not to argue that anything short of "deconstruction" or anything smacking of tolerance cannot be of intellectual interest. But the
multitrack approach of broadening out general education easily lapses
into the intellectually paralyzing cure-all which counsels that if only
women, or this or that minority, or Asian or African cultures would
be added to diversify the Atlanticist curriculum, everything would be
fine. It is not.

For a postmodernist like Geyer, committed to a quixotic notion of
destabilizing all forms of identity, the liberal faith in pluralism, diversity,
and tolerance are as alien as they are to Kramer and Kimball. Both sides
are against a "multitrack" approach since both have specific messages they
want general education to convey – one Western, canonical, confident
of the beneficent role of rationality and objectivity, oblivious to how
these words have been questioned or misused, the other anti-Western,
deconstructive, skeptical, anti-foundationalist. "One side needs the
other," notes Robert Hughes, "so that each can inflate its agenda into a
chiliastic battle for the soul of America."

In the context of this sterile opposition, the recent emergence of a
liberal critique of PC has been heartening. John Searle and Frederick
Crews in *The New York Review of Books,* Irving Howe and C. Vann
Woodward in *The New Republic,* Arthur Schlesinger, Jr. in *The
Disuniting of America,* David Bromwich in *Politics By Other Means,*
Robert Hughes in *Culture of Complaint,* Todd Gitlin in *Dissent,* and historian John Higham in *The American Quarterly* by no means agree completely with each other. Schlesinger and Higham defend assimilation and
universalism while Hughes, an outsider himself, emerges as a critic of ethnic separatism but an ardent proponent of diversity, a genuine openness
to other cultures. For Hughes, most self-proclaimed advocates of
"diversity" are simply practicing ethnic boosterism and identity politics in
disguise.

Thus, one of the prime effects of the PC controversy has been a
resurgence of liberal thought, rejecting both intimidation of the left and
the hysteria of traditionalists, aggressively defining its own values. The
same shift occurred in Paris in the wake of Marxism's failures. The
Heidegger controversy in France, the long-delayed reckoning over the
Vichy years, the de Man controversy in America, the exhaustion of post-
structuralism and the exposure of its political irresponsibility, the end of
the Cold War and the Reagan era, and finally the explosion of ethnic
hatred and cultural nationalism throughout the world have powerfully
demonstrated the need for despised liberal values like pluralism, tolerance,
and diversity, which never fared well in the apocalyptic atmosphere of

modernist culture.

The general opprobrium heaped on political correctness in the last two years doesn't mean that PC culture is a thing of the past. A whole academic generation that came of age in the seventies and eighties remains deeply invested in post-structuralist theory and the separatist politics of *différance*. A pointed display of the current generation gap can be found in Mark Edmundson's recent collection of autobiographical essays, *Wild Orchids and Trotsky*. Recoiling from the excesses of PC-style criticism, older contributors to the volume like J. Hillis Miller, Harold Bloom, Frank Lentricchia, Edward Said, and William Kerrigan shift to higher ground and renew their links to canonical writers like Milton, Arnold, and Eliot, while the younger critics seem shipwrecked in feminist rage and deconstructive hostility to dead white European males.

The same conflict is played out every day in debates within academic departments, with younger scholars opting for a theory-based, radically decentered, highly politicized curriculum reflecting current fashions in ethnicity, postmodernism, and gender politics, and older teachers retiring early, feeling depressed and beleaguered. In my own undergraduate department last spring there was a strong push to eliminate the whole core curriculum, including basic survey courses in English and American literature. At meetings I asked if there weren't at least a few writers all English majors should be required to read, Shakespeare perhaps? Not a chance.

Where the insurgents' motives weren't overtly political, they were anti-hierarchical and anti-elitist. "You're saying that some books are more important than others," I was told, "and therefore some people's courses are more important than others." Though the revisionists claimed to be devoted to history, they rejected the historical approach for a theoretical one, whether or not our students were equipped to handle it. They were determined to surround literary works with ideological markers, like road signs warning of dangerous terrain. Control of the curriculum meant shaping the mind of the next generation.

Through this whole debate, none of the proponents of a new curriculum said one word about their political motives, since political correctness is on the defensive today. Institutional power was the real issue yet the discussion remained on the highest educational plane. In other contexts one now hears remarks prefaced by, "I know this sounds like a really PC comment, but. . . ." A trace of bad conscience has infiltrated the ranks of PC. The end of the Cold War has exposed the hollow rhetoric of ersatz academic radicals. Many holding extreme views have moved back toward the center, while outright time-servers and academic careerists have changed their tune.

I'm struck by the fact that political correctness belongs to the secondary culture of academic and journalistic opinion, rarely to the primary culture of new novels, stories, and poems. Secondary cultures, whether cultures of publicity or of professionalism, feed on the creativity of others. Immensely trendy and conformist, they ebb and flow with the conventional wisdom of the moment. Genuine artists, on the other hand, like research scientists, work not from received ideas but from within or from observation. Depending on creative intuition, they are at once personal and objective.

We are in the process, I hope, of putting political correctness behind us, yet a whole academic generation has been brought up on it. PC will continue to have an enormous impact at the school level, where, as Nathan Glazer pointed out, the textbooks are rewritten every generation, propagating new myths, bolstered by strong political constituencies. Universities have an institutional investment in this outlook. Journals have been started, departments have been created, faculty have been tenured.

Multiculturalism itself is not the issue. Because the world is shrinking and America's population is changing, our future will be a multicultural one. But assimilation and economic striving should exert as strong a pull as ethnic pride. Once-excluded minorities will assimilate to America's corporate and professional cultures just as those cultures, themselves increasingly global and multinational, will be considerably altered to receive them. The result should be a more genuine diversity, not separatism and fragmentation.

There's no doubt that some of the influence of politically correct thinking has been good. We have become far more sensitive to the rights and needs of women, minorities, gays, the handicapped. My children's generation, which went to college in the 1980s, is probably the most color-blind and gender-blind in American history. I hope these virtues won't be lost in the inevitable backlash against PC but instead, free of dogmatism, will remain a vital constituent of a resurgent liberalism.

EUGENE GOODHEART

PC or Not PC

"Discourse," Paul Ricoeur reminds us, "consists in a series of choices by which certain meanings are selected and excluded." What does the pre-vailing "politically correct" discourse select and exclude? It selects the postcolonial agenda which reminds us of the destructive legacy of impe-rialism; it requires us to focus on the claims of particular groups, charac-terized by race, gender, and sexual orientation. Its politics are "identity politics." Difference has become sacrosanct. There are differences among those who subscribe to the prevailing discourse. New historicists may quarrel with Marxists over the importance of class as an explanatory cat-egory, Marxists with Foucauldians, and so on, but the prevailing dis-course excludes persons of conservative or even liberal persuasion who do not view all the evils of the modern world as springing from Western imperialism and who are concerned with the discovery of commonalities among people rather than differences. Exclusion means that these views are ignored or are treated with contempt as reactionary. To be excluded means not to be part of the discussion; it may mean not to be consid-ered seriously for a grant or for a job.

But if all discourse entails exclusions, why should the currently pre-vailing discourse incur the charge of censoriousness? A prominent expo-nent of the prevailing discourse reminded me that there was a time when literary critics were rebuked if they sought to determine an author's in-tention or if they promiscuously consulted their feelings in reading texts. The intentional and affective fallacies entered into "the speech codes" of the New Criticism. The analogy between then and now is false. It was always possible then to contest the intentional or affective fallacy with-out being made to feel that one was arguing a view that was politically or morally disgraceful. What characterizes the present situation is the way in which all differences have been politicized and transformed into ideo-logical encounters. Every community, no matter how generous and in-clusive its accommodation of political differences may be, has a view of what is outside the pale. An intolerance of Holocaust revisionism is not in itself a sign of general intellectual intolerance. We sense intolerance when what is viewed as outside the pale colonizes more and more the territory of possible differences. It is an irony that for all the talk about

difference, real differences of view are often not tolerated in cultural debate.

Though political correctness on the left is not limited to the
academy, the academy is where it is most at home. Political correctness
has not been associated with the right, but in the world outside the
certain sections of the media and in the highest government circles. The
ferocious, often mean-spirited satire of *Heterodoxy,* directed against the
cultural left and liberalism in general, has its own standards of PC. Its
language and animus are carryovers from the sixties (its editors David
Horowitz and Peter Collier were then editors of *Ramparts*) and are no
better than the worst instances that they take as their targets.

It is unfortunate that the idea of political correctness has been formulated along a right-left axis. It surely is possible to be a liberal or even
a person of the left and be severely critical of the ethos of political correctness. A First Amendment advocate like Nat Hentoff, a man of the
left, is allergic to any code that tries to regulate expression. It is also
possible that persons of conservative persuasion in politics may find political correctness congenial. Stanley Fish's conception of the authority of
the interpretive community (the current paradigm for PC) is a conservative idea. It does not provide a place for the rebel, the outsider, the individual who differs with the prevailing view. Political correctness is a
doctrine of opportunism. Since what constitutes the correct view
changes from time to time, the adjustment to it may have nothing to do
with principle. Such opportunism is not a matter of left or right.

The issue of political correctness has been trivialized by the debate
over speech codes, which may or may not be enforced by penalties. It
has produced cultural comedy. Short people are vertically challenged,
handicapped people differently abled. The comedy lies in the euphemistic
solemnity of the phrases. The perniciousness of political correctness lies
elsewhere – in the timidity of academics who know better and are fearful
about expressing their convictions, or whose convictions are frozen by
an anxiety not to offend.

It is politically correct to say that political correctness is an invention
of conservatives, or a self-ironizing device of the sophisticated left, or the
excess of extremists, and hence a marginal phenomenon. It is not true
that conservatives have invented the term, though they have gleefully
pounced upon it in order to insinuate its Stalinist implications.
(Communist Party members were required to follow the party line,
whatever reservations or disagreements they had with it.) The phrase has
been spoken ironically and self-ironically to disarm those who object to
the idea of political correctness. I recall that the first time I heard the
phrase was from the lips of a person of the left. She was characterizing

someone as a prelude to a critical judgment. "Her attitudes may be politically correct, but. . . ." The person who spoke the phrase was a
scholar of considerable intelligence and sophistication. She meant to say
that she had no objection to the attitudes of the person she was judging,
but that those attitudes were not enough to qualify that person.
Moreover, the tone of irony with which she spoke the phrase was intended to distance her from the vulgarity and tyranny implied by
"political correctness."

By now there is a consensus that "political correctness" exists, but
there are strong differences of opinion about how significant a phenomenon it is. Barbara Ehrenreich writes: "I have seen P.C. culture on
college campuses, chiefly among relatively elite college students and on
relatively elite college campuses. It amounts to a form of snobbery that is
easily made fun of by the right and even by students who are not on the
right. P.C. culture, as far as I can tell, is a limited phenomenon. The
major problems on American campuses are racial and sexual harassment,
alcoholism, and the anti-intellectualism of young white Republican
males." Ehrenreich writes from outside the academy (she is a *Time*
columnist), and her authority as a witness is suspect. "Chiefly among . . .
elite college students" – and what of the faculty that instructs them?
Why suddenly are Republican white males singled out in a culture noto -
rious for its anti-intellectualism across political lines? "Republican white
male" is a piece of inverted bigotry. It is not simply that Ehrenreich is
not to be trusted as a witness; she herself in the very passage in which she
dismisses PC as silliness exemplifies its absurdity or, should I say, its seriousness.

The least fruitful debates about political correctness involve charge
and countercharge based on anecdotal evidence. The debate degenerates
into bickering about the nature of the evidence and whether the evidence is marginal or central. It is rare that antagonists agree about the
topic of debate. Even an apparent agreement about a topic often involves misunderstanding. Take the issue of the "canon." The very word
itself is a misfortune, because as a theological trope it implies that the intellectual and literary tradition is fixed and unchanging. Tradition (as in
Eliot's "Tradition and the Individual Talent") has until recently been the
currency of discussion, and the idea of change and contestation is built
into the idea of tradition. The issue, it seems to me, is not whether
change should occur, but the nature and criteria of change. Advice: the
opponents of political correctness should change the terms of debate
from "canon" to "tradition."

The "canon bashers" or revisers, to use a more neutral term, want to extend and change the canon to include works by women and blacks that are worthy but have been ignored. On what basis is the worth determined? (Anxiety about political correctness makes me want to reassure my reader that of course I believe there are worthy books by women and blacks. My concern is directed to the standards of judgment.) Since the aesthetic category is under suspicion and value itself is insecure and contingent, the critic who "traditionally" had derived his confidence from a knowledge of the literary tradition, experience, taste, and intellectual capacity discovers or is told that his or her judgments are without foundation. The field is then left to politics, or to a certain kind of politics that determines what stays in, stays out, goes in, goes out. (The political or ideological category has yet to receive the kind of demystifying scrutiny to which the aesthetic category has been treated.) The revision of the canon does not necessarily entail exclusion: it may mean a new "understanding" motivated by suspicion of concealed motives of domination and by a passion for demystification. It discovers sexism in Rabelais, colonialism in Shakespeare, complicity with patriarchy in Jane Austen. The politically motivated critic whose view of texts is complex and literary will not reduce the meanings of Rabelais, Shakespeare, and Austen to sexism, colonialism, and patriarchy respectively. But the new ideological focus tends to produce a code of political correctness once one has decided to take this route. The temptation is strong to judge texts according to contemporary standards of decency. Even if one wishes to accept these standards, the burden of proof that Shakespeare is not colonialist or that his colonialist message may not be the most interesting thing about him becomes very heavy. Assuming the worst about sexism, colonialism, and patriarchy, such criticism tends to freeze all pleasure in the playfulness, irreverence, and irresponsibility of the imagination. It becomes blind and deaf to the possible truth in ideas and attitudes that do not satisfy contemporary standards of decency. "Political correctness" is hostile to the imagination.

Earlier I suggested that political correctness does not necessarily follow from a leftist politics. The content of a political position may be distinguished from an attitude taken toward it. One may advocate multiculturalism without dogmatic arrogance. If it simply meant a respect for cultural diversity, much of the controversy would be unintelligible. The debate concerns how multiculturalism is construed. Thus Diane Ravitch celebrates "the pluralistic nature of American culture" and "the new history . . . [which] demands an unflinching examination of racism and discrimination in our history." She accepts the raised "tempers" and "controversies" that accompany changes in historical perspectives, for we are now provided with "a more interesting and accurate account of American history." But she sets herself against "a new, particularistic multiculturalism" that "insist[s] that no common culture is possible or desirable." It should be noted that a particularist view does not necessarily represent the interests and desires of a particular group. There is the political question of who decides the identity of the group and its desires and interests.

Cultural particularism or separatism is a somewhat misleading phrase, for it implies that each group should be allowed to develop in its own fashion without interference from other groups. The particularist model is based on a binary opposition between dominant and subordinate groups. The effective goal is to invert the opposition, so that those who have dominated may feel what it means to be subordinate. For a "white male" (the favorite target of particularist resentment) to adopt the multicultural agenda, he may have to transform his own cultural interests. When he undertakes a study of the colonialized Other, he must be vigilant not to allow the prejudices or ideological preconceptions of his own culture to distort the object of his study. He may even be told that distortion is unavoidable and that he had best leave the study of the Other to the other, the notion being that one necessarily understands any experience better from the inside than one does from the outside. The epistemology that supports this notion is a subjectivism which allows no place for objectivity. Objectivity assumes that one can see with clarity and understanding by standing at a distance from the object. One need only reflect upon the inadequacies and failures of self-understanding that characterize most lives in order to see how vulnerable the subjectivist view is. In any case, the dominant subject finds himself in something of a bind. He must attempt to know the other but never presume to know it, because his knowledge, given his cultural position, is unreliable. He winds up mistrusting his own claims about the other and suspicious, indeed guilty, about his own social and cultural experiences.

His pleasure in Shakespeare may be diminished, if not destroyed, when he discovers a colonialist motive in the plays. His reading of *Heart of Darkness* may be an indictment of its putative imperialist imagination, which in turn may be a prelude to a decision that the text be eliminated from the canon. (*Heart of Darkness* remains a central text for its hostile critics, however, as a powerful negative example for ideological instruction.) Jane Austen's marriage plots are transformed from vehicles of delight and even fulfillment to structures for the oppression of women. What the particularist version of multiculturalism requires is not self-criticism, which is essential to education, but self-revulsion. The effect of particularist multiculturalism is to induce anxiety or guilt in "dominant" groups, which must expiate for their sins against subordinate and now-insurgent groups. I have characterized the situation in stark terms, but not hyperbolically, I believe, in order to explain what may sometimes appear as irrational defensiveness against a benign multiculturalism. Because diversity might mean separatism and the internecine belligerence that separatism breeds, thought must be given to an idea of community or solidarity beyond difference. The model that Ravitch proposes is one of dialogue rather than unresolvable conflict.

In recent years, dialogue under the sponsorship of Mikhail Bakhtin has been fetishized in theoretical discussion, but academic practice has confined the territory of dialogue to the politically like-minded, so that the differences which have been played out within the prevailing discourse have been small and esoteric. There has been no genuine dialogue, for instance, between radicals and conservatives, between radicals and liberals, or between liberals and conservatives. The metaphor for exchange between left and right has been "war," as in the phrase "the culture wars." Moreover, I think it unfortunate that an issue like multiculturalism has been formulated in left-right or liberal-conservative terms in which the critics of particularism are seen as persons on the right. One can argue the reverse: that a particularism which cannot entertain a conception of community beyond itself is reactionary. The failure of liberals to affirm the importance of a common culture that represents common interests as liberal doctrine reflects a failure of nerve. The terms of the debate and the political and moral significance of the oppositions need to be reformulated. We may be witnessing the beginnings of such a reformulation. Henry Louis Gates, Jr. and Cornel West, writers on the left, who have devoted themselves to the cultivation of African-American studies, have spoken forcefully against an invidious particularism. Ravitch's view is important because it is forward-looking. To go beyond particularism is not to deny the particular contributions of ethnic and racial groups.

What is to be done? I see no prospect of a return to the status quo ante, nor would it necessarily be desirable if such a return occurred. The dynamism of a liberal or conservative viewpoint must not depend upon a negative relation to cultural radicalism. The formulation of constructive alternatives is necessary, taking into account social and cultural changes that may be irreversible. Opponents of PC have a parasitic and negative relation to the topic, which puts them at a disadvantage. They spend much of their time and energy arguing against PC, but they offer little in the way of alternative conceptions of what is to be taught and of how one is to teach, as if the appropriate form and content of teaching had been decided long ago and in recent years corruption had set in. Assuming for a moment that the battle against political correctness has been won, what would higher or lower education become? It is a mistake to think that the ferment of the past several decades has produced nothing of value, which is the neoconservative view. The neoconservative attack rarely engages the arguments of the cultural left. It scorns them as nonarguments or arguments beneath contempt. On its side, it often commits the sin of exclusion in peremptorily declaring certain views to be beyond the pale, precisely what its adversaries do. There are contemptible arguments, but they should not be made to exhaust the range of thought and argument possible to liberal or left perspectives. The identification of the debasement of a position with the position itself does no service to the intellectual life.

The interest in cultural diversity, the emergence of the women's movement, the concern with the decolonization of the third world, the changing character of the student body: these are facts of our cultural life. There are a number of intellectuals who respect these facts and have been thinking and writing creatively and unfashionably about the current situation. Leszek Kolakowski and Tzvetan Todorov come to mind. What distinguishes their work is a rare combination of respect for difference and a belief in the idea of a common humanity. Both writers have experienced imperialist oppression, though not from the West, the agent of imperialism usually invoked in the academy. Their skepticism, which protects them against ideological dogmatism, is not of the radical kind that makes genuine conviction impossible. In their rethinking of the Enlightenment, they represent a belief in the values of reason, intellectual honesty and clarity as the foundation of our cultural life. They are signs of a possible future.

SUSAN HAACK

Knowledge and Propaganda: Reflections of an Old Feminist

> The philosophy which is now in vogue . . . cherishes certain tenets
> . . . which tend to a deliberate and factitious despair, which . . . cuts
> the sinews and spur of industry. . . . And all for . . . the miserable
> vainglory of having it believed that whatever has not yet been discov-
> ered and comprehended can never be discovered or comprehended
> hereafter.   – Francis Bacon

I have been a feminist since the age of twelve, when I got the top grade
in my first chemistry exam, and the boy who got the next highest grade
protested indignantly that it wasn't *fair:* "Everyone knows girls can't do
chemistry." And, since I have been working in theory of knowledge for
more than a decade now, I think I qualify as an epistemologist. So I
must be a feminist epistemologist, right? Wrong; on the contrary, I think
there is no such connection between feminism and epistemology as the
rubric "feminist epistemology" requires.

Perhaps you think that only someone of extreme right-wing political
views could possibly be less than enthusiastic about feminist epistemology.
If so, you are mistaken. The only thing extreme about my political views
is my dislike of extremes; and my reasons for thinking feminist epistemology misconceived are, in any case, not political but epistemological.

The last fifteen years or so have seen a major shift within feminist
philosophy: from a modest style which stressed the common humanity of
women and men, focused on justice and opportunity, and was concerned
primarily with issues in social and political theory; to an ambitious, imperialist feminism which stresses the "woman's point of view," and claims
revolutionary significance for all areas of philosophy, epistemology included. So, yes, the pun in my title is intentional; my feminism is of the
older-fashioned, modest stripe. But I shall take issue, here, only with the
imperialist ambitions of the new feminism with respect to the theory of
knowledge specifically.

Perhaps you think that only someone confined too long to the ar-
cana of contemporary philosophical analysis would care whether there is
such a thing as feminist epistemology. If so, you are again mistaken.

"Feminist epistemology" is a significant part of the rationale both of a fashionable kind of intellectual apartheid of the sexes and of the fashionable demand that inquiry be "politically correct." So if, as I believe, it is a mistake to suppose there is such a thing, it is a very consequential mistake.

Understandably reluctant to devote their time to a largely unrewarding body of literature, or understandably unwilling to take the risk that, if they criticize it, they will be perceived to be against women, my colleagues in the epistemological mainstream mostly hope that, if they ignore it, feminist epistemology will go away. I fear they overestimate the power of good ideas to drive out bad, and underestimate the power of the institutionalization of feminist epistemology, of the extent to which reputations and careers now depend on its legitimacy.

The rubric "feminist epistemology" is incongruous on its face, in somewhat the way of, say "Republican epistemology." And the puzzlement this incongruity prompts is rather aggravated than mitigated by the bewildering diversity of epistemological ideas described as "feminist." Among self-styled feminist epistemologists one finds quasi-foundationalists, coherentists, contextualists; those who stress connectedness, community, the social aspects of knowledge, and those who stress emotion, presumably subjective and personal; those who stress concepts of epistemic virtue, those who want the "androcentric" norms of the epistemological tradition to be replaced by "gynocentric" norms, those who advocate a descriptivist approach, and so on. Even apparent agreement, for example, that feminist epistemology will stress the social aspects of knowledge, masks significant disagreement about what this means: that inquirers are pervasively dependent on one another; that cooperative inquiry is better than individual inquiry; that epistemic justification is community-relative; that only a group, not an individual, can properly be said to inquire or to know; that reality is socially constructed, and so on.

The puzzlement is further aggravated by the reflection that neither all, nor only, females, or feminists, favor all, or indeed any, of the ideas offered under the rubric "feminist epistemology." Peirce, for example, is critical of what he calls the "vicious individualism" of Descartes' criterion of truth, and has a subtle conception of the social aspects of inquiry; yet he was neither female nor (to judge by his use of "masculine intellect" equivalently to "tough, powerful mind") feminist. John Stuart Mill surely qualifies as feminist if any male philosopher does; yet one finds none of the supposedly feminist themes in his epistemology – any more than one does in Ayn Rand's.

So: what is feminist about feminist epistemology? There seem to be two main routes by which feminism and epistemology are supposed to be connected, corresponding to two interpretations of the phrase, "the woman's point of view": as "the way women see things," or as "serving the interests of women." (These correspond also to two kinds of criticism of the epistemological mainstream: that it is androcentric, focusing exclusively on male ways of knowing, and that it is sexist, hostile to women's interests.)

Sometimes we are told that feminist epistemology represents women's "ways of knowing." This reversion to the notion of "thinking like a woman" is disquietingly reminiscent of old, sexist stereotypes. Still, there are disquieting truths, so this hardly settles the matter. But I am not convinced that there are any distinctively female "ways of knowing." All any human being has to go on, in figuring out how things are, is his or her sensory and introspective experience, and the explanatory theorizing he or she devises to accommodate it; and differences in cognitive style, like differences in handwriting, seem more individual than sex-determined.

The profusion of incompatible themes proposed as "feminist epistemology" itself speaks against the idea of a distinctively female cognitive style. But even if there were such a thing, the case for feminist epistemology would require further argument to show that female "ways of knowing" (scare quotes because the term is tendentious, since "knows" is a success-word) represent better procedures of inquiry or subtler standards of justification than the male. And, sure enough, we are told that insights into the theory of knowledge are available to women which are not available, or not easily available, to men. In all honesty, I cannot see how the evidence to date could be thought to speak in favor of this bold claim; what my experience suggests is rather that the questions of epistemological tradition are hard, very hard, for anyone, of either sex, to answer or even significantly to clarify.

Sometimes it is claimed that oppressed, disadvantaged and marginalized people are epistemically privileged in virtue of their oppression and disadvantage. If this were true, it would suggest that the truly epistemically privileged are not the affluent, well-educated, white, Western women who (mostly) rest their claim to special insight upon it, but the most oppressed, the most disadvantaged – some of whom are men. But, aside from appeals to the authority of Karl Marx on epistemological matters, is there any reason to think it is true? Kuhn observed that revolutionary scientific innovations are often made by persons who are at the margin of a discipline; but women, as a class, are not "marginal" in this sense. And one of the ways in which oppressed people are oppressed is, surely, that their oppressors control the information that reaches them. This argues, if anything, a cognitive disadvantage for "oppressed, disadvantaged, marginalized" people. So no such connection between feminism and epistemology as the rubric "feminist epistemology" requires is to be found under the first interpretation of "the woman's point of view," as "the way women see things."

Under the second interpretation of "the woman's point of view," as "serving the interests of women," the connection is supposed to be made by way of feminist criticisms of sexism in scientific theorizing. This would merge with the first connecting route on the assumption – which, of course, I do not accept – that sexism in scientific theorizing is the result of the exclusion of women, and hence of "women's ways of knowing," from the sciences. It is true, I think, that in the social sciences and biology theories which are not well-supported by the evidence have sometimes come to be accepted by scientists, most often male scientists, who have taken stereotypical ideas of masculine and feminine behavior uncritically for granted. (Perhaps I need to add that, by my lights, a theory is sexist – or rather, sexist against women – only if it is false as well as disadvantageous to women; that some women find it disturbing or offensive is neither sufficient nor necessary. Perhaps I also need to add that I am skeptical of claims that sexism has somehow infected theorizing in the physical as well as in the social sciences.)

Those who think that criticisms of sexism in scientific theorizing require a new, feminist epistemology insist that we are obliged, in the light of these criticisms, to acknowledge political considerations as legitimate ways to decide between theories. But on the face of it these criticisms suggest exactly the opposite conclusion – that politics should be kept out of science.

I can make sense of how things got so startlingly *aufgehoben* only by looking at feminist epistemology, not just as part of a larger development in feminism, but also as part of a larger development in epistemology. Here the last thirty years or so have seen a major shift: from the old romantic view, which took science to deserve a kind of epistemic authority in virtue of its peculiarly objective method of inquiry; to a new cynicism, which sees science as a value-permeated social institution; stresses the importance of politics, prejudice and propaganda, rather than the weight of the evidence, in determining what theories are accepted; and sometimes goes so far as to suggest that reality is constructed by us, and "truth" a word not to be used without the precaution of scare quotes.

My diagnosis is that the new cynicism in the philosophy of science has fed the ambition of the new feminism to colonize epistemology. The values with which science is permeated, it is argued, have been, up until now, inhospitable to the interests of women. Feminist criticisms of sexism in scientific theorizing, the argument continues, cannot be seen merely as criticisms of bad science; the moral to be drawn is that we must abandon the quixotic quest for a science that is value-free, in favor of the achievable goal of a science informed by feminist values. There would be a genuinely feminist epistemology if the aspiration could be achieved to legitimate the idea that feminist values should determine what theories are accepted.

The arguments offered to motivate the shift from feminist criticisms of sexism in scientific theorizing to feminist epistemology are of precisely the kind this diagnosis would predict. I can consider here only the two most important, each of which focuses on a notion dear to the hearts of the new cynics: underdetermination and value-ladenness.

The first appeals to "the underdetermination of theories by data," claiming that, since there is unavoidable slack with respect to what theories are accepted, it is proper to allow political preferences to determine theory choice. In one version, the appeal to underdetermination is intended only to point to the fact that sometimes the available evidence is not sufficient to decide between rival theories, and that in some cases (for example, with respect to theories about the remote past, "man the hunter" and all that) additional evidence may be, in practice, unobtainable. The proper response is that, unless and until more evidence is available, scientists had better suspend judgment – and that the lay public, philosophers included, should not be too uncritically deferential to scientists' sometimes unwarrantedly confident claims about what they have discovered. Underdetermination, in this sense, has not the slightest tendency to show that we may legitimately choose to believe whatever theory suits our political purposes.

In another version, the appeal to underdetermination is intended, rather, to rest on the Quinean thesis that there can be incompatible theories with the same observational consequences; theories, therefore, between which not even all possible evidence could decide. Fortunately it is not necessary to discuss whether the thesis is proven (though it may be worth noting that Quine himself at one point suggests that what he elsewhere describes as empirically equivalent but incompatible theories would really only be verbal variants of one theory). For in any case, if the thesis is true, it is true only of the genuinely theoretical (in the sense of "unobservable in principle"); it is irrelevant, therefore, to such questions as whether men's hunting or women's gathering mainly sustained prehistoric communities. And if it were relevant to such questions, the feminists' appeals to it would be self-defeating, since in that case it would undermine their presumption that we can know what theories conduce to the interests of women, or what those interests are.

The second line of argument from criticisms of sexism in scientific theorizing to feminist epistemology urges the untenability of the supposed boundary between science and values, and hence, again, the appropriateness of allowing feminist values to determine theory choice. In one version, the argument seems to be that the idea that feminist values could not constitute evidence with respect to this or that theory rests on an untenable distinction of descriptive versus normative. This argument is only as good as the reasons for thinking the required distinction untenable. What is at issue is not whether moral or political criticisms of priorities within science, or of uses of the findings of science, are ever appropriate; not whether some epistemic norms may turn out to be covertly of a descriptive, means-end character; but whether it is possible to derive an "is" from an "ought." I can find no argument in the literature that even purports to show this, and neither can I think of one. That it is false is manifest as soon as one expresses it plainly: that propositions about what states of affairs are desirable or deplorable could be evidence that things are, or are not, so.

In another version, the argument seems to rest on the claim, not that the distinction between fact and value is in principle untenable, but that in practice it is impossible entirely to exclude "contextual" (that is, external, social and political) values from scientific theorizing. In this version, the argument is a *non sequitur*. Even if it were true that scientists are never entirely without prejudice, even if it were impossible that they should entirely put their prejudices out of sight when judging the evidence for a theory, it doesn't follow that it is proper to allow prejudice to determine theory choice. (No doubt it is impossible to make science perfect; it doesn't follow that we shouldn't try to make it better.)

The failure of these arguments is symptomatic of the false presupposition on which the second attempt to connect feminism and epistemology depends: that, since the old romantic picture is not defensible, there is no option but the new cynicism. These are not the only options; the truth, as so often, lies between the extremes. The old romanticism overstresses the virtues, the new cynicism the vices, of science; the old romanticism focuses too exclusively on the logical, the new cynicism too exclusively on the sociological, factors that an adequate philosophy of science should combine. Science is neither sacred nor a confidence trick. It has been the most successful of human cognitive endeavors, but it is thoroughly fallible and imperfect — and, in particular, like all human cognitive endeavor, it is susceptible to fad and fashion, partiality and politics.

If my diagnosis is correct, though it is not inevitable that all the themes offered under the rubric "feminist epistemology" are false, it is inevitable that only those themes can be true which fail in their cynical intent. It is true, for example, that inquirers are profoundly and pervasively dependent on each other; but it does not follow that reality is however some epistemic community determines it to be. It is true that sometimes scientists may perceive relevant evidence as relevant only when persuaded, perhaps by political pressure, out of previous prejudices; but it does not follow that what evidence is relevant is not an objective matter. The misconception that it does, however, is so ubiquitous that it deserves a name. I call it "the 'passes for' fallacy," since it argues from the true premise that what passes for evidence, known fact, reality, and so forth, often is no such thing, to the false conclusion that the ideas of evidence, fact, reality, truth are humbug.

Once the "passes for" fallacy is seen as such, the epistemological significance of feminist criticisms of sexism in scientific theorizing is seen to be, though real enough, undramatic and by no means revolutionary. One traditional project of epistemology is to give rules, or, better, guidelines, for the conduct of inquiry; another is to articulate criteria of evidence or justification. One sub-task of the "conduct of inquiry" project is to figure out what environments are supportive of, and what hostile to, successful inquiry. One sub-task of this sub-task is to figure out how to minimize the effect of unquestioned and unjustifiable preconceptions in encouraging the acceptance of theories which are not well-supported by evidence. (One way, if there is diversity of preconceptions within science, is competition between prejudice and counterprejudice. But "diversity" here emphatically does not mean "proportional representation of women, blacks, Jews . . ." – an interpretation which rests on the assumption that all women, or all blacks, and so on, think alike; nor "equal representation for any and all ideas and approaches" – an interpretation which ignores the need for mechanisms, even if they are inevitably imperfect mechanisms, to exclude the crank, the crackpot, and the long-discredited idea.) Feminist criticism of sexist science, like studies of the disasters of Nazi or Soviet science, can be a useful resource in this sub-subtask of the "conduct of inquiry" project. But this is a role that requires the conception of theories as better or worse as supported by the evidence, and the distinction of evidential and nonevidential considerations, traditionally investigated in the "criteria of justification" project; not a role that allows us to abandon or requires us radically to revise the concepts of evidence or truth or reality.

I have argued that there is no such connection between feminism and epistemology as the rubric "feminist epistemology" requires. I have not denied that some themes presented under that rubric are true; and I have granted that some feminist criticisms of sexist science seem well-founded and have a bona fide epistemological role, albeit a rather modest one. So why, you may ask, do I make all this fuss about the label? Well, since the idea that there is an epistemology properly called "feminist" rests on false presuppositions, the label is at best sloppy. But there is more at stake than dislike of sloppiness; more than offense at the implication that those of us who don't think it appropriate to describe our epistemological work as "feminist" don't care about justice for women; more than unease at sweeping generalizations about women and embarrassment at the suggestion that women have special epistemological insight. What is most troubling is that the label is designed to convey the idea that inquiry should be politicized. And that is not only mistaken, but dangerously so.

It is dangerously mistaken from an epistemological point of view, because the presupposition on which it rests − that genuine, disinterested inquiry is impossible − is, in Bacon's shrewd phrase, a "factitious despair" which will, indeed, "cut the sinews and spur of industry." Serious intellectual work is hard, painful, frustrating; suggesting that it is legitimate to succumb to the temptation to cut corners can only block the way of inquiry.

I would say that inquiry really is best advanced by people with a genuine desire to find out how things are, who will be more persistent, less dogmatic, and more candid than sham reasoners seeking only to make a case for some foregone conclusion; except that, since it is a tautology that inquiry aims at the truth, the sham reasoner is not really engaged in inquiry at all. This should remind us that those who despair of honest inquiry cannot be in the truth-seeking business (as they should say, "the 'truth' racket"); they are in the propaganda business.

And this makes it apparent why the idea that inquiry should be politicized is dangerously mistaken, also, from a political point of view, because of the potential for tyranny in calls for "politically adequate research and scholarship." Think what "politically inadequate research" refers to: research informed by what some feminists deem "regressive" political ideas − and research not informed by political ideas at all, that is, honest inquiry. Have we forgotten already that in *1984* it was "thoughtcrime" to believe that two plus two is four if the Party ruled otherwise?

This is no trivial verbal quibble, but a matter, epistemologically, of the integrity of inquiry and, politically, of freedom of thought. Needlessly sacrificing these ideals would not help women; it would hurt humanity.

ROGER KIMBALL

From Farce to Tragedy

Nearly everyone who observes the contemporary cultural scene has had occasion to savor Marx's witty elaboration of Hegel's dictum about the important events and personages of history occuring, "as it were, twice." "He forgot to add," Marx quips, "the first time as tragedy, the second as farce." How much in our cultural life today qualifies as a farcical reenactment of half-forgotten tragedies! And yet the most ludicrously farcical of all recent cultural phenomena – the juggernaut of political correctness – seems poised to accomplish the revenge of Hegel on Marx, transforming an instance of farce into tragedy.

Egregious examples of political correctness have been so numerous (and the impotent, hand-wringing commentary that accompanies them so common) that it is easy to forget that the term gained currency only three to four years ago. It is even easier to forget that the epithet originated not with conservative commentators, as most academic radicals would have you believe, but with impatient college students. "Politically correct" described the self-righteous, non-smoking, ecologically sensitive, vegetarian, feminist, non-racist, sandal-wearing beneficiaries of capitalism – faculty as well as students – who paraded their outworn sixties-radicalism in the classroom and in their social life. Mostly, it was a joke. Who could take these people seriously? Thus it is that the acronym "PC" first won larger notice in a student cartoon strip out of Brown University, an institution still distinguished for its overweening quotient of political correctness if little else.

Some of the jokes preserve a residue of humor. Non-academics, at least, still chuckle when told about "Specific Manifestations of Oppression," a document that Smith College distributes to all incoming students in which the sin of "lookism" – the politically incorrect belief that some people are more attractive than others – is enrolled in the catalogue of punishable prejudices. The rub, of course, is "punishable." At colleges across the country, students (and staff and faculty) can be disciplined by campus diversity police not only for behaving in certain proscribed ways *but also for expressing forbidden opinions or exhibiting certain unpopular attitudes.* As the ethos of political correctness spread and codified, what seemed at first a disagreeable joke began to appear consider-

ably more ominous. The odor of totalitarian intolerance was unmistak-
able. And in this context it is worth noting that the proponents of political correctness have all along vociferously denied that they were politically correct: denial has always been a totalitarian specialty. But anyone
who has taken the trouble to observe what has happened in the academy
knows that over the last couple of years political correctness has evolved
from a sporadic expression of left-leaning self-righteousness into a dogma
of orthodoxy that is widely accepted, and widely enforced, by America's
cultural elite.

That was stage one. Stage two, the penetration of political correctness into public policy, is now underway. Future historians will look
back to the election of Bill Clinton as a defining event in this process.
As Hillary Clinton rattled on about "the politics of meaning" – what a
delicious phrase: so redolent of virtue, so empty of content! – her hus-
band set about filling (or at least attempting to fill) top government
posts with people distinguished chiefly for their championship of politically correct causes. The appointment of Donna Shalala, former
Chancellor of the University of Wisconsin, to the Clinton cabinet as
Secretary of Health and Human Services will surely be remembered as a
watershed. The woman who in 1989 insisted that "Covert racism [in
America] is just as bad today as overt racism was thirty years ago" now
presides over the single largest budget in the United States government.

Yet somehow even more disturbing is President Clinton's nomina-
tion of the marvelously named Sheldon Hackney, sometime president of
the University of Pennsylvania, to be the head of the National
Endowment for the Humanities. As I write, Mr. Hackney's appointment
is all but official: he was unanimously approved by the Senate Labor and
Human Relations Committee and now awaits only confirmation by the
full Senate. Barring divine intervention, that is sure to be forthcoming.*

Mr. Hackney has been much in the news of late. As president of the
University of Pennsylvania, he presided over some of the most noxious
examples of politically correct intolerance to capture the public's attention in years. There was, for example, the infamous Water Buffalo incident, in which a white male student was hauled up before a disciplinary
committee because in a moment of exasperation he had referred to some
black female students as "water buffalos" when they were making noise
outside his dormitory window. Would that Eveyln Waugh were present
to anatomize that incident!

Less funny, and even more disturbing, was the case of the missing stu-

---

*Divine intervention failed to intervene: Mr. Hackney has been duly appointed.

dent newspaper, which also made national headlines. This past April, a group of black activist students, unhappy about a conservative column in *The Daily Pennsylvanian,* set out to steal the entire press run of the newspaper. Breaking into various university buildings – the medical school, the university art museum, et cetera – they made off with nearly fourteen thousand copies of the newspaper. To most of us, this sounds like criminal trespassing and theft. But to Mr. Hackney and his politically correct administration the black students were engaged in "protest activity" – and so it was the security officers who intervened, not the students, who were held to be at fault.

In fact, as the columnist Charles Krauthammer aptly put it, the response of the administration was a "little piece of campus fascism." One security officer was reassigned to desk duty pending an investigation of his behavior. His crime? Apprehending two women he saw running out of the university art museum with three large plastic bags. Nor was that the end of the incident. The findings of the university panel appointed to study the theft has recently been released. As *The Wall Street Journal* reported, it absolves the students of all wrongdoing except failing to show their identification cards.

So Kafkaesque are its findings that, if one did not know better, one might think the university report was a surrealistic spoof. For example, the panel found that a security guard on duty at the medical school "behaved in a discourteous manner toward the students by ordering them to leave before determining who they were or giving them an opportunity to explain their presence." Poor babies! Presumably, what the guards should do the next time they encounter a trespasser is to tap him on the shoulder and inquire – politely – why he has broken in.

If, that is, there is a next time for those particular guards. Their conduct was to be "reviewed for possible disciplinary action." In a move that Chairman Mao would have smiled upon, the panel further recommended "that all security personnel receive training on working with people from diverse backgrounds" – as if apprehending thieves is an example of "working with people from diverse backgrounds"! Why worry about education when there is so much reeducation, so much consciousness-raising and sensitivity training, to be done! Like so many examples of political correctness, the entire episode at first strains credibility – then one realizes that what was simply incredible last week has now become business as usual. One might almost have thought one was at a White House retreat for Mr. Clinton's cabinet.

And it gets worse. In this summary, the panel concluded that the campus security officers "should have recognized" that the students' behavior was "a form of student protest and not an indicator of criminal behavior." Attend to the language:

> According to the University's "Emergency Procedures Protocols," "the [university police] should have contacted the Office of the Vice Provost for University Life as soon as it recognized that the students were involved in a form of protest. Once the VPUL was notified of the protest, Open Expression Monitors would have been dispatched to observe and monitor the students' actions, in compliance with the existing Open Expression Guidelines.

"Open Expression Monitors"? No wonder the adjective "Orwellian" is so often used to describe the rhetoric of political correctness. It is a perfect illustration of Orwellian "doublethink" and the principle enunciated in *Animal Farm* that "all animals are equal, but some are more equal than others." In order to appreciate this, one need only imagine what Mr. Hackney's response would have been had the students been white males pilfering a black student newspaper. Would he have agonized, "Two important university values now stand in conflict: diversity and open expression," as he did in this instance? I am happy to take bets. It is worth remembering, too, that this is the man who in 1990 denounced the attempt to stop federal funding of exhibitions of work by Robert Mapplethorpe and Andres Serrano. "I get very nervous when fundamental principles are at stake," Mr. Hackney preened. Ah, yes, supporting pornographic and blasphemous trash with taxpayers' money is a "fundamental principle," but protecting freedom of speech and law and order at his own university is up for grabs. Opportunism anyone?

The spectacle of Sheldon Hackney as the president of a great university was profoundly disturbing. The prospect of him heading the National Endowment for the Humanities is even worse. The NEH was founded to preserve and transmit what is best and most lasting about our culture. Under Mr. Hackney's rule, one can be certain that those ideals will be utterly forgotten in the name of cultural activism. Radical multiculturalism, "gender studies," Afrocentrism, wacko feminism: one can be sure that the entire politically correct smorgasbord of academic cultural offerings will henceforth occupy a prominent place in the NEH's roster of interests. This is bad enough in itself, but it is even more disturbing for what it says about the evolution of political correctness. For a brief moment around 1990, "the long march through the institutions" for which sixties radicals agitated seemed to be complete with the more or less total capitulation of most American universities and cultural organizations to the forces of political correctness.

Unfortunately, it now appears that the takeover of the universities and organizations like the Modern Language Association and the American Council of Learned Societies was only the first step. What Sheldon Hackney's appointment signals is the opening up of a new front: the aggressive application of political correctness beyond the cloistered purlieus of the academy to cultural life writ large. As Hillary Clinton has said, she doesn't want government simply to govern, she wants it to change people's lives. The cultural mandarins in the Clinton administration and their sympathizers in the academy and its satellites know what virtue is, and they want to force you to become virtuous.

It is said by some well-meaning commentators — even, on occasion, intelligent well-meaning commentators — that although the methods and, as it were, the manners of political correctness are deplorable, its "goals" are, at bottom, noble. For example, Martin Amis, in his *New Yorker* review of Andrew Motion's controversial new biography of the poet Philip Larkin, speaks of political correctness "at its grandest" as "an attempt to accelerate evolution." Make no mistake, Mr. Amis comes down very hard on the politically correct campaign against Larkin for his unenlightened views on women and blacks — a campaign, incidentally, that allowed an unnamed columnist for the British Library Association *Record* to suggest that Philip Larkin's books "should be banned." But Mr. Amis nevertheless insists that political correctness, since it is "against" nasty things like racism and sexism must, in theory if not in practice, be on the side of the angels. This is a conclusion as naive as it is dangerous. Recall the paving stones of the road to Hell. And recall that Robespierre and Saint-Just, too, were against tyranny and for "virtue" — so much so that they saw no problem employing tyranny to enforce virtue. The French Republic, Robespierre chillingly wrote, was to be founded on "virtue and its emanation, terror." In his view, the stroke of the guillo-tine kept track of the Republic's level of virtue. How much twentieth-century despots have learned from Robespierre! How much he could have learned from the sober wisdom of *The Federalist Papers,* which repeatedly warned against attempting to legislate virtue.

The history of political correctness to date has presented us with several crossroads. So far, most challenges to established standards of be-havior have been met by capitulation and pusillanimity. We are now at another crossroads, one at which the intolerance of political correctness threatens to spill over into our daily lives. Many people involved in the debate seem to be inured to the outrages the partisans of political cor-rectness perpetrate: what's one more student expelled because he took the wrong line on feminism or race or homosexuality? Why should they get involved, rock the boat, put their careers on the line? There are plenty of principled reasons, but there are practical reasons, too. Winston Churchill mentioned one when, in 1938, he wrote that the British people had before them the choice of shame or war. He feared that they would choose shame – and have war nevertheless. He was right.

HILTON KRAMER

Confronting the Monolith

The essential thing to remember about the political correctness movement at this point in our history is that in the realm of education, culture, and the arts the champions of PC have already achieved a decisive
victory. They have succeeded in changing the way books, ideas, and every intellectual and artistic endeavor are discussed and assessed. In the
classroom and in the media, in foundations and government agencies, in
arts organizations, critical journals, and public intellectual forums, the
consequences of censorship (and the wider phenomenon of self-censorship) in the service of PC are now so fully established that an entire generation of younger artists, writers, intellectuals, academics, and cultural
bureaucrats takes the rhetoric and indeed the philosophical premises of
political correctness for granted and conducts its affairs according to its
dictates.

Some of this is purely cynical, of course. It is a way of getting ahead
in a political environment that now anathematizes all dissent from PC
orthodoxy as racist, sexist, homophobic, and so on. But whether the
support for PC is cynical or genuine, the result is the same. At every level
of culture and the arts, PC has already altered the terms of employment,
the agenda of events, the patterns of patronage, the language of criticism, the choice of books to be published and accorded favorable notice,
and even the way bookshops stock their shelves and display their titles.
Careers are now made and unmade on the basis of PC criteria, and professional life is divided along PC lines. So, too, is the social scene that is
an important accessory to professional life.

There is resistance to political correctness, to be sure – I take this
symposium to be an example of it – but it is now resistance to an established order of power and belief. And such resistance as exists is greatly
impaired, if not entirely crippled, by a refusal, especially among liberals,
to examine the origins of PC in the illiberal doctrines and policies that
were given a liberal sanction as the movement was gathering its forces.
Foremost among these doctrines and policies is the concept of
"affirmative action," which, in establishing race-based and gender-based
criteria of employment and preferment, succeeded in demonizing traditional standards of merit in favor of "minority" quotas.

Once the policy of affirmative action was embraced and enforced as legitimate liberal doctrine, it was bound to have a shattering effect on liberalism itself. Acceptance of affirmative action entailed the dismantling of the meritocratic system that had long been the foundation of liberal culture. When the liberals caved in to the radicals on this issue, they surrendered their right to invoke any but a race- or gender-based criterion of judgment in the assessment of professional accomplishment. Their docile support of affirmative action thus guaranteed that liberals would be made politically hostage to the imperatives of the political correctness movement. For one of the purposes of the movement is, after all, to protect the beneficiaries of affirmative action from criticism based on what had once been the intellectual standards of the liberal meritocracy, and this protection racket soon degenerated into a programmatic effort to discredit all critical discourse – which means, in effect, all standards of cultural achievement – that are not based on race and gender. It is because of this history of liberal surrender to an illiberal ethos that the attempt lately made by certain liberals to mount their own attack on PC is so hollow, for it addresses only the effects of the political correctness movement and leaves its causes unexamined. Or else it takes refuge in the mendacious claim that PC militancy has somehow been caused by the actions of conservatives who have opposed political correctness from the outset.

It is worth recalling that it was undergraduate students at some of our most liberal universities who were the first to protest the hypocrisy of PC. The term "political correctness," in its current usage, was coined by these undergraduates to ridicule the kind of instruction they were receiving from faculty recruited through affirmative-action hiring practices. Such ridicule – almost always ascribed by PC *apparatchiks* to racist, sexist, or homophobic motives – had to be quelled, however, to allow the policy of affirmative action to complete the task of enforcing race- and gender-based quotas and the race- and gender-based teaching that followed in their wake. Hence the introduction of speech codes and other official prohibitions restricting the open expression of all opinion that could be construed as casting doubt on the new ideologies of race and gender. For the juggernaut of affirmative action to succeed in its mission, derision had to be made a punishable offense. In a great many areas of cultural life, it now is.

Opponents of PC should have no illusions about the obstacles to be surmounted in combating this ideological plague. They have to be prepared for a long and unremitting struggle if its devastating effects are ever to be repaired and reversed. The prospects for such a reversal are bleaker than ever, of course, with a PC administration in the White House and a

PC Congress now adding their considerable administrative and legislative weight to the PC orthodoxy already dominating the academy, the media, and the cultural bureaucracy. Coverage of the Senate hearings over the appointment of Sheldon Hackney for the chairmanship of the National Endowment for the Humanities was a reminder, if we needed one, that not much in the way of truth or judicious inquiry is now to be expected on these matters – even when they involve clear violations of the First Amendment! – from the journalistic establishment, which is itself hostage to affirmative-action hiring practices and the PC standards of reporting that accompany them. Between the views of a liberal militant like Senator Kennedy and those of the editorial page of *The New York Times* there is now no discernible ideological difference. Nor is there any longer a significant political difference between the way *The New York Times* and *The Nation*, for instance, report on PC issues. Opponents of PC thus face an ideological monolith that daily increases its power and prerogatives.

Still, I do not believe that opposition to the political correctness movement – or to multiculturalism, its bastard offspring – is by any means a lost cause. We are a long way from having become a totalitarian society, despite the success of PC militants in moving us in the direction of what the British writer Paul Johnson has called liberal fascism. The losses that we have incurred – not only in the freedom to call things by their right names, but in the way the language itself has been debased to serve coercive political purposes – have certainly been immense. Yet it is still possible to speak the truth if one is willing to take the flak. And speak we must, for nothing less than the intellectual and political achievements of our democratic society and a recognition of their specific roots in our Western cultural traditions are at stake in this struggle against falsehood.

As far as education, culture, and the arts are concerned, this battle must be waged on several fronts simultaneously. There must, first of all, be no temporizing about the task of identifying and deriding the lies and distortions that are now routinely invoked to misrepresent, misinterpret, and otherwise discredit the greatest of our intellectual and artistic accomplishments past and present, in the name of a politically sanctioned alternative "canon." The trashing of those accomplishments as the work of "dead white European males" must be called to critical account at every opportunity, and so must the promotion of newly sanctified mediocrities and nonentities simply because they meet the requisite criteria of race and gender. As Lionel Trilling once wrote about his criticism of Stalinism, with which the political correctness movement has so much in common, the unmaskers must themselves be unmasked – which in today's political climate entails fairly steady work.

Then, too, the war against some allegedly fixed and allegedly oppressive canon must be exposed as the political fraud that it is. The so-called canon, in art as well as in literature, has always been in flux. The revisions and modifications that have regularly occurred from generation to generation were not effected by political fiat – not, anyway, in democratic societies. They resulted from the creative thought of our leading artists and writers and the critical debate their work engendered. Eliot's elevation of the Metaphysical poets, Yeats's affinity for Blake, Picasso's appropriation of African sculpture, Matisse's use of Islamic design – these issued from profound artistic endeavors that effectively altered our understanding of the traditions upon which the life of art in our culture is based. Every great artist redefines the tradition in which he works. Even the classics are subjected to the tests of redefinition, and their power to survive such periodic tests through the ages is what makes them classics. To dismiss this rich process of revaluation as some kind of ongoing conspiracy on the part of white European males to secure their "hegemony" is, besides being intellectually contemptible, nothing but crass racial and sexual politics, and should be labeled as such.

Political attacks on literature and the arts from the PC brigades have to be met with the kind of political response that will effectively defend our accomplishments and our traditions from being politically trashed. But this is not the only task that is required of the opponents of PC, for they must not allow the PC movement to politicize their own critical judgments. To win this battle, it is equally important for the opponents of PC to persist in the work of judging art by artistic standards. Criticism must not be allowed to degenerate into a contest between one set of political criteria and another opposing set. Disinterested aesthetic assessment of the arts must remain a primary task, lest we too succumb to the practice of judging every aspect of our culture according to a political standard.

Finally, we must engage in a more vigorous examination of what the political correctness movement has done to language – to the language of criticism and theory, the language of politics and the law, the language of the classroom, the media, and the cultural bureaucracy. PC has been responsible for a corruption of our language on a truly Orwellian scale, yet we still lack a new Orwell who – if we are lucky – might someday give us a definitive account of the melancholy fate that language has suffered as a consequence of this atrocious assault on our culture. There is a lot to be done.

CHARLES KRAUTHAMMER

Defining Deviancy Up

In a recent essay in *The American Scholar* titled "Defining Deviancy Down," Daniel Patrick Moynihan offers an arresting view of the epidemic of deviancy – of criminality, family breakdown, mental illness – that has come to characterize the American social landscape. Deviancy has reached such incomprehensible proportions, argues Moynihan, that we have had to adopt a singular form of denial: we deal with the epidemic simply by defining away most of the disease. We lower the threshold for what we are prepared to call normal in order to keep the volume of deviancy – redefined deviancy – within manageable proportions.

For example. Since 1960 the incidence of single parenthood has more than tripled. Almost thirty percent of all American children are now born to unmarried mothers. The association of fatherlessness with poverty, welfare dependency, crime and other pathologies points to a monstrous social problem. Yet, as the problem has grown, it has been systematically redefined by the culture – by social workers, intellectuals, and most famously by the mass media – as simply another lifestyle choice. Dan Quayle may have been right, but Murphy Brown won the ratings war.

Moynihan's second example is crime. We have become totally inured to levels of criminality that would have been considered intolerable thirty years ago. The St. Valentine's Day massacre, which caused a national uproar and merited two entries in the *World Book Encyclopedia,* involved four thugs killing seven other thugs. An average weekend in today's Los Angeles, notes James Q. Wilson. More than half of all violent crimes are not even reported. We have come to view homicide as ineradicable a part of the social landscape as car accidents.

And finally there is mental illness. Unlike family breakdown and criminality, there has probably been no increase in mental illness over the last thirty years. Rates of schizophrenia do not change, but the rate of hospitalization for schizophrenia and other psychoses has changed. The mental hospitals have been emptied. In 1955 New York state asylums had 93,000 patients. Last year they had 11,000. Where have the remaining 82,000 and their descendants gone? Onto the streets mostly. In one gen-eration, a flood of pathetically ill people has washed onto the streets of

America's cities. We now step over these wretched and abandoned folk sleeping in doorways and freezing on grates. They, too, have become accepted as part of the natural landscape. We have managed to do that by redefining them as people who simply lack affordable housing. They are not crazy or sick, just very poor – as if anyone crazy and sick and totally abandoned would not end up very poor.

Moynihan's powerful point is that with the moral deregulation of the 1960s, we have had an explosion of deviancy in family life, criminal behavior, and public displays of psychosis. And we have dealt with it in the only way possible: by redefining deviancy down so as to explain away and make "normal" what a more civilized, ordered and healthy society long ago would have labeled – and long ago did label – deviant.

Moynihan is right. But it is only half the story. There is a complementary social phenomenon that goes with defining deviancy down. As part of the vast social project of moral leveling, it is not enough for the deviant to be normalized. The normal must be found to be deviant. Therefore, while for the criminals and the crazies deviancy has been defined down (the bar defining normality has been lowered), for the ordinary bourgeois deviancy has been defined up (the bar defining normality has been raised). Large areas of normal behavior hitherto considered benign have had their threshold radically redefined up, so that once innocent behavior now stands condemned as deviant. Normal middle-class life then stands exposed as the true home of violence and abuse and a whole catalog of aberrant acting and thinking.

As part of this project of moral leveling, entirely new areas of deviancy – such as date rape and politically incorrect speech – have been discovered. And old areas – such as child abuse – have been amplified by endless reiteration in the public presses and validated by learned reports of their astonishing frequency. The net effect is to show that deviancy is not the province of criminals and crazies but thrives in the heart of the great middle class. The real deviants of society stand unmasked. Who are they? Not Bonnie and Clyde but Ozzie and Harriet. True, Ozzie and Harriet have long been the object of ridicule. Now, however, they are under indictment.

The moral deconstruction of middle-class normality is a vast project. Fortunately, thousands of volunteers are working the case. By defining deviancy up they have scored some notable successes. Three, in particular. And in precisely the areas Moynihan identified: family life, crime, and thought disorders.

First, family life. Under the new dispensation it turns out that the ordinary middle-class family is not a warm, welcoming fount of "family values," not a bedrock of social and psychic stability as claimed in conservative propaganda. It is instead a caldron of pathology, a teeming source of the depressions, alienations, and assorted dysfunctions of adulthood. Why? Because deep in the family lies the worm, the 1990's version of original sin: child abuse.

Child abuse is both a crime and a tragedy, but is it nineteen times more prevalent today than it was thirty years ago? That is what the statistics offer. In 1963: 150,000 reported cases. In 1992: 2.9 million.

Now, simply considering the historical trajectory of the treatment of children since the nineteenth century, when child labor – even child slavery – was common, it is hard to believe that the tendency toward improved treatment of children has been so radically reversed in one generation.

Plainly it hasn't. What happened then? The first thing that happened was an epidemic of over-reporting. Douglas Besharov points out that whereas in 1975 about one-third of child abuse cases were dismissed for lack of evidence, today about two-thirds are dismissed. New York state authorities may have considered it a great social advance that between 1979 and 1983, for example, reported cases of child abuse increased by almost fifty percent. But over the same period, the number of substantiated cases actually declined. In other words, the 22,000 increase of reported cases yielded a net decrease of real cases.

Note the contrast. For ordinary crime, to which we have become desensitized, we have defined deviancy down. One measure of this desensitization is under-reporting: nearly two out of every three ordinary crimes are never even reported. Child abuse is precisely the opposite. For child abuse, to which we have become exquisitely oversensitized, deviancy has been correspondingly defined up. One of the measures of oversensitization is over-reporting: whereas two out of three ordinary crimes are never reported, two out of three reported cases of child abuse are never shown to have occurred.

The perceived epidemic of child abuse is a compound of many factors. Clearly, over-reporting is one. Changing societal standards regarding corporal punishment is another. But beyond the numbers and definitions there is a new ideology of child abuse. Under its influence, the helping professions, committed to a belief in endemic abuse, have encouraged a massive search to find cases, and where they cannot be found, to invent them.

Consider this advice from one of the more popular self-help books on sex abuse, *Courage to Heal*. "If you are unable to remember any specific instances [of childhood sex abuse] . . . but still have a feeling that something abusive happened to you, it probably did." And "if you think you were abused and your life shows the symptoms, then you were."

If your life shows the symptoms. In a popular culture saturated with tales of child abuse paraded daily on the airwaves, it is not hard to suggest to vulnerable people that their problems − symptoms − are caused by long-ago abuse, indeed, even unremembered abuse. Hence the *reductio ad absurdum* of the search for the hidden epidemic: adults who present themselves suddenly as victims of child abuse after decades of supposed amnesia − the amnesia reversed and the memory reclaimed thanks to the magic of intensive psychotherapy.

Now, the power of therapeutic suggestion is well known. Dr. George Ganaway of Emory University points out − and, as a retired psychiatrist, I well remember − how fiction disguised as memory can be created at the suggestion of a trusted therapist whom the patient wants to please.

Why should the memories of child abuse please the therapist? Because it fits the new ideology of neurosis. For almost a century Freudian ideology located the source of adult neuroses in the perceived psychosexual traumas of childhood. But Freud concluded after initial skepticism that these psychosexual incidents were fantasy.

Today Freud's conclusion is seen either as a great error or, as Jeffrey Masson and other anti-Freudian crusaders insist, as a great betrayal of what he knew to be the truth. Today's fashion, promoted by a vanguard of therapists and researchers, is that the fantasies are true. When the patient presents with depression, low self-esteem, or any of the common ailments of modern life, the search begins for the underlying childhood sexual abuse. "Some contemporary therapists," writes Elizabeth Loftus, professor of psychology at the University of Washington, "have been known to tell patients, on the basis of a suggestive history or 'symptom profile,' that they definitely had a traumatic experience. The therapist then urges the patient to pursue the recalcitrant memories."

This new psychology is rooted in and reinforces current notions about the pathology of ordinary family life. Rather than believing, as we did for a hundred years under the influence of Freud, that adult neurosis results from the inevitable psychological traumas of sexual maturation, compounded by parental error, and crystallized in the (literally) fantastic memories of the patient, today there is a new dispensation. Nowadays neurosis is the outcome not of innocent errors but of criminal acts occurring in the very bosom of the ordinary-looking family. Seek and ye shall find: the sins of the father are visible in the miserable lives of the children. Child abuse is the crime waiting only to be discovered with, of course, the proper therapeutic guidance and bedtime reading. It is the dirty little secret behind the white picket fence. And beside this offense, such once-regarded deviancies of family life as illegitimacy appear benign.

So much for the family. Let us look now at a second pillar of everyday bourgeois life: the ordinary heterosexual relationship. A second vast category of human behavior that until recently was considered rather normal has had its threshold for normality redefined up so as to render much of it deviant. Again we start with a real offense: rape. It used to be understood as involving the use of or threat of force. No longer. It has now been expanded by the concept of date rape to encompass an enormous continent of behavior that had long been viewed as either normal or ill-mannered, but certainly not criminal.

"Some 47 percent of women are victims of rape or attempted rape . . . and 25 percent of women are victims of completed rape." So asserts Catherine MacKinnon on a national television news special. Assertions of this sort are commonplace. A Stanford survey, for example, claims that a third of its women have suffered date rape. The most famous and widely reported study of the rape epidemic is the one done by Mary Koss (and published, among other places, in *Ms.* magazine). Her survey of 6,159 college students found that fifteen percent had been raped and another twelve percent subjected to attempted rape. She also reported that in a single year 3,187 college females reported 886 incidents of rape or attempted rape. That is more than one incident for every four women per year. At that rate, about three out of every four undergraduate women would be victims of rape or attempted rape by graduation day.

If those numbers sound high, they are. As Neil Gilbert points out in *The Public Interest,* the numbers compiled by the FBI under the Unified Crime Reporting Program and suitably multiplied to account for presumed unreported cases, yield an incidence of rape somewhere around one in a thousand. As for the college campus, reports from 2,400 campuses mandated by the Student Right-to-Know and Campus Security Act of 1990 showed fewer than 1,000 rapes for 1991. That is about one-half a rape per campus per year. Barnard College, a hotbed of anti-rape and Take Back the Night activity, released statistics in 1991 showing no reports of rape, date or otherwise, among its 2,200 students. Same for Harvard, Yale, Princeton, Brown – and Antioch, author of the strictest, most hilarious sexual correctness code in American academia.

How does one explain the vast discrepancy – 1 in 2 differs from 1 in 1,000 by a factor of 500 – between the real numbers and the fantastic numbers that have entered the popular imagination? Easy. Deviancy has again been redefined – up. Rape has been expanded by Koss and other researchers to include behavior that you and I would not recognize as rape. And not just you and I — the supposed victims themselves do not recognize it as rape. In the Koss study, seventy-three percent of the women she labeled as rape victims did not consider themselves to have been raped. Fully forty-two percent had further sexual relations with the so-called rapist.

Now, women who have been raped are not generally known for going back for more sex with their assailants. Something is wrong here. What is wrong is the extraordinarily loose definition of sexual coercion and rape. Among the questions Koss asked her subjects were these: "Have you given in to sexual intercourse when you didn't want to because you were overwhelmed by a man's continual arguments and pressure?" and "Have you had sexual intercourse when you didn't want to because a man gave you alcohol or drugs?" The Stanford study, the one that turned up one out of every three female students as victims of date rape, rests on respondents' self-report of "full sexual activity when they did not want to."

It is a common enough experience for people (both men and women) to be of two minds about having sex, and yet decide, reluctantly but certainly freely, to go ahead even though they don't really want to. Call that rape and there are few who escape the charge.

The cornerstone of this new and breathtakingly loose definition is the idea of verbal coercion. Consider this definition from the "Nonviolent Sexual Coercion" chapter in *Acquaintance Rape: The Hidden Crime* (John Wiley, 1991): "We define verbal sexual coercion as a woman's consenting to unwanted sexual activity because of a man's verbal arguments, not including verbal threats of physical force." With rape so radically defined up — to include offering a drink or being verbally insistent — it is no surprise that the result is an epidemic of sexual deviancy.

Of course, behind these numbers is an underlying ideology about the inherent aberrancy of all heterosexual relations. As Andrea Dworkin once said, "Romance . . . is rape embellished with meaningful looks." The date rape epidemic is just empirical dressing for a larger theory which holds that because relations between men and women are inherently unequal, sex can never be truly consensual. It is always coercive.

"The similarity between the patterns, rhythms, roles and emotions, not to mention acts, which make up rape (and battery) on the one hand and intercourse on the other . . . " writes MacKinnon, "makes it difficult to sustain the customary distinctions between pathology and

normalcy, violence and sex." And "Compare victims' reports of rape
with women's reports of sex. They look a lot alike . . . . In this light,
the major distinction between intercourse (normal) and rape (abnormal)
is that the normal happens so often that one cannot get anyone to see
anything wrong with it." Or as Susan Estrich puts it, "Many feminists
would argue that so long as women are powerless relative to men,
viewing 'yes' as a sign of true consent is misguided." But if "yes" is not a
sign of true consent, then what is? A notarized contract?

And if there is no such thing as real consent, then the radical feminist
ideal is realized: all intercourse is rape. Who needs the studies? The
incidence of rape is not twenty-five percent or thirty-three or fifty. It is
one hundred percent. Then Naomi Wolf can write in *The Beauty Myth*
that we have today "a situation among the young in which boys rape
and girls get raped *as a normal course of events.*" (Her italics.)

Date rape is only the most extreme example of deviancy redefined
broadly enough to catch in its net a huge chunk of normal, everyday behavior. It is the most extreme example because it is criminal. But then
there are the lesser offenses, a bewildering array of transgressions that
come under the rubric of sexual harassment, the definition of which can
be equally loose and floating but is always raised high enough to turn
innocent behavior into deviancy. As Allan Bloom wrote, "What used to
be understood as modes of courtship are now seen as modes of male
intimidation."

So much then for the family and normal heterosexual relations. On
now to the third great area of the new deviancy: thought crimes.

This summer, I was visited by an FBI agent doing a routine background check on a former employee of mine now being considered for
some high administration post. The agent went through the usual check-
list of questions that I had heard many times before: questions about financial difficulties, drug abuse, alcoholism. Then he popped a new one:
Did this person ever show any prejudice to a group based on race, ethnicity, gender, national origin, etc.? I assumed he was not interested in
whether the person had been involved in any racial incident. The FBI
would already have known about that. What he wanted to know was
my friend's deeper thoughts, feelings he might have betrayed only to
someone with whom he had worked intimately for two years. This was
the point in the interview at which I was supposed to testify whether I
had heard my friend tell any sexist or racist jokes or otherwise show signs
of hidden prejudice. That is when it occurred to me that insensitive
speech had achieved official status as a thought crime.

Now, again we start with real deviance – racial violence of the kind once carried out by the Klan or today by freelancers like the two men in Tampa recently convicted of a monstrous racial attack on a black tourist. These are outlawed and punished. So are the more benign but still contemptible acts of nonviolent racial discrimination, as in housing, for example. But now that overt racial actions have been criminalized and are routinely punished, the threshold for deviancy has been ratcheted up. The project now is to identify prejudiced thinking, instincts, anecdotes, attitudes.

The great arena for this project is the American academy. The proliferation of speech codes on campuses, restrained only by their obvious unconstitutionality, was an attempt by universities to curtail speech that may cause offense to groups designated for special protection. A University of Michigan student, for example, offers the opinion *in class* that homosexuality is an illness, and finds himself hauled before a formal university hearing on charges of harassing students on the basis of sexual orientation.

The irony here is quite complete. It used to be that homosexuality was considered deviant. But now that it has been declared a simple lifestyle choice, those who are not current with the new definitions, and have the misfortune to say so in public, find themselves suspected of deviancy. There is, of course, the now-famous case of the Israeli-born University of Pennsylvania student who called a group of rowdy black sorority sisters making noise outside his dorm in the middle of the night "water buffaloes" (his rough translation from the Hebrew *behemah*). He was charged with racial harassment. A host of learned scholars was assigned the absurd task of locating the racial antecedents of the term. They could find none. (They should have asked me. I could have saved them a lot of trouble. My father called me "behemah" so many times it almost became a term of endearment. I don't think he was racially motivated.) Nonetheless, the university, convinced that there was some racial animus behind that exotic term and determined not to let it go unpunished, tried to pressure the student into admitting his guilt. Penn offered him a plea bargain. Proceedings would be stopped if he confessed and allowed himself to be re-educated through a "program for living in a diverse community environment."

Consider: the psychotic raving in the middle of Broadway is free to rave. No one will force him into treatment. But a student who hurls "water buffalo" at a bunch of sorority sisters is threatened with the ultimate sanction at the disposal of the university – expulsion – unless he submits to treatment to correct his deviant thinking.

This may seem ironic but it is easily explained. Under the new dispensation it is not insanity but insensitivity that is the true sign of deviant thinking, requiring thought control and re-education. One kind of deviancy we are prepared to live with; the other, we are not. Indeed, one kind, psychosis, we are hardly prepared to call deviancy at all. As Moynihan points out, it is now part of the landscape.

The mentally ill are not really ill. They just lack housing. It is the rest of us who are guilty of disordered thinking for harboring — beneath the bland niceties of middle-class life — racist, misogynist, homophobic, and other corrupt and corrupting insensitivities.

Ordinary criminality we are learning to live with. What we are learning we cannot live with is the heretofore unrecognized violence against women that lurks beneath the facade of ordinary, seemingly benign, heterosexual relations.

The single parent and broken home are now part of the landscape. It is the Ozzie and Harriet family, rife with abuse and molestation, that is the seedbed of deviance.

The rationalization of deviancy reaches its logical conclusion. The deviant is declared normal. And the normal is unmasked as deviant. That, of course, makes us all that much more morally equal. The project is complete. What real difference is there between us?

And that is the point. Defining deviancy up, like defining deviancy down, is an adventure in moral equivalence. As such, it is the son of an old project that met its demise with the end of the Soviet empire. There once was the idea of moral equivalence between the East and the West. Even though the Soviets appeared to be imperialist and brutal and corrupt and rapacious, we were really as bad as they were. We could match then crime for crime throughout the world.

Well, this species of moral equivalence is now dead. The liberation of the Communist empire, the opening of the archives, the testimony of former inmates — all these have made a mockery of this version of moral equivalence.

But ideology abhors a vacuum. So we have a new version of moral equivalence: the moral convergence within Western society of the normal and the deviant. It is a bold new way to strip the life of the bourgeois West of its moral sheen. Because once it becomes, to use MacKinnon's words, "difficult to sustain the customary distinctions between pathology and normalcy," the moral superiority to which bourgeois normalcy pretends vanishes.

And the perfect vehicle for exposing the rottenness of bourgeois life is defining deviancy up. After all, the law-abiding middle classes define their own virtue in contrast to the deviant, a contrast publicly dramatized by opprobrium, ostracism, and punishment. And now it turns out that this great contrast between normality and deviance is a farce. The real deviants, *mirabile dictu,* are those who carry the mask of sanity, the middle classes living on their cozy suburban streets, abusing their children, violating their women, and harboring deep inside them the most unholy thoughts.

Defining deviancy up is a new way of satisfying an old ideological agenda. But it also fills a psychological need. The need was identified by Moynihan: How to cope with the explosion of real deviancy? One way is denial: defining real deviancy down creates the pretense that deviance has disappeared because it has been redefined as normal. Another strategy is distraction: defining deviancy up creates brand-new deviancies that we can now go off and fight. That distracts us from real deviancy and gives us the feeling that, despite the murder and mayhem and madness around us, we are really preserving and policing our norms.

Helpless in the face of the explosion of real criminality, for example, we satisfy our crime-fighting needs with a crusade against date rape. Like looking for your lost wallet under the street lamp even though you lost it elsewhere, this job is easier even if not terribly relevant to the problem at hand. Defining deviancy up creates a whole new universe of behavior to police, and – a bonus – a higher class of offender. More malleable, too: the guilt-ridden bourgeois, the vulnerable college student, is a far easier object of social control than the hardened criminal or the raving lunatic.

These crusades do nothing, of course, about real criminality or lunacy. But they make us feel that we are making inroads on deviancy nonetheless. A society must feel that it is policing its norms by combating deviancy. Having given up fighting the real thing, we can't give up the fight. So we fight the new deviant with satisfying vigor. That it is largely a phantom and a phony seems not to matter at all.

LEONARD KRIEGEL

Imaginary Others:
Blacks and Jews in New York

Is it the ultimate PC high, this way we have of casting victimization into acceptable and unacceptable modes? In the New York City I live in, suffering is no longer an evil in itself but a source of analogy. Donne's bell may toll for each of us, but before we can allow ourselves to heed its call the sound must be approved. Suffering must be made politically correct if it is to be meaningful, its victims framed not by their pain and anguish but by the extent to which that pain and anguish can be acknowledged by others.

Every man is a piece of the continent, a part of the main.

"Empowerment" is the fashionable PC word of our times, but acknowledgment is what the times demand. Ethnic successions, gender ultimatums, the right of individuals to infringe upon the larger society through graffiti or boom boxes or personal hygiene – the dissatisfied "I" demands, the politically correct listen. "Look at me!" The cry echoes throughout the city. Presence commands acknowledgment.

Even style, traditionally the domain of the young and rebellious, accepts the fiat of the politically correct and the socially acceptable. A golden ring in ear or nose is a cultural statement; graffiti and orange spiked hair are decorative arts. Yet style is neither freewheeling nor spontaneous. Style, too, must prove itself correct. It toes the line – a cautious daring, a calculating defiance.

And therefore never send to know for whom the bell tolls. It tolls for thee.

And it tolls for your moment in the New York sun. Hard times feed the city's growing sense of itself as ultimate victim in a nation of victims. And the only question we allow ourselves to ask is, whose suffering is acceptable?

Has there ever been a time when political life in New York seemed so tired and brittle? A city in which the sense of victimization is a source of identity is not going to feel very patient with the meliorative compromises of politics. Even our politicians view themselves as victims. Their world is too ordinary. Like poetry, it possesses too many real toads in too many real gardens. All choose to be victims. Dinkins and Stein, Woody and Mia, the cop on the beat and the faro dealer in the street — everyone is eager to serve. In the court of PC, to be a victim justifies the self in its manifold needs.

A buck for fear and conscience.
"I'm too proud to steal, mister," the man in the torn gray shirt says. "Can you give me something?"

Maybe it's always been like this in New York. Only now, the entire city seems to view victimization as a source of true legitimacy. The old struggle for social justice gives way to the demands of the unregenerate "I." If there is any such thing as a New York growth industry, it is the victimization we New Yorkers are willing to live with. Everyone suffers. The trick is to suffer for a purpose.

"I suffer for you," says Malamud's grocer to his young assistant. But in the city of the politically correct, Morris Bober would be forced to take a means test to prove his worth as a sufferer. And Morris would have so much in the way of competition. Politicians, opera stars, ballplayers earning five million per — all eagerly join the victim's swim. "Everybody dies," says John Garfield, playing the defiant boxer in *Body and Soul*. But not everybody dies with his sense of victimization intact.

I suffered, I was there.

A heavy black woman in her forties argues with a young Puerto Rican assistant manager in my local supermarket. They stand face-to-face outside the manager's office. The woman's hands grip the rim of a small two-wheeled shopping cart she holds in front of her as if she wanted to lift it and then smash it down like a club on the man's head. Anger visible, growing, face enveloped by a rage for justice.

Justice, Justice, shalt thou pursue.

In the shopping cart, an explosion of what looks like strands of spaghetti bursts through a torn brown paper wrapping. I bend low in my wheelchair, pretend to search for a flyer listing the weekly specials. In this New York, one trains oneself to eavesdrop on the conversations of strangers — mind plumbing for the significance of nuance, trying to decipher the twists and cuts that lie like booby traps behind shifts in tone or narrowing eyes. These two are not discussing unemployment or crime or teenage suicide or the prospects of the Mets and Yankees. Any supermarket in New York in May of 1993 is going to be a gallery of accusation and counter-accusation.

The black woman wants to return a mop she purchased six weeks earlier but has not used. The Puerto Rican assistant manager refuses to take it back. The woman's anger grows more visible. The assistant manager's demeanor grows more obdurate, his face grim, determined. The woman threatens to bring the supermarket to small claims court if he refuses to give her back the money. Lips pressed together, the assistant manager shrugs. Visibly straining for control, he stands there, determined not to be bullied by this woman.

Suddenly, he raises his hand, as if to strike her. Then he blurts out contemptuously, "You bought it six weeks ago and have no receipt!" As if voicing the objection affords him the relief of a painful boil surgically lanced, he repeats, "You bought it six weeks ago and you have no receipt! *Now* you want me to take it back."

The woman's eyes level him. If looks could kill, he is dead. Then she cries out, voice one decibel short of a scream, "It's 'cause I'm black! It's 'cause I'm black!"

Customers turn in the aisles. Just as quickly, they turn away. My own interest, which had begun to flag, is renewed. Race is the New York dimension, life in black and white. My eyes shift from woman to man. And brown.

He frowns. "It has nothing to do with your being black, lady," he says, exasperation in his voice. He has been put on the defensive. He knows it, she knows it.

"Yes, it does!" she says triumphantly. "I know."

"It's not race, lady," the assistant manager pleads, wholly on the defensive now.

"Yeah!" she says, gleefully slapping the shopping cart rim. "And I'm fucking Snow White. If I was some fucking little old Jewish lady, you'd take it back. It's 'cause I'm black. Black. I'm no little old Jewish lady. I'm black."

Mirror image absorbed, reality strikes. This exchange in a neighborhood supermarket between Puerto Rican man and black woman takes on the intimacy of an old threat. The invisible yet omnipresent Jew, this time in the shape of a "fucking little old Jewish lady," dropped like a lead weight into a confrontation between black woman and Hispanic man. No longer is this a mere squabble. Until now, the argument did not threaten. All has changed – the Jew thrust forward, the Jew card played. A shower of anger needles into rage. Rising within me, Melville's old grudge.

Memory demands witnesses. The assistant manager is my subaltern Jew in New York, symbolically singled out, like the narrator of a story by John Berryman. Only unlike "The Imaginary Jew," the person imply- ing the manager is partial to Jews is not a bullying white man in Union Square at the end of the Depression but a large black woman standing like an Old Testament Deborah in a Chelsea supermarket in 1993.

A minor incident? Admittedly. Were I to relate it to my black col- leagues at City College, it would merely embarrass them. (Embarrass most of them, anyway. Among the faculty is that racist harlequin, Leonard Jeffries, holding forth with Stephen Fetchit asininity about the Sun People and Ice People and the humanizing effects of melanin be- neath the skin.) Yet it gnaws at my mind. For days, I can focus on little else. It forces me to think about what I do not want to think about – blacks and Jews in New York.

Not *a* New York subject but *the* New York subject – and yet, the more written about, the more shrouded in nuance and accusation, the less real it is. As if blacks and Jews were simply rival claimants for the prerogatives of suffering. As if the lives of New Yorkers were lent mean- ing by an equal emotional physics, each group demanding exclusive pos- session of the mirror in which its victimization is reflected.

How difficult to look in that mirror today. Is that why this super- market encounter embodies my sense of caution in writing about blacks? Am I simply one more white liberal PC'd out on guilt, starching mind and insight with the fear that I, too, may be tattooed with the dreaded label "racist"? Is this what makes it so difficult for me to write that in today's New York, blacks seem at least as racist as they accuse whites of being? A note more and more whites in this racially obsessed city have begun to sound – but sound with caution, among themselves. Even childhood fantasies get sucked into race, echoing in the mind like those scratchy old blues records still known as "race music" in the 1930s.

And race matters, as Cornel West recently reminded us. In Princeton, where West teaches, race matters. But in New York, race overwhelms. Race is the raw energy of life in this city – structuring lives, dictating the schools to which we send our children, making suburbs of swamps and swamps of streets. Race defines our relationship to the landscape, even as we pace Melville's deck in the open air. Race echoes with tremors of the past. Jews become whites and blacks choose as the visible symbol of their rage this blood brother to Berryman's "imaginary Jew" of fifty years ago.

Racism in New York threatens to become as much a white problem as a black problem. Andrew Hacker might disagree. Since I possess neither the statistics nor the attitudinal surveys social scientists demand as "proof" of such an assertion, I can offer only a grab bag of personal observation. That is not proof, and writers are not social scientists. Nor does a lifetime in this city make me an expert on race matters.

A writer speaks for himself alone. Yet like the child who cannot help seeing that the emperor has no clothes, I, too, cannot help seeing what I see. Experience may be a casual teacher, its lessons to be approached warily. But in race matters, experience remains the only record one has. It is where one invariably begins. That woman in the supermarket may have believed she was shafted because she was black. And the imaginary Jew was somehow involved in that shafting. In her eyes, that abstraction of the ages, *the Jew,* stood behind the assistant manager's refusal to take back the mop and return her money. Invisible in a supermarket staffed by blacks and Puerto Ricans, the Jew had become her stand-in for whites in New York.

That supermarket is in a housing co-op in Chelsea built by the ILGWU, one of the last bastions of Jews in New York who "have politics" (as the cautionary phrase, tempered by still-fresh memories of McCarthy, put it back in May of 1962, when the co-op opened). The population is a curious amalgam of trade unionists and people like me and the head of the ACLU, both of whom arrived here in our twenties, determined to raise families in this city rather than join the growing white middle-class exodus to suburbia.

The union members arrived with a tradition of political activism. In their forties and fifties in 1962, they have aged with a curiously intense factionalism which, in these post-Cold War years, seems as exotic as a taste for eighteenth-century porcelain. "I'm a union man!" fiercely insists the eighty-seven-year-old who reminds me each time he sees me of how he stood shoulder to shoulder with my uncle (now dead) on Seventh Avenue when the cops rode down on furriers massed in the street as far as the eye could see in the fur strike of 1926, the horses black and brown, the cops dressed in blue. Only both cops and workers were white in 1926. An old furrier remembers how he stood with "the oppressed." Christian fundamentalists have Jesus as Lord, old Jewish radicals "the oppressed" as salvation.

Is that why first he calmly denies the existence of and then bitterly rages against black anti-Semitism? In one breath, an impassioned denial that blacks can ever be anti-Semitic; in the next, a cry of anguish, an equally impassioned *geshrei* to the sour heavens. The Cossacks, the Germans, the Poles — *they* were the anti-Semites. That blonde blue-eyed beast never roamed the streets of Harlem. Anti-Semitism is white. White.

Victims all.

And yet, he has heard it as I have heard it, that older cry, *the Jew* again singled out. Union man or not, this old man has discovered that he, too, is white. Indeed, for many blacks in this city, he has become *the* white man, definite article and all. An ironic fate, enough to make a man struggling with the shopworn euphemism "progressive" grind toothless gums together in the middle of the night. To be an "oppressor" is not the destiny he and his kind envisioned back in 1926. That God he has spent a lifetime denying not only wants the last word, he turns out to be a Woody Allen wannabe — master not of the universe but of the urban *shtick,* where life sidesteps logic for the perverse depths of the comic imagination. Blacks and Jews, Jews and blacks. Who's oppressing whom? *Gevalt!*

Life imitating politics is a subject beyond anyone's endurance. As if they were living inside the pages of a Malamud story, these old Jews keep coming back to the text, rereading lines, seeking connections. Do Italian-Americans or Irish-Americans or Greek-Americans in this battered city torture themselves with these endless racial permutations? Blacks and Jews, Jews and blacks. Who did what for whom? To whom? On whom? At whom?

Yet the subject demands attention. Can one conceive so distorted a view of history being made about the relationship between blacks and Koreans in Los Angeles or blacks and Cubans in Miami, as the film *The Liberators* puts forth? How striking that its creators assumed Jews would embrace the film, would love it for the sentiment behind its creation. As if the intent of "healing the rift" between blacks and Jews lent one immunity from history. Or as if suffering were worthwhile only after it was nickel-and-dimed into a high school civics lesson. If history gets in the way, then history can be altered. *The Liberators* is spiritual Krazy Glue, meant to rebind blacks and Jews to each other. Dance off into the sun, children.

Together again.

But history as a morality play is either childishly silly or blatantly obscene. As if the purpose of those fleshed skeletons were an hour of brotherhood talk at the Apollo. "Don't talk me no brother talk!" cries the boy in Shirley Clark's *The Cool World*. Smart boy. Reality is simpler than brother talk. Blacks and Jews during the Second World War each had enough *tsooris*. They were, after all, blacks and Jews. They didn't need to serve as the other's savior. To believe that one can react to those skeletal bodies with a celebration of brotherhood is the most blatant obscenity of all.

Even for the politically correct, fear is a reality reminder. The reaction of a Jew to the Holocaust — even one of those PC *gauleiters* trying to convince himself and others that the World Trade Center bombing was a Mossad plot, alone at night with a touch of indigestion forcing him to sound the hollows of his heart — is going to be different from the reaction of a black. Just as the reaction of a black to the horrors of the Middle Passage is going to be different from the reaction of a Jew. Not that we can or should remain oblivious to the other's pain and suffering. But fifty years after the Holocaust, Jews should realize that it is one thing to blind ourselves to the fate of others by saying "never again," quite another to make history trivial by universalizing it. The Holocaust was no more or less universal than African slavery or the nightmare committed on Armenians by Turks. But it happened to Jews *because they were Jews*. That is its enduring lesson. Jews may have created Hollywood (a feat embroidered in the sinister imaginations of black academic idiots), but the cavalry never made it over the hill in time to rescue them.

One of the minor legacies of our insistence on political correctness is that in the "gorgeous mosaic" of David Dinkins's city, social problems are personal problems. One offers group suffering on the altar of PC. Virtue and vice are sanitized and made acceptable, while the suffering, we tell ourselves, holds us together. But the reality of life in this city suggests different agendas. The fate of blacks and Jews is no longer tied together, nor does there any longer exist a political symbiosis between the groups. But each side continues to have expectations of the other. "If blacks behaved like Jews," another of those aging union men tells me in the street, finger fronting me like a mugger's pistol, "they would be a lot better off." We are forever instructing the other's *them*. And if the other refuses to listen, we assume disaster — for *them* and for us.

A few months ago, I sent an essay about my love affair with the American South to an editor who, like me, is a Jew from the Bronx. Accepting the essay, the editor wondered why it contained nothing about blacks. Didn't I realize blacks were Southerners, too? The question caught me off guard. I had simply never thought of blacks as Southerners.

I knew, of course, that the culture blacks carried to New York was rooted in the South, just as I knew that the Eastern European Yiddish *shtetl* had provided the rhythms to which I and my friends danced into adulthood. But cultural lineage didn't make us Eastern Europeans any more than cultural lineage makes blacks Southerners. New York conditions its offspring to take what they are given, however raw and angry and filled with grievance what they are given makes them. Then it teaches them to thrust their idea of self into what they have taken. New Yorkers are forever choosing up sides on issues. "Getting even," we called it as children. Is today's city merely a showcase for blacks and Jews to get even with each other? Is the meaning of suffering to be reduced to what is or is not considered politically correct at a particular moment?

The blacks I knew were New Yorkers, not Southerners. Like me, they wanted different fates. Memories of race matters root to memories of physical resurrection. Between September 1946 and May 1950, I was taken twice each week in a station wagon into the heart of Harlem, for physical therapy at the Joint Disease Hospital on Madison Avenue and 123rd Street. The driver of that wagon, Mr. Cooper, was a black man in his mid-fifties, who smoked cigars and drove cautiously.

Every Monday and Wednesday morning, the leftist pieties of my adolescence were tested by Mr. Cooper's anger toward his fellow blacks. "Damn loafers!" he would testily mutter, eyes splaying a group of boys and young men hanging out on a street corner. Like a hooked trout webbed in the terror of my crippledness – a fat adolescent with useless brace-bound legs being driven through streets threatening him not because they were filled with dark people but because those people, like the people in his Bronx neighborhood, could walk and run and jump – I took it upon myself to serve as defender of the blacks.

A fat crippled Jewish adolescent transforming himself into an imaginary normal – can one conceive of a more natural role for a New Yorker? And why not me? God knows, I had enough time on my hands to argue the case of those "damn loafers" with Mr. Cooper. Society had lined its heavy guns up against those boys; they were correct in assuming they were going nowhere; he himself was giving aid and comfort to the enemy. Throughout my tirade, Mr. Cooper would sneer at me. Then he would smile and blow smoke out the driver's window. "I'm a Republican, boy," he would say, a signal he had heard enough from me as defender of the blacks. Enraged, I shut up.

Oh, my America, my new found land.

"Mulatto" is no longer an acceptable word in the city of the politically correct. But it was a word whites and blacks both used in 1948,
when my physical therapy consisted of swimming for half an hour in a
heated pool and then lying on a tile slab, submitting my polio-ravaged
dead legs to the finger-subtle touch of a beautiful copper-haired
"mulatto" therapist whose NYU class ring hung like life's promised
medallion in her cleavage, nipples outlined in the wet gray bathing suit.
My session with my therapist was over by noon. But the station wagon
didn't pick me up for the trip back to the Bronx until 3:00.

Winter afternoons would find me in the hospital lobby, fantasizing
about Mrs. R. or else reading pulp magazines and historical novels that
allowed me to dream of different Mrs. R.'s (white, black, yellow – my
fantasy life formed its own rainbow coalition). In search of those fantasies, I would burrow myself near the office where hospital social workers interviewed young black mothers holding onto their small children.
They were no more capable of paying for the services the state rendered
them than my own mother was. During the spring and fall (therapy was
not offered to outpatients in summer), I would wander to Mount
Morris Park across Madison Avenue or to the drugstore on 124th Street.
I talked to old black men on park benches and those young black
"loafers" hanging out at the drugstore luncheonette.

Victims together.

A curious osmosis, this assumption of imaginary blackness.
Sometimes, a patrol car would cruise through the street and I would instinctively stiffen with fear. Wedged against a lamp post on my braces
and crutches, body rigid, as if I were a suspect in a movie lineup being
filmed by one of Leonard Jeffries's invidious Hollywood Jews. A crippled
white adolescent was the last person in the world who had anything to
fear from cops in Harlem. I knew that. But so what? Imaginary men
learn to suspend disbelief.

"*I yam what I yam,*" says the narrator of *Invisible Man*. Three years
before Ellison's great novel was published, I chorused my own very personal "Amen!" to that.

To become an imaginary other is to assume the weight of the other's fantasies, even when those fantasies are conspiratorial. It happens to
blacks who assume knowledge of *the Jews;* it happens to Jews who as -

sume expertise on what *they* want. By reading ourselves into the other, we read the other out of existence. Imagining the other, blacks and Jews, serve the cause of their own sense of victimization.

For it is suffering itself which has now become politically correct in this city. There was a time when we New Yorkers were expected to re - sist suffering, our own and everybody else's. Today, we seek to create the hegemonies of suffering with which to battle against each other's claims. "I suffered, I was there!" is turned into, "We suffered, we are here!" An added codicil: "You had better acknowledge our suffering." As if suffering is definition. Even in PC-land, suffering must have its limits. Why make it the defining aspect of any group's humanity?

Neither professors of pigmentation at City College nor that middle-aged woman in my local supermarket are the first blacks to find in the imaginary Jew the demonic presence behind black problems in New York. "Georgia has the Negro and Harlem has the Jew," Baldwin wrote around the time I was fantasizing about my mulatto therapist and pursuing my own imaginary blackness in Mount Morris Park. In the years to come, Baldwin himself would move uncomfortably close to framing the Jew as the source of black difficulty in New York. "The Jew, in America, is a white man," he decided. In Baldwin's eyes, white was sin enough, the one color beyond the rainbow.

Georgia may no longer have the Negro, but Harlem still has the Jew. And not merely Harlem. The imaginary Jew is a decisive presence in the minds of so many black New Yorkers, from that middle-aged woman in my local supermarket to the "activist" Sonny Carson and the lawyer Alton Maddox and the preacher Al Sharpton. If there are still Jews – not all of them aged trade unionists – who guard their vision of "the oppressed" with a passion so fierce they simply cannot admit, either to themselves or to others, that black anti-Semitism exists, there are considerably larger numbers of Jews who now look at blacks as their Italian-American and Irish-American and Greek-American peers look at them – from a distance made even more formidable by fear and suspicion.

Obsessed with the imaginary other, Jews and blacks nurture not the actual other but the other's image. A curious legacy of looking in the mirror to see how the other carries his pain. By now, the reflection in that mirror has grown distorted. And there is something tired in all those voices demanding exclusive possession of that mirror, just as there is something tired in those endless discussions of what blacks and Jews "owe" each other. If we owe each other anything, it is not political correctness. It is honesty.

One begins to wonder whether blacks and Jews in New York

wouldn't be better off if they simply sought a quiet divorce. In a more optimistic racial climate, the dancer Bill Robinson called his namesake, the baseball player Jackie Robinson, "a Ty Cobb in Technicolor." Is it to be our destiny – particularly we Jews, we creators of Hollywood who have recently found ourselves drummed out of the ranks of the politically correct – to discover that black anti-Semitism is hatred in Technicolor? Or that Jewish racism is hatred in black and white?

New racial permutations may pass the test of PC, but they will soon prove as empty as the old. Blacks and Jews would be doing themselves and this city a favor simply by refusing to imagine the other. Isn't it time both groups sought that benign yet skeptical indifference which Freud – himself now so politically incorrect – speaks of as true maturity? Faced with the prospect of seeing the other, warts and all, perhaps both blacks and Jews can finally learn to say "Enough already!" A little slack in the rope is probably the best blacks and Jews can offer each other in 1993. And politically correct or not, distance rather than justification is all that each of us has finally earned from the other.

EDITH KURZWEIL

Political Correctness in German Universities

Multiculturalism in Germany is different from multiculturalism in America, and what in America is subsumed under "politically correct" does not exist there, at least not yet. Instead, German concerns about taking correct positions are always about avoiding the pitfalls of another totalitarianism. Thus by using such terms indiscriminately we tend to jump to faulty conclusions. Basically, in America, an immigrant country, so-called multiculturalism started in the universities, whereas in Germany, a more homogenous country, it is rooted in political culture; in America it ends up celebrating ethnic differences, whereas in Germany it describes and attempts to solve the problem of integrating foreign nationals into the mainstream. Thus PC in America is a negative force, whereas in Germany it could be a positive one. But when professors and the media focus on the similarities alone, they – deliberately or unintentionally – confuse the public, sometimes to promote their own political biases.

For instance, an article in a special issue (March 1993) of *Der Spiegel,* Germany's lively, left-oriented equivalent of *Newsweek* or *Time,* misconstrues what goes on in American universities. There, an American (Hungarian-born and "politically correct") political scientist, Andrei Markovits, enthuses about the inordinate success of our system of higher education. He highlights its openness, range of options, diversity, and endless versatility; he describes "the feminization and totally transformed discourse since the 1970s," the visible multiculturalization even of our most respected intellectual stronghold, Harvard; and he praises dedicated American professors and their eager students. By totally ignoring our widespread public polemics about the sorry state of student achievement – that many students manage to get degrees for little more than "life experiences," and the fact that standards in general have reached an all-time low – he appears to ignore the *Spiegel* study's aim; that is, to rank universities in line with students' achievements and "satisfaction." For in the preface the editors state: "The German university is growing and growing – and keeps getting weaker. Semester after semester classes get larger; professors are discouraged or can't meet demands and flee into research. Possible solutions to the misery have been debated for years, so far without success." *Der Spiegel* initiated a complicated rating scheme of professors by students and colleagues, of conditions deemed optimal by professors, and of learning situations deemed acceptable in the various disciplines, in order to determine which of the sixty-nine German universities might serve as models for the rest of them.

Professor Markovits, however, started out by contrasting the alleged glories of American universities to our elitist, expensive and inadequate health care system, our unmanageable bureaucracy, our weak business enterprises, economy and party structure, and our neglected cities and families, which, he assures us, President Clinton and his team will fix – despite "twelve years of neglect, brutality and cynicism." Although he supplies the top twenty-five American rankings (of our 3,600 institutions), he declares at the outset that ranking has been "fetishized . . . into its use as a commodity just like most things in our capitalist economy," and thus avoids assessing what he is asked to rank – that is, optimal conditions for student learning. By rejoicing that the "anti-intellectual days of Reagan-Bush cynicism and their neglect of the university system are gone," and failing to question how the inordinate successes he describes could have occurred during that time, Markovits also undercuts his own argument. Ultimately, he trusts that President Clinton will listen ever more attentively to our professors, and will appoint them (including Markovits?) to Cabinet-level positions.

I have given the gist of this long article because it is the only one on America in this potpourri of German surveys, and the only one on a positive note. It also demonstrates that an American professor – this time one of the politically correct variety – can be put (accidentally or purposefully) into the position of influencing policy in another society. Certainly, most *Spiegel* readers cannot know Markovits's aims, even if they may be puzzled by the fact that German students when admitted to U.S. universities get advanced placement or know more than their privileged American-educated classmates – in languages, mathematics and nearly every other field.

Superficially, professors' and students' complaints are as interchangeable as Visiting Professorships. Yet because German professors read *Der Spiegel* and also American academic journals, I was asked during a recent stay in Berlin to advise them on "doing the politically correct thing." "God forbid," I quipped, before beginning to explain that their helplessness in "correctly" integrating "foreigners" and "asylum seekers" from many cultures can in no way be compared to what is subsumed in America as "political correctness," such as the antics of a Leonard Jeffries, some of the textual exegeses by literary scholars, or the public accusations of sexual harassment made by a former assistant of a nominee to the American Supreme Court.

Clearly, the instant domestication of what happens elsewhere on the globe, of unique, often freakish and variform happenings, of industrial leaps and inventions via media packaging, and the general bent to instantly translate events in other cultures by generalizing from our own – a practice we unconsciously emulate as we watch the nightly news – tends to simplify, distort and assume that we comprehend what we often misunderstand. Thus we downplay the influence selective reports may superimpose onto the perceptions (or even the policies) of well-meaning people in other countries. For within our own cultures we all know more or less what underlying assumptions our intellectuals and commentators share or dispute. But we are less savvy in assessing those of other nationals.

That is the primary reason why Germans (and others) are bound to miss the hidden component of what has become a shorthand for a concatenation of political stances, in the case of "political correctness." That the connections among the culture and the university, the culture *of* the university, and political and economic culture everywhere, vary in line with traditions and institutional linkages, nevertheless makes for amalgams that frequently defy distinctions. And because professors are entitled to make connections of thought as well as of substance, meanings get mixed up, and differences are ever harder to discern. Yet, comparisons of specific, concrete problems emanating from each society are needed as heuristic devices, or as road maps, to explain matters to the uninitiated. Inevitably, on both sides of the Atlantic, though differently, simplistic conceptions of East versus West, such as Kohl-Reagan versus Brandt-Honecker or Schmidt-Honecker, though pushed into the collective unconscious by the original euphoria of the "victory" of democracy over Communism, have a way of hanging on both in the so-called left and the right.

Because nearly all German universities are state institutions (the state – at the *Länder* levels – not only finances them but is involved in such matters as professorial appointments, et cetera), they are entrusted with a more immediate responsibility for the evolution of both intellectual and political culture than are their American counterparts. This direct link to government, though infused on every level with mediating input, with bureaucratic and financial manipulation, and with specific, personal histories, nevertheless holds faculty members and administrators more immediated instead of "reunification," because this de facto situation is assumed and discussed as the temporary evil nearly everyone hopes to eradicate: it avoids implying that the former Bundesrepublic [BDR] dominates the former German Democratic Republic [GDR].) As it is, even the most dedicated and insightful German professor, while trying to do the right thing in the true, practical sense, also brings along his or her former political baggage, his or her long-held "right-leaning" or "left-leaning" convictions and disillusions. Like professors everywhere, they are expected to arouse the students' moral conscience, to help turn them into trustworthy and active citizens who will ensure the survival of democratic culture.

Nowhere did I hear anyone suggest that professors help "make the world safe for democracy." But this is precisely what the debates are all about, what the professoriate is expected to accomplish, even though in the former West academics had been sharply divided between the Christian Democratic Union (CDU) and the Social Democrats (SPD), and in the East had been employed by the Unity Party (SED) to "make the world safe for communism," or for what its promise had become. As we know, the euphoria following the demise of the GDR was symbolized by the storming of the Berlin Wall (actually a strip of no man's land and a bulwark, reinforced with electrified barbed wire and manned by strutting soldiers), and institutionalized by Chancellor Kohl's management of the so-called *Wende* – which the growing number of detractors liken to annexation. But whatever it was, and whether or not it could have been better handled through delay, arranged more equitably, or with fewer negative consequences, is a moot issue. Germany is reunited. Now, Germans not only are forced to deal with the economic consequences – with massive unemployment, the absorption of hordes of immigrants into the West from the GDR, Poland, Turkey and further East, as well as with the repatriation of German nations, some of whom don't even speak German – but also with *their* multiculturalism. In the process not only the Communist utopia but all utopia is being repudiated – because the long-desired freedom instead of bringing greater riches has introduced new insecurities, along with other languages, cultures and competitors.

As noted by the sociologist Hermann Strasser of the University of Duisburg (which was ranked as number one in the *Spiegel* survey), multiculturalism is the result of immigration and immigrants are part of German reality. However, unlike America or Israel, Germany for years has granted residency without citizenship to its immigrant work force. Thus many workers have been in the country for a few decades, have German-born children but continue to be Turkish or Polish nationals. As long as unemployment did not loom as large – that is, until the *Wende* –

ethnic unrest was kept within bounds, or remained an issue that did not result in the sort of violence that reminds Germans of the hatred that allowed for their culpability in the Holocaust, for the murderous impulses many are seeing resurge in the violence against foreigners. Whereas Professor Strasser tries to analyze the increase in arson by the new breed of skinheads (especially against Turks) which the government so far has been able more or less to control, and describes the (admittedly limited) political options, writers address the prevalent cultural malaise. The Swiss-German writer, Urs Widmer, in *Der Freibeuter* (#55, 1993), states the pervasive sentiments rather elegantly:

> Now that houses inhabited by Turks or Vietnamese are burning, those who speak of hating people with different skin color, who speak another language, have other rituals of prayer and other histories, run the danger of closing the door upon our listeners. Good will and moral assurances no longer are enough. . . . Each of us in our own way has thoughts of the foreign within us, and we are aware of how strongly we are capable of projecting our anxieties, dislikes, dreams and desires. "You black – I white!" We know how relieving such a process of splitting can be, and how questionable. "We" are not the ones to set fires. We don't even watch you with approval from far away. . . . But what do we make of the multicultural confusion that too frequently remains a monocultural proximity? . . . We too are swimming in an ocean of fears and are trying, rather helplessly, not to drown.

Professors and students in German universities, in every discipline, share these fears. Some of the children of "established" immigrants as well as those of asylum seekers are in their classes. In addition, professors in the former West are expected to help reeducate their colleagues from the former East. (That many of the latter lost their jobs and are being replaced by more competent "Wessies" is yet another major issue for conflicts.) But even if it were possible to transform into cosmopolitan polymaths people accustomed to rigid Marxist thinking after decades of being deprived of all other texts, how could professors deal with and explain the inevitable clashes brought about by the ferocious competition for jobs that often don't exist and for apartments most people no longer can afford – at a time when wages have become totally inadequate to ensure survival and Communism has turned out to have been a nightmare rather than nirvana?

The future of Germany is particularly frightening due to the ideological and emotional remnants of the Nazi past. Whereas citizens in the former West were pushed to deal with this past, however inadequately, their counterparts in the former GDR never came to terms with it. Now, they are expected to do so while, simultaneously, facing their considerable compromises with the totalitarian aspects of Communism. How this will be done, in what for them is central to their "political correctness," remains an open and much-debated question. Since it apparently had been almost impossible to escape cooperating with the immense net of the secret police (Stasi), citizens – and university professors among them – have to confront the consequences of their former collusion before they can become productive, democratic individuals. The recent firebombings and other terrorist behavior by the far right, which obviously needs to be fought on *all* levels, have induced fear and paranoia, denunciations of the government and its leaders. This new type of terrorism does indeed require urgent attention and legislation. Although all Germans are quick to blame the government in Bonn for not stopping these frightening incidents, university professors as well are expected to help eradicate them.

The universities themselves, as the *Spiegel* study demonstrates, are as much the problem as the solution. Already in a previous survey, in 1989, German universities' rankings were exceedingly differentiated by both students and professors, and it had been considered imperative by all that classes nearly everywhere – become smaller and students receive more attention. Instead, the reverse has happened. Once again, it seems, younger universities fare better than older ones, and smaller ones better than larger ones; the natural sciences and technical subjects are in better shape than the humanities and social sciences; and most students study for too many years and under anomic conditions. Among them, students in the former GDR rank lowest. The most pessimistic of the *Spiegel* experts maintain that German universities cannot ever be reformed.

What is to be done in view of the fact that German society must rely upon these universities to teach citizens from both sides of the former Wall the necessary tolerance for cooperation, as well as the skills for evolving technocratic jobs? In what way can change be brought about without having it come from administrators who themselves are from the former West and thus will be attacked as enforcing democracy by authoritarian methods? How will it be possible, as Professor Strasser asks, to build upon the *nation* as "the mightiest moving force in all of history," to forge the necessary social bonds, interpersonal warmth and cultural roots that make for cooperation, while at the same time nurturing tolerance of the other in the multicultural society Germany – however unconsciously – already has been for some time?

Inevitably, to be politically correct in Germany means to integrate immigrants, to create what in America used to be called a melting pot. Germans and "strangers" as well appear to realize that this cannot happen at the expense of Western cultural traditions, either by replacing the former communist enemy with fundamentalist Islam, by decree from above, by turning the country into a vast counterculture, or by the McDonaldization of the world. In 1813, the German writer Moritz Arndt declared that "the German Fatherland is wherever the German tongue is heard." Now, however, other languages and other nationals will have to be granted equal status. We can only hope that this will happen before gangs of skinheads attack more innocent Turks and other foreigners, before hatred engulfs a society that over the past forty-five years has been building an exemplary democracy. But what the Germans do not need is to import our version of political correctness.

MARY LEFKOWITZ

Multiculturalism, Uniculturalism, or Anticulturalism?

Not long ago a student I'd never seen before walked into my office and said to me politely, "I hear you're against multiculturalism." It turned out that she was working as an assistant to a local television producer, who was eager to interview people who were opposed to Afro-American studies. She had heard (though she hadn't read it herself) that I'd published an article in *The New Republic* that (as she put it) attacked Afrocentric historians. I explained to her that in fact I fully supported the idea of studying the history of Africa, ancient and modern, and had voted for Wellesley's multicultural requirement, which asks students to take one course of their choice about a non-European culture. After a pleasant chat about her work with the television producer, I gave her a copy of the *New Republic* article and never heard from her again.

At the time I didn't think much about this incident, but in retrospect it seems highly representative of the central issues in the multicultural debate. What exactly do people mean by "multicultural"? The student equated the terms "multicultural" and "Afrocentric," whereas I understood "multicultural" to mean "learning about many different cultures." For the student, at least, multiculturalism was not simply a general commitment to making the curriculum more inclusive. Evidently she associated the term with the particular "culture" that she (and her producer or the producer alone) wanted to promote.

But although I think university curricula and the syllabi of individual courses should become more inclusive of subjects and points of view that have traditionally been excluded or ignored, I wish the proponents of particular interest groups or "cultures" would use a term other than "multicultural" to describe what they have in mind. For it seems clear to me from my conversation with the student and with some of my colleagues, that "multicultural" to them really means "unicultural," and even "anticultural," when the cultures involved are those that have traditionally been studied in university curricula.

Since uniculturalists think of themselves as multiculturalists, it is perhaps not surprising that they suspect that the inclusive multiculturalism that I have been talking about is merely a facade for my own brand of uniculturalism. Thus recently, on a radio program, Molefi Kete Asante explained to the audience that I had built a career on promoting the superiority of Greek and Roman civilizations. Presumably Asante thought that I was using the same methods that he and other Afrocentric writers have been, to demonstrate through research the superiority of African cultures. In *Kemet, Afrocentricity and Knowledge,* Asante rightly states that "a proper attitude toward human discovery and human knowledge depends on views that do not cast aside others' ways of thinking." But at the same time he argues that Afrocentric methodology is not only different, but also more effective than Eurocentric methods. According to Asante, "Africalogists" depend on the "soul of method," which works from matter outward and does not depend on prior classifications, like much European thought. "Soul of method" enables researchers to focus on what is natural, rhythmic, and organic. Eurocentric thought, by contrast, imposes structures and prejudices, and thus leads to misapprehension. There is considerable truth in Asante's general observations, but to be fair to Europeans, he should also point out the positive side of classification, categories and structures, which provide the underpinning for philosophical and scientific thought, and, indirectly, of all scientific progress.

In discussions of political organization of societies, it is possible to discern a similar tendency to point out what is good about Africa and bad about Europe, but not what is good about Europe and bad about Africa. Clinton Jean, in *Behind the Eurocentric Veils,* describes how African "values" permit people to live together in greater social harmony than in Europe, with its class struggle and interest group politics. African warfare, Jean argues, was ritualized, culminating in peaceful exchange of bodies and of gifts. Surely everyone on earth could profit from adopting the traditions of the Kung, who avoid war because it is dangerous and depend instead on expert defusers of quarrels. But there are also African practices everyone would be better off avoiding, such as the violent antagonism between the sexes among the Kamba and Pokot of Kenya. African religious beliefs, however differently expressed, can be just as damaging to their adherents as those of any Western religion, as in the case of the prophecy which led the Xhosa in the mid-nineteenth century to kill all their cattle.

It is possible to respond to my objections to uniculturalism by arguing that European historians from Herodotus to the present have treated their own civilizations as the norm, against which the civilizations of foreigners may be compared, usually unfavorably. In a famous passage, Herodotus writes that because the Egyptians have a sky and a river different from those of other peoples, "they have established for themselves customs and laws different from those of other human beings; for instance, women buy and sell in the marketplace, and the men sit at home and weave." In *The Disuniting of America* Arthur Schlesinger, Jr. argues for the superiority of Western civilization by mentioning African customs that would seem particularly obnoxious to his readers, like female cir-cumcision. But how can the damage done by writing with a pro-European bias be undone by African writers adopting the same tech-niques against Europe? Certainly it makes better sense to follow Asante's advice and try "not to cast aside" other peoples' ways of thinking, but rather to understand and appreciate them in their full social context.

It is also possible to remark in these discussions a tendency to gen-eralize about the whole on the basis of a selection of parts. Understandable as this practice may be, when such wide-ranging topics are under discussion, the result is rhetoric rather than history. Is it really possible to deduce, on the basis of a few remarkable customs such as those described by Herodotus, that the Egyptians are fundamentally dif-ferent from other people in all respects? If in Egypt men carried burdens on their heads, and women used their shoulders (in contrast to the stan-dard practice in Greece), what can that observation tell us? It can be used as evidence that Egyptian women had greater freedom to move about than Greek women, and that they could own property. But such a difference in custom cannot be used to argue that Egyptian minds worked differently from those of Greeks. Certainly Herodotus did not think so.

But arguments about differing "mentalities" are frequently produced as an argument for unilateral multiculturalism. As we have seen, Asante believes that as a result of their different customs, Africans think about their relation to objective reality differently from Europeans. In some respects, as Asante argues, this "African" notion that mankind is con-nected with the world, rather than set apart from it, will be advanta-geous; it could, for example, suggest that Africans instinctively had a greater respect for the environment than Europeans, and closer bonds to their immediate communities. But it also could be used to imply that Africans were unlikely to practice or instinctively uninterested in "classifying," that is, uninterested in scientific thought – a premise which is demonstrably untrue.

Rather than examine the premise on which such arguments are based, those of us who find ourselves on the defensive side of the multi-cultural debate too often respond to our opponents' arguments simply by denying that we are doing what we have been accused of. For exam-ple, when Asante stated that I had built a career on pointing out the su-periority of the Greeks, I replied that I was not trying to say that those civilizations were superior but rather interesting and significant, and that it would be hard for any modern person to applaud certain of their practices, such as the Athenian treatment of women and of slaves.

In calling attention to some of the flaws in the civilization I have spent my life studying, I was doing nothing unusual. Since the early seventies classical scholars have become increasingly interested in the "non-canonical" texts that were not on our graduate school reading lists: fourth-century speeches about contested wills and the lives of prostitutes, letters of ordinary people describing domestic crises, and the like. More work has been done on the history of women in the last twenty years than in all the centuries preceding. As a result, classicists can now present a picture of the ancient world that is at once more complete and therefore more honest than any that were presented in the past. Classical scholars readily acknowledge that many qualities nineteenth-century European scholars admired in the Greeks were basically reflections of the values of their own society and had little or no basis in ancient reality. In recent years, for example, it has been shown that even the Greek aristocrats did not compete in the games simply for the joy of amateur competition, as had long been supposed. The prizes offered even in the minor games made victory worthwhile in financial terms.

But to admit, or rather to advertise, that the Greeks shared the faults of other peoples, had a low as well as a high culture, and criminals as well as statesmen, is not a reason for removing the study of Greek civilization from the curriculum. Such limitations as they had are not unique or peculiar to Europeans: as we have seen, certain African peoples also practice misogyny. Yet in the process of cutting the Greeks down to size, it has become possible and even natural to lose sight of the qualities for which their civilization has justifiably been prized by later European societies. It is in this sense, I would argue, that the uniculturalism known as "multiculturalism" is also anti-cultural, because the claims in favor of cultures that have not been included in the curriculum are almost always made at the expense of the cultures on which European education has tended to concentrate.

This new anticulturalism has led to absurd claims that are easily refuted: that Europeans are "ice" people, cold, calculating, and destructive, and Africans are "sun" people, warm, natural, and peaceful; that Plato and Aristotle "stole" their philosophy from Egypt, when there is no ancient evidence that the Egyptians might have produced philosophical discourses that the Greek philosophers might have copied. But anticulturalism also encourages more subtle attacks on Greek "values" that can be substantiated by partial presentation of the evidence, or by citations

taken out of context. For example, some have interpreted as an illustration of Athenian misogyny the metopes on the Parthenon that depict
the defeat of the Amazons by the Athenian hero Theseus, as examples of
men defeating women who try to behave like men. That argument has
attractions, but only if other possibilities are ignored. Why not suppose
that the Amazons represent the East, especially if the Parthenon celebrates
the triumph of Athens over the Persians? And how are we to interpret
the depiction on the Parthenon of the Lapiths defeating the Centaurs?
Using the line of reasoning that represents Amazons as women, it would
be possible to argue that the Greeks despised horses – when in fact they
valued them highly.

Anticulturalism has also led to some bizarre reconstructions of the
history of European religion. The Olympian gods are believed to be the
inventions of male invaders, replacing the indigenous Mother Goddess of
the Aegean. The principal evidence for this claim is the Greek myth of
creation, in which the Goddess Earth comes into being before the male
gods. But again, it is equally possible to argue that it is only natural for
the myth to give priority to the female, since it is the female who gives
birth. The revisionist interpretation of the ancient myth, although perhaps more persuasive for being crude and schematic, prevents modern
readers from actually seeing what the ancient poet has written in favor of
females: in all the stories of father-son rivalry among the gods, it is the
goddesses who intercede and restore justice and order, and the god who
manages to remain in power, Zeus, does so in large part by giving the
various goddesses powers and honor. The female is always subordinate,
but the force of her moral reasoning cannot be ignored, nor can her
ability to upset world order by withholding her power to create life.

Since anticultural views have obscured the positive aspects of the
treatment of women in ancient Greek society, it seems almost natural to
countenance and even to believe many unwarranted criticisms, and to
undervalue or to overlook some of the Greeks' most astounding and
original contributions. In retrospect, before insisting that I did not think
that the Greeks were "superior" to other civilizations, I should have
asked Professor Asante whether superiority was in fact the issue. Ancient
Greek civilization has been included in the curriculum not because it has
been judged to be superior to Egyptian or any other African civilization.
Rather, the Greeks have been included in the curriculum because their
ideas have made a lasting contribution to later European civilization.

True multiculturalism (as opposed to uni- or anticulturalism) would
then require us to try objectively to appreciate them and their achievements, to praise or criticize different aspects of their legacy to us, and to

point out that they are like us in some ways, and very unlike us in others. For one thing, the ancient Greeks did not think of themselves as Europeans, since Europe literally had not yet come into existence. According to the myth, Europa, the Phoenician woman for whom the continent was later named, only got so far as the island of Crete. Until the conquests of Alexander, their notion of the civilized world extended only as far west and north as Sicily and Italy. What we think of as "European" civilization derives from the Christian Roman Empire.

Almost certainly the Greeks' most important accomplishments could not have taken place if their religion had been monotheistic and had codified in writing correct and incorrect ways of thinking, like the Jews and after them the Christians. The Greeks' polytheistic religion permitted them to question the behavior of gods, and to account for conflicts and problems by supposing that one god's plans had been opposed by another. It is here – in the nature of Greek religion – that we should look for an explanation of "the Greek achievement," since it is a religion that encouraged inquiry. By asking questions about traditional stories about the gods, known as myths, the Greeks came to ask questions about how the world came into being and about the origins of mankind, and to provide different and conflicting answers to their questions. The Greek word *historia* literally means "inquiry," and what Herodotus wanted to find out is how the Greeks came to quarrel with their Eastern neighbors.

The Greeks were not the only people who have in the course of history developed democracies, but they were the first people to theorize about the best systems of government. This kind of abstract theorizing is perhaps their most distinctive achievement. Here as in many other cases the Greeks could not have developed their theories without the work of their predecessors. The complex arithmetical and mathematical calculations on which Greek theories were based were invented by Egyptians and the Babylonians, but it was the Greeks who articulated the abstract principles behind them. Similarly, although surely other Aegean peoples had spoken persuasively and eloquently, it was the Greeks who developed and taught the art of rhetoric, which is arguably their most lasting legacy to Western civilizations. They gave names to the figures of speech and oratorical techniques that are still in use today.

If the discussion is framed in this way, so as to focus on analyzing and defining the nature of European civilization, it will be clear why the Greeks are included in the curriculum and why they ought to stay there. It probably is also necessary to add that one does not come to understand European cultural values simply by being European, but rather that one needs to assess the virtues and limitations of the European heritage by subjecting it to extensive study and criticism. In the process, it would be fair to ask whether the present debate about the meaning of multiculturalism could ever have taken place without the ancient Greeks and their legacy of inquiry and discussion. We could also learn from them that the ultimate value of the inquiry is the discussion, not any one particular answer to a particular question.

"I know," says Glaucon in Plato's *Republic*, "that [this ideal republic] exists in words, but I do not think it will ever be found on earth." "No," replies Socrates, "but it exists as a model in the sky for anyone who wants to see it and after seeing it to found one himself. It doesn't matter whether or not it ever existed or will exist." Clearly Plato expects his audience to have learned something from the exercise of imagining it (though it is fortunate that it has never actually come into existence, at least from the point of view of women and people in the lower strata of Plato's imaginary society). But we might never have been able so clearly to recognize and articulate its limitations if Plato had not devised his methods of inquiry. Anticulturalists try to make creations like Plato's *Republic* seem intentionally destructive, and uniculturalists would not approve of Plato's reluctance to describe and enforce the values of his ideal system. But real multiculturalism encourages the kind of debate Plato sought to foster, by promoting inquiry and discussion, and not permitting any particular point of view to prevail for very long. That's why I'm not opposed to real multiculturalism, and why I think real multiculturalism would always have a place for the Greeks.

DAVID LEHMAN

The Reign of Intolerance

Political correctness has a history: Leninists used it approvingly to indicate
proper party-line behavior, though soon enough it was used against
them to denote knee-jerk fidelity to the god that failed. The return of
the phrase suggests that people active in the resistance to the new multicultural order discern in it yet one more variant on the old Marxist-
Leninist model of radical social change.

Premise: Political correctness is to the 1980s and 1990s what fellow
traveling was to the 1930s and 1940s. Is this rhetoric, or is this truth? A
bit of both. To the extent that it is an exaggeration, the analogy suggests the intensity of the anxiety provoked by multiculturalism. ("All of
the passions lead to exaggeration," said Chamfort. "That is why they are
passions.") But the analogy does have the virtue of logically conjoining
two equally current academic phenomena: on the one hand, the battle
over free speech on campus; on the other, the prevalence on campus of a
nostalgically sentimental view of Marxism in general and "the New Left"
in particular.

In retrospect, it certainly seems that the seminal text for understanding the rise of political correctness is that New Left classic, Herbert
Marcuse's *Critique of Pure Tolerance*. According to the revolutionary
logic that countless campus cadres derived from Marcuse, tolerance was
repressive. Deconstruct ethical values and norms of conduct such as tolerance, open-mindedness, civility, and courtesy, and these would be seen
not as discourse-enabling virtues but as ruses that favor the perpetuation
of the status quo. A policy of exclusionary intolerance was one way to
trap the powers that be. The classic humanist would feel constrained to
act in a manner accommodating to his adversaries; the insurgent, committed to an adversarial posture, would feel no such obligation. The
former, by hiring the latter, would conspire in his own downfall.

What else is political correctness but a massive case of intolerance –
the inability or unwillingness to tolerate a rival point of view? The reign
of intolerance is ever in need of theoretical justification. The latest attempt has been made by the attention-grabbing Stanley Fish, in his new
book *There's No Such Thing as Free Speech, And It's a Good Thing, Too*.
Upon such a rock is founded the church of political correctness.

Political correctness stems from the drive to cast all matters of culture and intellect in political terms. Politics has triumphed in the academy to the precise degree that it is commonly accepted, without much dissent or debate, that everything from sexual behavior and the life of the nuclear family to the meaning of poems and paintings is political. Not only does everything have a political dimension; more emphatically, everything is primarily (and structurally) political before it is anything else.

Defenders of the PC faith take it for granted that they have justice on their side. They tend to sound righteous, aggrieved. "I consider 'political correctness' to be a term created by the European American far right in order to maintain its position of power and privilege in this society, a position achieved by a long legacy of racial and sexual oppression," writes Velina Hasu Houston in her introduction to *The Politics of Life,* a collection of four plays by Asian-American women. Hers is the rhetoric of special pleading, the language of victimization, and it is routinely used in committee meetings when grants and fellowships in the arts are decided. Advocates of multiculturalism act as if a discussion of merit is beside the point in the case of a candidate with the right demographic credentials. Committee members critical of a work on the ground that it is meretricious or superficial or technically incompetent are themselves denounced on the ground that they are incapable of responding to the "non-linear" thinking or the "anti-Western metaphysics" in the work in dispute. This is smokescreen talk, owing something to warmed-over Derrida and other gurus of the moment. It is meant to disguise the fact that artistic works are being judged not by real critical criteria but by something else, something resembling touchy-feely boosterism.

It is assumed that the enlightened citizen of the intellectual world is highly political in nature, strongly leftist in orientation, and willing to purchase the whole package of contemporary academic opinion with its many deep prejudices and its deconstructive bent. The citizen is enlightened, in other words, to the exact extent that he or she holds the right opinions. If that is at the heart of political correctness, it is not exactly a novel phenomenon. Flaubert anticipated it (though not the specifically political form it has taken) in his *Dictionary of Received Ideas*.

The idea of systematically subjecting opinions, political and otherwise, to standards of correctness depends on a Manichaean conception of the social world: history consists of an unbroken series of incidents pitting victims and oppressors, us and them, the enlightened and the benighted. It is not terribly sophisticated; victims and villains are substituted for the heroes and bad guys in the shoot-em-ups targeted for the preteen audience. This vision of a stark and simple dualism in the universe, this science of victimology, is one thing that Marxism has to offer. Taken together with other fashionable *isms* and *ologies* of our moment, it, the old reliable, can teach you how to line yourself up unerringly on the right side of any given issue.

There is a plethora of Marxisms on college campuses, and they differ from one another in numerous particulars, but it seems as if each of them is conceived as a speculative model rather than as a series of wretched historical cases. Spreading from the English department to the social sci-ences and law faculties, the fetish of literary theory – the popularity of the idea that everything is finally textual – has helped foster an atmo-sphere in which the adept can avoid reckoning with the historical par-ticulars that would wreck a utopian thesis. There is no truth; there is only discourse. Knowledge has little to do with fact, everything to do with theory. Thus the romance of the left has continued unabated de-spite the fall of the Berlin Wall, the collapse of Communism in Eastern Europe, and the incontrovertible proof that Marxism in practice is ru-inous economically and tyrannical politically, bringing nothing but mis-ery to the peoples who have lived under its yoke.

The romance of the left rests on that rusty old tenet of romanticism, the identification of poverty with virtue. (Poverty had previously been associated with vice, as you can see if you check the etymology of words like "scamp" and "rascal.") Mary McCarthy, in *The Groves of Academe* (1952), describes a "true liberal" as one "who could not tolerate in her well-modulated heart that others should be wickeder than she, any more than she could bear that she should be richer, better born, better look-ing than some statistical median." There is something of this sentimental-ity in the behavior of the politically correct – as in, for example, their well-documented, much-lampooned deployment of euphemisms, which work by a process of linguistic wish-fulfillment, obfuscating inconvenient facts, so that "fat" becomes "circumferentially challenged" and "handicapped" turns into "handicapable." The speed with which the politically correct bureaucrat will reach for a euphemism – or for the censor's scissors – argues a certain belief in the power of words, of rhetoric. Whoever controls the discourse, controls everything: the influ-ence of Michel Foucault has been as considerable as that of Jacques Derrida.

A generous view: when idealism goes academic it turns into ideol-ogy, and when ideology hardens into doctrine, political correctness re-sults. The road to political correctness is paved with good intentions. A severe view: it is a symptom of bad faith and inauthenticity and should be treated within the larger context of the "treason of the clerks." An ironist's view: the use of "diversity" to describe the politically charged atmosphere on college campuses proves the deconstructionist's point that a word can mean its own opposite. An educational reformer's view: political correctness is part and parcel of the entire syndrome of academic snobbism, the fear of being wrong, the terror of associating with one's intellectual inferiors. Academics decry hierarchies but have an acute awareness of them, precisely because their own institutional structures are among the most hierarchical in our society. The desire to please one's powerful elders comes as second nature to climbers of tenure ladders. If you really want to strike at the very roots of political correctness, begin with a system that reduces assistant professors to sniveling grovelers — scrap tenure.

Premise: "correctness" has more to do with conformity than with a sense of rectitude. It is curious that the urge to conform should be so strong in the land of Emerson and Thoreau. It is doubly curious that professors who want to "teach students to think for themselves" should be so susceptible to an anxiety about being (or being thought to be) different. There is very little real deviation from accepted norms of thought in the academy. The self-styled radical is in actual behavior as much an organization man as the "other-directed" members of David Riesman's *The Lonely Crowd* — a book written on the eve of the 1950s. Yet valedictorians do laud the virtues of individualism and originality, and a great hue and cry will always be made over figures who seem to embody a "new" and putatively revolutionary spirit. The mimetic compulsion assures that any true or apparent maverick will instantly be copied; that the copies will circulate with terrific speed via the technological media; and that in time the ever-proliferating copies of copies will swamp the market denuded of whatever substance inhered in the original. It is all like a media junkie's version of the parable of Plato's cave. The process turns heroes into "role models" and, in the realm of ideas, reduces convictions into theoretical propositions to be entertained and abandoned. Intellectual discussion is definitely "academic" to the precise extent that it is weightless, of no real consequence, running no risks.

When the long hair and beards of the 1960s succeeded the crewcuts and flattops of the 1950s, many thought that the change was a symbolic representation of a change in social values. When jocks of the 1970s began to sport mustaches and filled the locker room with hair dryers, it was becoming clear that the hirsute revolution signaled a change in style only. The handlebar mustache on the mug of the ace relief pitcher signified less than the mustache Marcel Duchamp contributed to the face of the Mona Lisa. But in time Duchamp's gesture was canceled out by its own ubiquitousness – it had been reduced to the status of a reproducible image, empty of meaning. The obsessive concern of American academic intellectuals with matters of style and fickle fashion seems irreversible. Back in 1972, in his essay "Discipline and Hope," Wendell Berry cited "an intellectual fashionableness" as an instance of consumer mentality. "The uniformity of dress, hair style, mannerism, and speech is plain enough," he wrote. "But more serious, because less conscious and more pretentious, is an intellectual fashionableness pinned up on such shibboleths as 'the people' (the most procrustean of categories), 'relevance' (the most reactionary and totalitarian of educational doctrines), and 'life style.' "

The resort to political considerations, in the context of the critical evaluation of works of art, implicitly devalues art, though this is not usually acknowledged in the committee rooms of foundations and government agencies. Scholars, who can afford to be somewhat more candid, will grant that the emphasis on the political goes together with an antipathy to the moral and aesthetic dimensions of experience. In advanced circles, works of art are approached as cultural "products" deemed to be of interest because they reinforce certain political suasions and tendencies. Art requires demystification. It is a front, a camouflage, diverting the concerned citizenry from some sort of power play or ploy. It is as if works of art operated on principles akin to those of television commercials: paid for, they are charged with the task of propagandizing for a particular platform. And if art is no better than and no different from an editorial or an advertisement, how else to judge it except on the basis of the message it expresses or the political gesture it makes? The subordination of art to politics, almost always a surefire prescription for artistic disaster, is the risk run by high-minded philanthropic enterprises, let alone by the attempts of clumsy bureaucrats to use art, culture, and higher education as arenas in which to pursue agendas of social justice.

The reign of intolerance and political correctness has had other consequences as well, many of them deleterious. Grade inflation by itself seems a minor enough thing to worry about until you remind yourself that it is a function of groupthink, closed-mindedness, and a priori argumentation. "A lot of grade inflation in the humanities is due to the fact that many courses now have an ideological basis," Harvard Professor William Cole observes. "Where once you had a course in, say, nineteenth-century French literature, now the course will be something like 'The Repression of Women by the Dominant Discourse of Nineteenth-

Century French Literature.' Students who enroll will all agree with its premise, that literature acts in a certain way to marginalize women. It's curious that the same academics who most vociferously promote diversity wind up with the most monolithic classrooms. The teacher is surrounded not by students but by disciples. And hey – you give your disciples A's."

Overheard on a cactus university campus: "Historically," said the graduate student, "we've gotten to the point that irony is immoral." The attitude is unfortunate, but it is easy to understand. In dreary earnest, the politically correct tend to distrust the anarchic, uncontrollable impulses of mirth and humor. Irony and wit are casualties of this distrust. But irony is also the rhetorical trope for the attempt of the mind to accommodate conflicting points of view. The very phenomenon of political correctness militates against this trope, this habit of thought. The politically correct mind has had enough of complexity, nuance, contradiction, uncertainty, irony. The politically correct mind yearns to know where it stands and would seem to be willing to put up with tyrannical limitations on its own freedom – simply in order to enjoy the satisfaction of being always in the right.

DORIS LESSING

Unexamined Mental Attitudes
Left Behind by Communism

While we have seen the apparent death of Communism, ways of thinking that were born under Communism or strengthened by Communism still govern our lives. The very first place this is evident is in our language. It is not a new thought that Communism debased language and with language, thought. There is a Communist jargon recognizable after a single sentence. Few people have not joked in their youth about concrete steps, contradictions, the interpenetration of opposites, and all the rest. The first time I saw that mind-deadening slogans had the power to take wing and fly far from their origins was in the fifties when I read a leader in the *Times* and saw them in use: "The demo last Saturday was irrefutable proof that the concrete situation . . . " Words that had been as confined to the left as corralled animals had passed into general use and, with them, ideas. One might read whole articles in the conservative and liberal press that were Marxist, but the writers didn"t know it.

There is an aspect of this heritage that is much harder to see. Even five or six years ago *Izvestia, Pravda,* and a thousand other Communist papers were written in a language that seemed designed to fill up as much space as possible without actually saying anything – because, of course, it was dangerous to take up positions that might have to be defended. Now, all these newspapers have rediscovered the use of language. But the heritage of dead and empty language these days is still to be found in some areas of academia and particularly in some areas of sociology, psychology, and some literary criticism.

Recently, a young friend of mine from North Yemen saved up, with much sacrifice, every bit of money he could to travel to that fount of excellence, Britain, to study the branch of sociology that teaches how to spread Western know-how and expertise to benighted nations. It cost him £8000, and that was five years ago. I asked to see his study material, and he showed me a thick tome, written so badly and in such ugly empty jargon it was hard even to follow. There were several hundred pages, and the ideas in it could easily been put into ten pages. This kind of book is written by people who were Marxists or have been taught by Marxists. Students come from "backward" and closed countries to be taught how to write in this debased language. I have seen people, in Zimbabwe this time, introduced to the English language in this pedantic, empty jargon. They will believe that this is the English language and that this is how they should write and speak it.

Yes, I do know the obfuscations of academia did not begin with Communism, as Swift, for one, tells us, but the pedantries and verbosity of Communism had their roots in German academia. And now it has become a kind of mildew blighting the whole world. One may spend a morning in the kind of bookshop that sells student textbooks and only with difficulty find books that are fresh and alive. How to stop this self-perpetuating machine for dulling thought? For sometimes I do see it as one of those mechanisms set to revolve forever inside a vacuum within a sealed glass case. How to break the glass and let in the air? Perhaps this will be accomplished by the ideas themselves concealed in the dead language, for they can be useful and full of insights. As I pointed out before, work is being done in the research departments of universities that could, if we let it, transform our societies. Full of insights about how the human animal actually does behave instead of how we think it does. These are often presented for the first time in unreadable language. This is one of the paradoxes of our time.

Powerful ideas affecting our behavior can be visible in brief sentences or even a phrase. All writers get asked by interviewers this question: "Do you think a writer should . . . ?" The question always has to do with a political stance. Note that the assumption behind the words is that all writers should do the same thing, whatever that may be. There is a long history behind this. Let us go no further back than the nineteenth century in Russia, where there were great critics: Belinsky, Dobrolubov, Chernyshevsky, and the rest. They wanted writers to be concerned with social problems. All the great writers that we now describe as belonging to the golden tradition of Russian literature had to endure criticism from this point of view, some of it on a very high level. Donald Fanger has noted that the Russian novel contains in itself all areas of sociology and social criticism. But I do believe that this is because this is what the writers were like and not because of what the critics were saying. As we say in Britain, "The proof of the pudding is in the eating." In all these great writers' work there is no moment when there is that dull thump that comes when writers have been writing because they felt they ought to. All these writers continued to write from a much older tradition than their critics. If a writer writes truthfully out of individual experience, then what is written inevitably speaks for other people. For thousands of years storytellers have taken for granted that their experiences must be general. It never occurred to them that it is possible to divorce oneself from life or to "live in an ivory tower." It will be seen that this view of storytelling ends the interminable debate about form and content that still bedevils literature in some provincial universities. If these writers in Russia had not claimed their right to an individual conscience rather than a collective one, we would not now be remembering and reading Gogol, Tolstoy, Dostoevsky, Chekhov, Turgenev, and all the rest of that dazzling galaxy.

We saw what happened when this formula, that writers must write about social injustice, took power in 1917. It became socialist realism. Anyone who had the misfortune to read through a lot of that stuff, which I did in London early in the fifties for a Communist publisher, knows that socialist realism created novels written in a language as dead as the books that are a product of academia. Why? Writers know instinctively that a recipe for writing dead books is to write because you ought. This is because you are writing out of a different area of your mind. I shall never forget an exchange between a writer and an interviewer on television. The interviewer said, "Among the influences that shaped your work, would you say that Heidegger was the most important?"

The writer replied, "You don't understand. When you describe a scene, let's say at the breakfast table, you have to know what your hero is eating. Bacon and eggs? Pancakes? Is it a cold morning? Is the sun shining in? Is there a smell of burning leaves? Did he sleep with his wife last night? Does she love him? What color shirt does he have on? Is the dog there waiting for tidbits? You have to know all this even if you don't describe it because this is what brings the scene to life."

"Oh, I see, then you describe yourself as a realist?"

Never the twain shall meet. And they can't meet because it's two different parts of the mind speaking. One is the critical part; the other one is the holistic part which is probably situated somewhere in the solar plexus. Two parallel lines: the writer is talking about "the fine delight that fathers thought," in Hopkins's wonderful phrase. The critic is talking out of the same spirit that pervaded socialist realism and before that the nineteenth-century Russian critics. I am sure the mindsets of Communism were patterned by religion, Christianity and the dialectics of Judaism. A biography of Cervantes tells us he had the Inquisition breathing down his neck all his life. The questions: "Should a writer. . . . Ought writers to . . . ?" have a long history that seems unknown to the people who so casually use them. Another is "commitment" – so much in vogue not long ago. Is so-and-so a committed writer? Are you a committed writer? "Committed to what?" the writer might ask.

"Oh well, if you don't know, I can't tell you," comes the reproof, full of moral one-upmanship. A successor to commitment is "raising consciousness." This is double-edged. The people whose consciousness is being raised may be given information they most desperately lack and need, may be given moral support they need. But the process nearly always means that the pupil gets only the propaganda the instructor approves of. Raising consciousness, like commitment, like political correctness, is a continuation of that old bully, the Party Line.

A very common way of thinking in literary criticism is not seen as a consequence of Communism, but it is. Every writer has the experience of being told that a novel, a story, is "about" something or other. I wrote a story, *The Fifth Child,* which was at once pigeonholed as being "about" the Palestinian problem, genetic research, feminism, anti-Semitism, and so on. A journalist from France walked into my living room and before she even sat down said, "Of course *The Fifth Child* is about AIDS." An effective conversation-stopper, I do assure you. But what is interesting is the habit of mind that has to analyze a literary work like this. If you say, "Had I wanted to write about AIDS or the Palestinian problem, I would have written a pamphlet," you tend to get bafffled stares, such an unfamiliar thought has it become. That a work of the imagination has to be "really" about some problem, is, again, an heir of socialist realism, of the infamous Zhdanov. To write a story for the sake of storytelling will not do; it is frivolous, not to say reactionary. Whole literary departments in a thousand universities are in the grip of this way of thinking, and yet the history of storytelling, of literature, tells us that there has never been a story that does not illuminate human experience in one way or another. The demand that stories must be "about" something is Communist thinking and, further back, comes from religious thinking, with its desire for improving books as simpleminded as the messages on samplers. "Little birds in their nests agree." "Good children must, good children ought, do what they are told, do what they are taught." I found that on a wall in a hotel in Wales.

If, for example, a writer should timidly remark, "My book, *Eternal Springs,* is not at all about water shortage in the Middle East," the reply is that the writer has no idea at all of what he or she is "really" writing about. A great deal has been said and is being said about political correctness, but I think we might usefully note that this is yet again self-appointed vigilante committees inspired by ideology. Of course, I am not suggesting that the torch of Communism has been handed on to the political correctors. I am suggesting that habits of mind have been absorbed, often without knowing it. There is obviously something very attractive about telling other people what to do. I'm putting it in this nursery way rather than in more intellectual language because I think it is nursery behavior, very primitive stuff. Deep in the human mind is the need to order, control, set bounds. Art, the arts in general, are always unpredictable, maverick, and tend at their best to be uncomfortable. Literature in particular has always inspired the house committees, the Zhdanovs, the vigilantes into, at best, fits of moralizing, and at worst into persecution. It troubles me that political correctness does not seem to know what its exemplars and predecessors are; it troubles me a good deal more that they may know and do not care.

Does political correctness have a good side? Yes, it does, for it makes us re-examine attitudes, and that is always useful. The trouble is that, as with all popular movements, the lunatic fringe so quickly ceases to be a fringe; the tail begins to wag the dog. For every woman or man who is quietly and sensibly using the idea to look carefully at our assumptions, there are twenty rabble-rousers whose real motive is a desire for power over others. The fact that they see themselves as antiracists, or feminists, or whatever does not make them any less rabble-rousers.

Political correctness did not invent intolerance in universities, which is an evident child of Communism. If intolerance, not to say despotism, governed universities in Communist countries, then the same attitude of mind has infected areas in the West and often sets the tone in a university. We have all seen it. For instance, a professor friend of mine describes how when students kept walking out of classes on genetics and boycotting visiting lecturers whose points of view did not coincide with the students' ideology, he invited them to his study for discussion and the viewing of a video that factually refuted such ideology. Half a dozen youngsters in their uniform of jeans and T-shirts filed in, sat down, kept silent while he reasoned with them, kept their eyes down while the video was shown and then, as one, walked out. The students might very well have been shocked to hear that their behavior was a visual representation of the closed minds of young Communist activists.

Again and again in Britain, we see in town councils and in school councils that headmistresses or headmasters or teachers are being hounded by groups and cabals of witch-hunters, using the dirtiest and often cruel tactics. They claim their victims are racist or in some way reactionary. Again and again, an appeal to higher authorities proves that the campaign tactics have been unfair. This happened to a young friend of mine in Cape Town, whom the fanatical Moslems and the hardline Communists joined forces to expel. They had done the same to her predecessor, and doubtless they are now at work on her successor. The victims were white. Were they racists? They were not. Unlikely bedfellows? Not at all. I am sure that millions of people, the rug of Communism pulled out from under them, are searching frantically, perhaps without even knowing it, for another dogma. Some have already found a home with the fanatical Moslems.

The next point seems to have on the face of it little connection with the others, but I think it underlies them all. It is excitement, pleasure in strong sensations, a search for ever-stronger stimuli. What could be more pleasurable when in one's twenties - the age at which millions of young people have tortured or murdered others in the name of the forward march of mankind - than the excitements of being the only possessors of the truth? Revolutionary politics, the house committees, the vigilante slogans, are intoxicating drugs. In Spain not long ago I met a youth, of the same stuff as Byron, who said it was the great regret of his life that he was too young to have been in Paris in '68. I asked why, when that revolution had been a failure? He was amazed I could ask. It must have been so exciting, said he. Bliss in that dawn to be alive. Bliss being the point, being turned on, getting a buzz, a high, a thrill, a fix. This set of mind was summed up by one of our political commentators thus: he was talking about demonstrations that seem to have little point, that is, from the point of view of actually achieving something. He said: A large part of left-wing politics these days has nothing to do with ends. The ends are not the point. The means are the point.

There must be hundreds of thousands of people, now middle-aged and in positions of authority, whose most vibrant experiences were the events of '68. Like a war for soldiers, '68 was a high point of their lives. No, Communism did not invent demonstrations, riots, marches, petitions, or even revolutions. The nineteenth-century was full of them, 1848 being only part of it and before that the French Revolution, that great mother of so many of our mind-sets. We can't really blame Jean Jacques. He didn't invent sensation and excitement and bliss; he didn't invent the worship of sensibility and elation. He merely mirrored these ideas in books that are still instructive. Exciting ideas have always swept across countries, nations, the world. There have always been people high on ideas. They used to be religious emotions, a fact we might usefully keep in our minds. (They still are religious in some areas, and spreading fast.) But in all our minds are patterns which we do not examine that govern our behavior.

It was, at least until very recently, taken absolutely for granted that revolution is a nobler thing than the ballot box. It was and often still is taken for granted that the right place for a serious young person is with the revolutionaries in Cuba or Nicaragua, with dissidents, or protesting the suffering of the underprivileged, or on a picket line anywhere at all. We have watched successive waves of young people from the West traveling to the scenes of new revolutions, to Gdansk, or Czechoslovakia, or Berlin at the fall of the Wall – anywhere at all where there is strong popular emotion. If half of a certain stratum of youth has been off seeking thrills on the road to Katmandu, then the other half has been getting high on a revolution somewhere or other. The last thing they ever think of is staying at home and working for the good of their own country – even to suggest it bores them, inspires a yawn. For one thing, their own countries are judged as being beneath contempt and not worth their attention. Thus arose the paradox that countries, like those of Western Europe, seen to people suffering under Communism as unreachable paradises of freedom and plenty, were continually being represented as unendurable by young Westerners in search elsewhere for the good and the truth. Because of this unrecognized need to experience suffering, persecution, oppression, successive political movements have invented or exaggerated the oppression in Western countries.

This phenomenon has been analyzed, but I wonder what are the psychological mechanisms underlying the need to denigrate one's own country and seek eternally for paradises somewhere else? I think one reason is that few people on the left – and far beyond the left – have not been soaked in tales of persecution from other countries. Many have spent happy years fantasizing about being in prison and enduring it all with fortitude and heroism, being tortured by interrogators and outwitting them – being clever enough to immediately identify the good and the bad interrogators. Yet these are people who will never be in prison for political reasons, unless they work really hard at it. The secret minds of these Walter Mittys of revolution are landscapes of disaster, tyranny, torture, prison, car bombs, Semtex, and heroic suffering. I personally believe that these hidden landscapes have and do contribute to the continuation of torture and oppression; that they are the reason why ordinary social or political efforts in peaceful and democratic countries have proved so uninviting to so many young people. They yearn for the madder music and for the stronger wine of revolution.

My next point is a development of the last. It is that a great many people love violence and killing. Of course they have always existed and always will, but I think, under ideal conditions, only as a minority. One result of our history of two centuries of revolution, that is, of violence sanctified by high motive, is that there are many people you would not expect to identify with killing and torture who do. In Europe that type of person classified by the sociologists as "tender-hearted" - who hates capital punishment, flogging, bad prison sentences, and the sufferings of the underprivileged and who continues to agitate against these things – often accepts terrorism for good causes. The romance of violence, which began in our time in the French Revolution, was enhanced by the Russian Revolution and then the Chinese Revolution. The result is that the left wing and liberals - millions of people - have schizophrenia. You can see it easily in the tolerance, not to say worship, of the I.R.A. murderers or the Red Brigades in Italy. Few people of a certain age group in Italy have not had friends in the Red Brigades, or even for a time were not themselves in the Red Brigades. It was the chic thing to do. Hundreds of young people with the highest possible motives supported murder for political reasons. Most in the Red Brigades were not deprived people. What they all had in common, of course, was the war just behind them. Granted it was a bad and ugly war in Italy, though we tend to forget that, and war brutalizes all of us. But these were "the tender-hearted," dreaming of gentle, fruitful and noncorrupt futures. Those that remained in the organization became merciless and brutal killers, even if most have now had reverse conversions and become good citizens. They were and are still sometimes admired precisely for their brutality. There are people on the left who still defend them. Why? I think the reason is, again, revolutionary romanticism.

And now my last point, but I am leaving out a dozen other ways, of which we are hardly aware, by which I think our minds have been set by Communism. I think that the left-wing, the social, even liberal movements of Europe have been terminally damaged because the progressive imagination was captured by the Soviet experience. The Russian Revolution, the Soviet Union, was a paradigm, whether seen as a success or as a failed experiment which we could better. For decades, for half a century, for three-quarters of a century, all the "tender-hearted" people longing for better things were preoccupied with the Soviet Union. With its history of assassination, mass murder, show trials. A history, and this I'm sure is the important thing in the long run, of failure. The entire "progressive" movement of Europe has had its imagination in thrall to the Soviet experience, an experience in fact irrelevant to Europe.

It would easily be possible to make an alternative reality, a history of a Europe that had made a decision to develop socialism, or even a just society, without any reference at all to the Soviet Union. We must remember, I think, that because of the Soviet Union it has been impossible even to consider creating a just society that is not either socialist or Communist. We did not have to identify with the Soviet Union, with its seventy-odd years of logic-chopping, of idiotic rhetoric, brutality, concentration camps, pogroms against the Jews. Again and again, failure. And, from our point of view, most important, the thousand mind-wriggling ways of defending failure. I think the history of Europe would have been very different. Socialism would not now be so discredited, and above all, our minds would not automatically fall into the habit of "capitalism or socialism."

The story of the Soviet Union in the last eighty years has been a tragedy, for the Russians and the other Communist nations now free. It has also been a tragedy, on a somewhat smaller scale of course, for Europe. Europe has been corrupted by it in obvious and not so obvious ways, to what an extent it is too early to say. It has been corrupted because we've allowed our imaginations to be totally preoccupied with other peoples' experience and not with our own, for one reason or another. I think that it has been suggested many times that there are reasons that have not yet been examined. My conclusion is that until we know the patterns that dominate our thinking and can recognize them in the various forms they emerge in, we shall be helpless and without real choice. We need to learn to watch our minds, our behavior. We need to do some rethinking. It is a time, I think, for definitions.

MARK LILLA

Only Disconnect. . . .

It is a sign of the provincialism reigning in American letters today that no one has noticed how closely our culture wars have been observed and commented upon by Europeans. Over the past year one could hardly pick up a publication on the Continent without finding an article on the latest American hysteria. The French have led the way here. Besides journalistic treatments in magazines like *Le Nouvel Observateur,* there have also been long and revealing analyses of our present situation in more serious reviews. *Esprit* has published articles on "les défis du multicultural-isme" and "Le *political correct* aux États-Unis," while *Le Débat* ran a special dossier that included an interview with historian François Furet titled "L'utopie démocratique à l'américaine," certainly the most lucid discussion of this issue in any language. A recent number of the distinguished *Merkur* is titled "Gegen-Moderne? Über Fundamentalismus, Multikulturalismus, und Moralische Korrektheit," showing that the Germans have also begun to pay attention (perhaps for reasons of their own). And in Italy the leading left-wing review *MicroMega* has contributed articles with titles like "Assalto alla cultura occidentale," while Umberto Eco in *L'Espresso* has publicized "il Khomeiniismo" in the American university.

What strikes one first in reading these European war dispatches is that, no matter whether the authors are on the political left or right, they are almost uniformly critical of any attempt to delegitimize the great works of the Western mind. If anything, the European left has reacted the most vigorously against ideas like multiculturalism, which it considers incompatible with the universalist aspirations of traditional progressive politics. (The European right, perhaps remembering Joseph de Maistre's remark that in his life he had met Frenchmen, Italians, and Russians, "mais quant à l'homme, je déclare ne l'avoir rencontré de ma vie," seems rather less disturbed by the new ethnic particularism.) The reason it is difficult to put the issue in right-left terms, though, is that European intellectuals see it instead in light of the long-standing cultural struggle between Europe and America. In their view, the real culture war is a transatlantic one over the nature of democracy, and they are right.

In recent decades Europeans were the more aggressive party in this skirmish as they tried to erect economic barriers against a democratic popular culture they mistakenly considered to be a uniquely American product and weapon. But today Americans are the cultural protection-ists, defending their shores against the undemocratic ideas allegedly pro-fessed in, or implied by, the works of "dead" Europeans. (Nothing, it seems, is less democratic than the voice of the dead.) This cultural war is not a nationalistic one; it is, as it were, cultural. It pits a once-aristo-cratic Old World accustomed to making distinctions when thinking about itself and others – distinctions between "high" and "low," "us" and "them" – and an incorrigibly democratic New World suspicious of distinctions in any form. Europeans believe that most other cultures make these very same distinctions, that they offer a key to understanding "them," and that they might have something to teach us; Americans do not. Europeans do not believe that political democracy is incompatible with intellectual or aesthetic hierarchy; Americans do. Americans believe passionately in the simplicity and universality of the democratic project, therefore in the impossibility of wanting to live outside it or limit its scope. Hence our passionate romanticization of the "other" that surrep-titiously turns "them" into embryonic democrats. Hence, too, our pas-sionate demonization of those who defend a cultural hierarchy at home as enemies of democracy itself. No wonder Europeans have concluded that our multiculturalism is nothing of the sort, that it is only a new, sinister form of puritanical democratic boosterism. Multiculturalism is an Americanism.

In many respects, the Europeans' objections to American multicul-turalism echo those made stateside by our conservatives and neoconserva-tives. The difference is that, having said *A*, culturally aristocratic European intellectuals are willing to say *B*. If Americans succeed in level-ing relevant distinctions in literature and the arts in the name of democ-racy, perhaps that means that democracy (or at least its American variant) has certain built-in limits. Q.E.D. But American conservatives and neo-conservatives refuse to draw this obvious conclusion from what they see. Stung by the "blame America first" attitude they believe dominates American intellectual life, they have convinced themselves that a political defense of American liberal democracy can be reconciled with a defense of high culture – *indeed, that the two are really the same thing.* This ex-traordinary assertion rests on two presuppositions, both of which are mistaken. The first is the nativist belief that Europeans themselves are to blame for our culture wars, since they exported the ideas which are thought to lie behind PC and multiculturalism. There is indeed a story to be told here, but it is an American story, not a European one. The French thinkers who inspired the various schools of "post-structuralism" never drew the leveling, democratic conclusions regarding culture which their American disciples have.

The second, and more revealing, presupposition is that the attacks on intellectual and cultural distinctions over the past twenty-five years represent a sharp historical deviation from traditional American practice. These attacks are said to be led by a "cultural elite" against "the American people," who, we are repeatedly assured, are "basically all right." Of course, nothing could be further from the historical truth, as we learn by turning back to the bible on these matters, Richard Hofstadter's *Anti-Intellectualism in American Life*. Reading Hofstadter's thirty-year-old book today is certainly the best antidote I know to the fevers brought on by our present culture wars. Not that the book gives comfort; it does not. It focuses attention instead on our real problems, which are the cultural consequences of the American democratic project itself.

As Hofstadter's earlier readers will remember, the book was written out of the McCarthy experience and the political attacks on "eggheads" in the 1950s. Hofstadter refused to accept that American intellectuals were destined to remain forever alienated from their country. The bulk of his book documents the development of that alienation by focusing on four different sources of the American anti-intellectual impulse: religion, democratic politics, business, and democratic education. But in the conclusion, titled "The Intellectual: Alienation and Conformity," Hofstadter ends on a somewhat upbeat note. It is true that "intellectuals in the twentieth century have found themselves engaged in incompatible efforts: to be good and believing citizens of a democratic society and to resist the vulgarization of culture which that society constantly produces." Yet that effort was getting easier, not harder. Whereas American intellectuals near the turn of the century fled our native provincialism for spiritual liberty on the Continent, this migration had reversed direction with the rise of European fascism in the thirties, making America the natural home of those who held dear the life of the mind. The arrival of these émigres was then followed after the war by the arrival of New York intellectuals in the rapidly expanding universities and other mainstream institutions like the press and the foundations. Even the late Irving Howe, who scolded his fellow intellectuals for their "conformism" in the fifties, spent four years during this period writing for the mass-market *Time*. In fact, there had been a slow rapprochement between "our country" and "our culture" since the thirties, Hofstadter insisted, despite the superficial effects of McCarthyism. Historically considered, America in the postwar decades had been remarkably open to the lives of intellect and art, and to the cultural distinctions and standards they implied. "Anti-intellectualism in various forms continues to pervade American life," he concluded, "but at the same time intellect has taken on a new and more positive meaning and intellectuals have come to enjoy more acceptance and, in some ways, a more satisfactory position."

Neoconservative nostalgia for this postwar period of high intellectual seriousness may be exaggerated, but it is perfectly understandable. What passes for literary criticism, art criticism, and historical writing in America today simply cannot be compared – certainly in style and sensibility – to what was written during those years. But if one looks back at that period with the perspective Hofstadter himself employs, and in light of what has happened since, one begins to see what an exception it was in American history. What we are experiencing in the name of multiculturalism and PC today is alien to the highbrow spirit of the fifties, of that there is not doubt. But it is perfectly consistent with the anti-intellectualism that preceded it. What we face today is not a European-inspired or elite-driven cultural deviation from American democratic practice; what we face is the traditional cultural expression of Americans' understanding of democracy.

Were we to add a chapter to Hofstadter's book on the anti-intellectualism of our time, we would surely have to remark important differences. While religion and business were once the most important sources of American hostility to high culture, today we would have to explain how the institutions nominally charged with propagating that culture, and especially the university, have in many ways abdicated their responsibilities. But even here we would have to remark a more profound continuity in American attitudes toward democratic education. A reader today cannot but be struck by the evidence Hofstadter accumulates to document Americans' enduring hostility to the discipline of learning and to its potential for producing social distinction. Every American believes in education for self-improvement; few Americans believe that those improved through education are in any sense superior to those without it. Hofstadter shows that Americans' indifference to the study of history and foreign languages, and their belief that education should be practical and psychologically reassuring, have very long histories. "The appearance within professional education of an influential anti-intellectualist movement is one of the striking features of American thought." He was speaking of the 1870s, but it might as well have been the 1970s. This is old news.

But the university was always different from the public school system, we will be told. In the postwar years, perhaps. But no one the least bit acquainted with the American university's history before this period – with its provincialism, moralism, and hostility to Jews and other immigrants – will want to make an exemplar of it. (One only has to read the shocked letters and memoirs of the émigre scholars who found themselves in this stale environment in the thirties to return oneself to earth.) As for the period since the mid-sixties, the most important change the university suffered was its own absorption into the mass-education establishment, where it inevitably fell victim to the anti-intellectual impulses already present there. The fact that every university today promotes a multicultural education, yet few demand the real mastery of a single foreign language, is just one more sign that the university is being driven by the same democratic passions that have traditionally hobbled American secondary education. While American high schools have always been forced to prove the "practicality" of their offerings to the average student, today the university must prove that its offerings "reflect" the diverse "sensibilities" of its average students. The university, for better or worse, is being massified and Americanized.

So where does that leave us? Does it mean that PC, multiculturalism, and the culture wars are not threats to American intellectual life today? On the contrary, they are our most pressing problems. But it is very important that we understand how they have arisen before we consider how to respond. The European critics of these developments echo what our own history teaches us: American democratic culture remains in profound tension with the life of the mind. That tension may have slackened in the postwar period, but now it is as strong as it has ever been. One can rebel against the current anti-intellectualism and attack it head-on; we don't lack pamphlets that do just that, and we should be grateful for most of them. But there are dangers in letting oneself be drawn too deeply into these debates, and not simply because people will stop listening. The danger is that one will forget that the destiny of intellect is not that of democracy in America, and that the pursuit of the first may at times require a studied indifference to the latter. At the end of his book, Hofstadter rightly reminds us that "dogmatic predictions about the collapse of liberal culture or the disappearance of high culture may be right or wrong; but one thing about them seems certain: they are more likely to instill self-pity and despair than the will to resist or the confidence to make the most of one's creative energies." Do we not see ourselves in this portrait?

Let us be frank. Polemics against the anti-intellectualism of our day, however satisfying, will not produce one more novel, one more poem, one more painting, or one more work of history or philosophy. American artists and writers facing the provincialism of earlier eras understood this and left for Europe; their work mattered more to them than a democratic culture they could not hope to tame. They resigned themselves to the fact that America will always be America. This should be our attitude today, even if our emigration is internal and psychological rather than physical.

So let this be the last symposium on the culture wars. Let us turn back to our work, back to speaking to the happy few still capable of discussing the arts, literature, and ideas in a language that will forever remain alien to that of populist democratic politics. If we accomplish nothing else, we can at least keep that language alive. Either American political and educational institutions will come to their collective senses or they will not; it will depend on the profound social dynamics that move democratic societies, and not on anything we write or say. America is rediscovering its provincial, nativist, anti-intellectual roots. This is a passionate rediscovery, and passionate nations, like passionate people, are notoriously deaf to the voice of reason. *Sauve qui peut:* it is time to disconnect.

GLENN C. LOURY

Self-censorship

Political correctness is an important theme in the raging "culture war" that has replaced the struggle over Communism as the primary locus of partisan conflict in American intellectual life. Starting on the campuses – over issues like affirmative action, multicultural studies, environmentalism, radical feminism, and gay rights – the PC debate has spread into news-rooms, movie studios, and even the halls of Congress. Critics, mainly on the right, claim that only the "correct" views on these and other sensitive issues can be expressed – on campus, in print, on film, or in electoral politics – without provoking extreme, stifling reactions from activists seeking to make their opinions into an enforced orthodoxy. Liberals call these charges overblown, and they insist that their efforts to hold people accountable for what they say and write are justified by legitimate moral concerns.

Unlike much that has been written on this topic, I will not spend time telling "horror stories" about the excesses of PC zealots or lamenting their influence on the campuses. (This ground has been well covered by Dinesh D'Souza in his book, *Illiberal Education*.) Rather, my aim is to "lay bare" the underlying logic of political correctness – to expose the social forces which create and sustain movements of this sort. Though PC is often seen as a threat to free speech on the campuses (which is indeed the case when it leads to legal restrictions on open expression, as with formal speech codes), the more subtle threat is the voluntary limitation on speech which a climate of social conformity encourages. It is not the iron fist of repression but the velvet glove of seduction that is the real problem. Accordingly, I treat the PC phenomenon as an implicit social convention of restraint on public expression, operating within a given community. Conventions like this often arise because: 1) the community needs to assess whether the beliefs of its members are consistent with its collective and formally avowed purposes; and 2) scrutiny of their public statements is an efficient way to determine if members' beliefs cohere with communal norms. The need to police group members' beliefs in order to ferret out deviants, along with the fact that the expression of heretical opinion may be the best available evidence of deviance, creates the possibility for self-censorship: Members whose beliefs are sound but who nevertheless differ about some aspect of communal wisdom are induced by fear of ostracism to avoid the candid expression of their opinions.

Despite the attention given recent campus developments, the PC phenomenon, understood as an implicit convention of restrained public speech, is neither new nor unusual. Pressuring speakers and writers to affirm acceptable beliefs and to suppress unacceptable views is one of the constants of political experience. All social groups have norms about the values and beliefs appropriate for members to hold on the most sensitive issues. Those thought not to share the consensus suffer low social esteem and are sanctioned by their colleagues in various ways for their apostasy: Heretics are unwelcome within the councils of the faithful. Communists and their sympathizers paid a heavy price for their "incorrect" views during the early Cold War. "Uncle Toms" – blacks seen as too eager to win favor with their white "overlords" – are still treated like pariah by other blacks who greatly value racial solidarity. Jews critical of Israel or Muslims critical of Islam may find that they "can't go home again." A persuasive account of our current problems with PC should be broad enough to address these related phenomena. I argue that such an account emerges naturally from a conception of political communication which stresses strategic considerations.

In his fine essay, "Politics and the English Language," George Orwell states:

> The great enemy of clear language is insincerity. When there is a gap between one's real and one's declared aims, one turns as it were instinctively to long words and exhausted idioms, like a cuttlefish squirting out ink. . . . Thus political language has to consist largely of euphemism, question-begging and sheer cloudy vagueness.

The skepticism is justified, for political communication – the transmission of ideas and information about matters of common concern with the intent to shape public opinion or effect policy outcomes – is, indeed, a tricky business. Those sending and those receiving messages have to be wary. To be effective, both parties must behave strategically. Naive communication – where a speaker states literally all that he thinks, or an audience accepts his representations at face value – is rare, and foolish, in politics. Because political rhetoric engages interests, expresses values, conveys intent and seeks to establish commitment to certain courses of action, the risk of manipulation is particularly great in political argument. When someone addresses us "in the forum," we must consider what he will do if he gets power; we must decide whether he can be trusted; we must wonder, "What type of person is it who would speak to me in this way?"

Strategic listeners will look behind what is spoken or written, in an effort to discern all that is implied by the act of speaking or writing in a given way. The sender of a public message intended to shape opinions and influence policy may have ultimate aims which are not apparent to his audience. And yet, because the sender's values, ideals, and intentions will shape the strategy he adopts in the forum, a proper decoding of his message requires knowledge of his ultimate aims. For this reason, interpretation of political expression involves, in an essential way, making inferences from the expressive act about the sender's motives, values, and commitments.

At the same time, being aware that his speech act is subject to such interpretation, and wanting to create a desired impression, a skillful speaker will structure his message in a way that is mindful of the inferences which listeners are inclined to make. He will try to use the patterns of inference established within a given community of discourse to his advantage. He will avoid some expressions known to elicit negative judgments or associations, and he will deploy others known to win favor with his audience or to cast him in a positive light. He will edit or censor his speech if he wants to be effective.

From this strategic perspective a regime of political correctness can be understood as a pattern of expression and inference within a given community where listeners (readers) impute undesirable qualities to speakers (writers) who express themselves in an "incorrect" way and, as a result, most speakers avoid such expressions. If known enemies of progressive ideals regularly make a certain argument, then one who wants to be seen as standing on the right side of history cannot make a similar argument without the risk of being labeled a "reactionary." When there are some real racists in our midst, if proponents of diversity insist that blacks be referred to as African-Americans, and American Indians as Native Americans, then a speaker who eschews that terminological fashion in the course of an otherwise admirable argument about diversity invites the conclusion that he is intolerant of ethnic difference. His more prudent course is to use the PC terms, though he may prefer not to. In a south Florida enclave, where hatred of Castro is universal, to argue that the normalization of relations with Cuba should be studied amounts to announcing that the arguer cares nothing whatever about remaining in good standing with his fellows. And in a nearby precinct, where reaction against the Cuban immigration runs high, to question the wisdom of making English the state's official language has a similar meaning-in-effect.

Ad hominem reasoning lies at the core of the political correctness phenomenon. A speaker's violation of protocol turns attention from the worth of his case toward an inquiry into his character, the outcome of which depends on what is known about the character of others who have spoken in a similar way. When sophisticated speakers are aware of this process of inference, many of them will be reluctant to express themselves in a way likely to provoke suspicion about whether their ultimate commitments conform with their community's norms.

Though *ad hominen* inference is denigrated by the high-minded, it is a vitally important defensive tactic in the forum. Knowing a speaker shares our values, we more readily accept observations from him which have unpleasant implications, or which are contrary to our initial sense of things, because we are confident that any effort on his part to manipulate us is undertaken to advance ends similar to those we would pursue ourselves. Hence, whenever political discourse takes place under conditions of uncertainty about the values of participants, a certain vetting process inevitably occurs, in which we cautiously try to learn more about the larger commitments of those advocating a particular course of action. This process encourages the conformity of expressed opinion which we associate with PC.

The self-censorship which results is the hidden fact of political correctness. For every act of aberrant speech seen to be punished by "thought police," there are countless critical arguments, dissents from received truth, unpleasant factual reports, or nonconformist deviations of thought which go unexpressed, or whose expression is distorted, because potential speakers fear the consequences of a candid exposition of their views. As a result, the public discussion of vital issues can become dangerously impoverished. I offer two examples which serve to illustrate the broad scope of this phenomenon.

Phillipp Jenninger, once the president of Parliament in the former West German Republic, was forced to resign in November of 1988, following a speech he gave at a special parliamentary session marking the fiftieth anniversary of Kristallnacht. An uproar was created by the fact that many in his audience construed Jenninger's brutally frank account of prevailing attitudes among Germans in the 1930s as a disguised defense of National Socialism. This was so despite the fact that Jenninger was regarded as an opponent of totalitarianism of all stripes, a fierce anti-Nazi, and an arch supporter of Israel. No one accused him of being anti-Semitic. Still, even before his speech had ended, there were demonstrations of anger from some in the audience who, finding his words profoundly offensive, rushed ashen-faced from the chamber. Virtually all reviewers who examined Jenninger's speech concluded that he had said nothing untrue, malicious or defamatory; he simply said things that some people did not want to hear in a manner that they were unwilling to accept. Jenninger had spoken "incorrectly."

This incident illustrates a complex social reality. Jenninger's personal sentiments, as evidenced by a lifetime in politics, did not cause his downfall. Quite the contrary, his liberal reputation led him to believe he could get away with such a graphic "truth-telling." And, though everyone acknowledged the literal truth of his claims, in the end this seemed not to matter. Many even affirmed the importance of his evident goal in the speech — encouraging modern Germans to look candidly at their history, the better to avoid repeating it. But by violating a taboo against any expression which might be construed as sympathetic with this period in German history, by offending an etiquette of discourse that prevents the full truth of the period from being faced, by failing to limit himself to the platitudes which, though showing due deference to collective sensibility, cannot possibly advance the moral discussion, he committed an unforgivable offense.

Jenninger, it could be said, suffered the wrath of political correctness. And his case illustrates one problematic aspect of the PC phenomenon: *The effective examination of fundamental moral questions is often impeded by the superficial moralism of expressive conventions. If exploring an ethical problem requires expressing oneself in ways that raise doubts about one's basic moral commitments, then people may opt for the mouthing of right-sounding but empty words over the risks of substantive moral analysis.* The irony is exquisite. For though the desire to police speakers' morals underlies the taboo, the sanitized public expression that results precludes the honest examination of history and current circumstance, from which genuine moral understanding might arise. Discussion of racial issues in the United States, it seems to me, is plagued by a similar problem.

In the mid- to late 1980s, we all knew that solidarity with the struggle of blacks in South Africa required the United States government to impose trade sanctions against that nation and American universities to divest themselves of stock in companies doing business there. Nobel laureate Desmond Tutu, Rev. Allen Boesak, spokesmen for the African National Congress, and black American anti-apartheid activists repeatedly said so. People genuinely committed to justice did not become entangled in arcane technical arguments about the effects of economic boycotts. Nor were they unduly concerned about the possible deleterious impact of sanctions on black South Africans, since the most visible proponent of *that* argument was the racist government. Remarkably, even those South Africans who had spent a lifetime fighting apartheid, but who opposed sanctions because they thought the policy would do more harm than good (Helen Suzman for example), were not taken seriously by

American activists.

Consider the dilemma of a politically liberal university president during this period. Whether or not he believed in the efficacy of the sanctions policy, he could not credibly claim to be ignorant of it. If he nevertheless chose to resist student demands for radical change in univer- sity investment policies, saying: "Divestment is a well-intentioned but unwise policy for our university; there are better ways for us to pro- ceed," then he would risk having the students draw the inference that he was an obstructionist of doing the "progressive" thing. Most college administrators and trustees dubious about the morality or wisdom of di- vestment found the prospect of this reaction from students to be un- palatable.

In the end, "resistance to the policy" became an accurate signal of "lack of commitment to the cause," since the "truly committed" who doubted the virtues of the policy had censored themselves, while those who continued openly to oppose the policy were identified as the "truly uncommitted." This process took place not just on campuses, but in leg- islatures and on op-ed pages as well.

In effect, the constraints of PC obviated the rational discussion of the many complex ethical and political considerations raised by the sanc- tions policy and by the tactics used to promote it. Decisions were made without the benefit of a full analysis and debate. I am not arguing that the sanctions policy was disastrous, merely that it was pursued without due consideration of its objective consequences or, on occason, in spite of what were thought to be the likely results. Perhaps as important to the universities, decisions about the handling of student protests on behalf of the policy were colored by a concern for the negative symbolism that applying discipline in that context was sure to have. The inaction of those years set precedents which have outlived the sanctions "debate."

There are some general features of the climate of tacit censorship that political correctness encourages. One important aspect of such an environment is that an individual cannot break the grip of a taboo against the candid expression of his thoughts with a declaration such as "Despite my violation of the norm, please understand that my values are pure." Conventions of tacit restraint in public expression are made more durable by the fact that they do not themselves easily become objects of criticism, since it is often the "truly deviant" who have the greatest in- terest in criticizing them. Those, for example, who genuinely value racial equality know that, even if they harbor reservations about affirmative ac- tion, in the interest of supporting a good and decent policy they ought not to utter their reservations. If one wants to maintain his reputation as a good liberal, he will not only abstain from criticizing affirmative ac- tion, but he will also not complain about not being able to express his criticisms. Under a convention of restrained public expression, "progressive" people do not protest for the right to say "reactionary" things.

Another general consequence of a PC regime is the use of ambiguous and imprecise speech. Orwell, in the essay mentioned earlier, was withering in his denunciation of this practice. He noted that "words . . . are often used in a consciously dishonest way. . . . The person who uses them has his own private definition, but allows his hearer to think he means something quite different." With a euphemism, well chosen for its vagueness, a speaker can say palatably (that is, in a manner consistent with extent communal norms) what, if said more incisively, might offend some listeners. The circumlocution may be intended to *deceive,* or merely to *obscure,* but in either case the result is a debasement of the currency of public discourse.

Consider, for example, some uses of the term "minorities" in contemporary American public speech. The speaker may actually mean "blacks" but find that term embarrassingly specific. (This is usually the case when the reference is to some aspect of urban life which has negative connotations.) Or, as in the phrase "women and minorities," the speaker may hope by the use of words alone to create a coalition of interests in the listener's mind, when none exists in fact. Or finally, consider a recent addition to the progressive lexicon, "disadvantaged minorities." One finds this phrase used in educational philanthropy circles when the speaker really means "non-whites, excluding Asians." Never mind the fact that many Asians are disadvantaged! Imagine the uproar were a foundation to candidly announce a scholarship program intended to help "non-white persons belonging to groups that perform poorly on standardized tests." So the strategic speaker sacrifices honesty and accuracy by declaring instead that the program is aimed at "disadvantaged minorities." (A variation on this theme is the "under-represented minority" – though talk of any minority group being "over-represented" is unheard of!)

Such linguistic imprecision impairs analysis. But that is often its purpose. The person who utters the phrase "women and minorities" may want not to reckon with the fact that the majority of women, married to white men, share significant resources and fundamental interests in common with their putative oppressors. An advocate for "diversity" may prefer not to be explicit about which differences are included and which (religious and political beliefs, for example) are excluded from that advocacy. No sane person could relish the task of explaining to poor but studious Vietnamese immigrants why they do not qualify for some "minority" scholarships. And if one wants to accommodate more "under-represented" black and Hispanic students at a university by admitting fewer whites, but not fewer Asians, then one surely would rather not dwell on the statistical "over-representation" of the latter.

Yet another feature of censured public speech is that *standing to address an issue becomes restricted to a certain class of persons who have what I will call "natural cover."* These are people who, because of their group identity, are not immediately presumed to have malign motives for expressing themselves in a potentially offensive way. Thus blacks, but not whites, can make movies or report news stories on the problem of skin color prejudice which continues to affect African American society. Women, but not men, can publicly question whether in a given case the crime of date rape has been manufactured on the morning after by a "victim" who wishes she had made a different decision about sexual intimacy the previous night.

When the effective meaning of some expression is contingent on both the speaker and the audience, the rules of permissible expression in "mixed company" will generally differ from those applicable to homogeneous gatherings. Men talking among themselves have rules concerning what can decently be said about women, but these are generally less restrictive rules than the ones governing a mixed conversation. Moreover, in such environments prudent speakers must be sure to remember to whom they are speaking at any moment. And they must also worry about how an expression made in one context will "sound" in another. Indeed, a common source of the political gaffe is the rendering in public by the news media of a remark made privately, in a setting where different rules applied.

Sometimes it is the insiders, not the outsiders, who are specifically forbidden to voice certain opinions or address certain issues in "mixed company." "Washing dirty linen in public" refers to injudicious speech by an insider which is taboo in mixed company, but which would be appropriate if no outsiders were present. This can be speech – criticism of one's group, especially – in which outsiders routinely engage. The taboo may derive from a concern that outsiders will misinterpret the information, a fear that the insider's words will be exploited by outsiders against the group's interest, or a worry that outsiders will feel legitimized in their own criticism of the group, once an insider has confirmed it. For these reasons, groups often try to discourage insider criticism by punishing the members who engage in it – a tendency which has important implications for the ethics and efficacy of public discourse.

I am often struck by the intensity of critical debate among black Americans over such issues as the social problems of the "underclass" – when that debate takes place out of the hearing of whites. The same theme being explored by a black speaker in mixed company causes other blacks to severely sanction the deviant. If, for example, a white gives voice in mixed company to his fear of criminal victimization, he may be perceived as criticizing blacks. (And that may be his intent.) This perception will be enough to keep some, but not all, whites from expressing their fear. But if a black in that audience supports or confirms the white's feeling, when everyone knows that complaint over the "criminal element" has racial connotations, he courts serious trouble with other blacks. So does the black who worries publicly about the fairness of affirmative action.

Both are expressing themselves in ways that cause their fellows to question their basic commitments. By departing from the convention of restrained expression they are seen as violating a cardinal principle of group loyalty. (However, as Albert Hirschman has noted in his influential book, *Exit, Voice and Loyalty,* the willingness to deviate in the face of sanction for the sake of the group's welfare, as one understands it, might be seen as an expression of true loyalty.) It is therefore not surprising that *these deviants are often accused of being racially inauthentic.* Breaking of the no-group-criticism-in-mixed-company taboo raises in the minds of "blind loyalists" the question of whether the critics are "genuinely" black. The problem here, as Michael Walzer has observed in his study of social criticism, *The Company of Critics,* is that serious political analysis in a democracy cannot take place in private, among one group alone, out of others' hearing. So, by making racial authenticity contingent on rhetorical conformity, the "blind loyalists" succeed in diminishing the vitality of the American political forum.

A final general feature of the PC climate which I will mention is the notion of "forbidden facts." Jean-François Revel, lamenting the difficulty of keeping the truth about the Soviet Union before the West European public, observed, "It is around the circulation of facts that the taboos are strongest in the evolution of public information and debate into national policy. . . . As a rule, concern that a fact might influence public opinion in a way we dislike overrides our curiosity about it and our honesty in making it known." If some truth about the world is inconsistent with a firmly held communal value, listeners may punish the messenger who asserts that truth, reasoning that only someone who disdains the value would act so as to undermine it. Anticipating this punishment, investigators will not only be dissuaded from saying what they know, but also from asking questions which might have unpleasant answers. When rhetoric about facts comes in this way to signal one's values on an important ethical matter, the identification and analysis of significant social problems can be impeded. This is, to my mind, the most damaging consequence of the development of a regime of political correctness in the universities.

Thus, scientists looking into the genetic basis, if any, for gender or racial differences in behavior have met with vocal opposition from "women and minorites" who regard the very act of such speculation to be evidence of bigotry. The search for biological factors influencing violent behavior has been denounced as racist, though this plausible hypothesis has no evidently racial connotation. Yet the speculation that sexual preference *is not* rooted in biology has been denounced as well, and by the very same people! James Coleman, perhaps the world's leading scholar of educational policy, recalls that in 1976 the president and a number of prominent members of the American Sociological Association tried to have him censured for the "crime" of discovering, and announcing, that city-wide busing for school desegregation purposes caused white flight. This had been vehemently denied prior to Coleman's research; far-reaching social policies had been erected on the presumption that it was not true. But, as we now know, Coleman was right. The "taboos around the circulation of facts" then prevalent among American sociologists have had seriously deleterious consequences. Yet, when presenting his work at the ASA meetings that year, the corridors outside of the lecture hall, and the wall behind the podium from which Coleman had to speak, were covered with posters displaying, along with his name and the title of his talk, Nazi swastikas and other epithets suggesting that he was a racist. In 1985, when Richard Herrnstein and James Q. Wilson tried to lecture on their important treatise *Crime and Human Nature,* in the shadow of Harvard University, they were drowned out by students chanting, "Wilson, Herrnstein, you can't hide. You believe in genocide!"

Researchers identifying with certain groups advocate approaches to their disciplines said to reflect their group's perspective – a feminist, or black, or "gay" approach to history, sociology, economics, anthropology, et cetera. This fragmentation (now well advanced and seemingly irreversible, whatever one may think of it) is closely connected with the fact that *public rhetoric in many areas of the social sciences is self-consciously undertaken as strategic political expression.* The disciplines are no longer insular venues of discourse governed by internal norms of scholarly expression accepted by all who have been trained to do research in the field. Social scientists not only address each other, they participate in a larger discussion with extra-scientific implications. Perhaps it was ever thus, though growth of the regulatory and welfare state, and the now greater emphasis on cultural politics, have enlarged the extent to which scholarly expression has political consequences.

The notion of "objective research" – on the employment effects of the minimum wage, say, or the influence of maternal employment on child development – can have no meaning if, when the results are reported, other "scientists" are mainly concerned to pose the *ad hominem* query: "Just what kind of economist, sociologist, et cetera, would say this?" Not only will investigators be induced to censor themselves, the very way in which research is evaluated and consensus about "the facts" is formed will be altered. If when a study yields an unpopular conclusion it is subjected to greater scrutiny, and more effort is expended toward its refutation, an obvious bias to "find what the community is looking for" will have been introduced. The very way in which knowledge of the world around us is constituted has become dependent upon the strategic expression of ideologically motivated researchers.

These are matters of great seriousness, raising ethical as well as political questions. Who, we must ask, will speak for compromise and moderation in negotiations, when to speak in this way is seen to signal a weak commitment to "the struggle"? Who will declare "the emperor" to be naked, when a leader's personal failings hurt the movement? Who will report the lynchers, known to everyone in town despite their hooded costumes? Who will expose the terrorists, or denounce the haters, once lynching, terror and hatred have become "legitimate" means of political expression? Who will insist that we speak plainly and tell the truth about delicate and difficult matters which we would all prefer to cover up or ignore? How can a community sustain an elevated and liberal political discourse, when the social forces which promote tacit censorship threaten to usher in a dark age?

One of the finest statements ever written on these questions, I believe, is Vaclav Hável's essay, "The Power of the Powerless." Confronting the overarching repression of the "post-totalitarian system," Havel describes the existential and ideological features of late Communism that gave the dissidents their power. "Between the aims of the post-totalitarian system and the aims of life there is a yawning abyss," he writes. While life moves toward "fulfillment of its own freedom," the system demands "conformity, uniformity and discipline." The system is permeated with lies: workers are enslaved in the name of the working class; the expansion of empire is depicted as support for the oppressed; denial of free expression is supposed to be the highest form of freedom; rigged elections are the highest form of democracy. For the system to continue, individual citizens must make their peace with these lies; they must choose to "live within a lie." The dissident, who quixotically refuses to go along with the program, is profoundly subversive: "By breaking the rules of the game, he has disrupted the game as such. He has exposed it as a mere game. . . . He has said that the emperor is naked. And because the emperor is in fact naked, something extremely dangerous has happened." Thus the struggle between the "aims of the system" and the "aims of life" takes place not between social classes, or political parties, or aggregates of people aligned on either side, for or against the system, but rather *within* each human being:

> The essential aims of life are present naturally in every person. In everyone there is some longing for humanity's rightful dignity, for moral integrity, for free expression of being and a sense of transcendence over the world of existences. Yet, at the same time, each person is capable, to a greater or lesser degree, of coming to terms with living within the lie. Each person somehow succumbs to a profane trivialization of his or her inherent humanity, and to utilitarianism. In everyone there is some willingness to merge with the anonymous crowd and to flow comfortably along with it down the river of pseudo-life. This is much more than a simple conflict between two identities. It is something far worse: it is a challenge to the very notion of identity itself.

Truth, Hável concludes, has its own special power in the post-totalitarian system: "Under the orderly surface of the life of lies, therefore, there slumbers the hidden sphere of life in its real aims, of its hidden openness to truth."

While I certainly do not intend to compare the constrained expressive environment of a politically correct college campus with the systematic extirpation of dissent characteristic of the totalitarian state, I nevertheless find the moral dimensions of Havel's argument relevant to the dilemmas faced by individuals in our own society. Conventions of self-censorship are sustained by the utilitarian acquiescence of each community member in an order that, at some level, denies the whole truth: By calculating that the losses from deviation outweigh the gains, individuals are led to conform. Yet by doing so they yield something of their individuality and their dignity to "the system." Usually this is a minor matter, more like the small sacrifices we make for the sake of social etiquette than some grand political compromise. But, as I hope to have made clear in the foregoing exposition, circumstances arise when far weightier concerns are at stake. The same calculus is at work in every case.

How then are the demagogues and the haters to be denounced? How can reason gain a voice in the forum? How can the truth about our nation, our party, our race, our church come to light, when the social forces of conformity and the rhetorical conventions of banality hold sway? How can we have genuine moral discourse about ambiguous and difficult matters – like racial inequality in our cities or on our campuses –

when the security and comfort of the platitudes lie so readily at hand? Though it may violate the communal norms of my economics fraternity to say so, I believe these things can be achieved only when individuals, first a few and then many, transcend "the world of existences" by acting not as utilitarian calculators, but rather as fully human and fully moral agents, determined at whatever cost to "live within the truth."

HEATHER MAC DONALD

The Diversity Principle

When President-elect Clinton announced his intention to form a Cabinet that "looked like America," he put the power of the presidency behind the diversity principle. He needn't have bothered. With or without presidential backing, the diversity movement has already transformed American society.

It is impossible to overstate the strength of the movement. Every day, another organization comes under attack for its demographic composition. Research science, mathematics, medicine – all must now scramble to come up with a satisfactory number of minorities and women. Public officials, business leaders, educators, and arts administrators are all expected to proclaim their commitment to diversity upon taking office. Public employees at every level of government are being sent to "diversity training" at taxpayer expense, and governments are adding yet another layer of bureaucracy to monitor their racial and gender mix.

The diversity principle is nonpartisan. The Reagan Labor Department pioneered the practice of race-norming, whereby the general aptitude employment test scores of minorities are adjusted upward – leapfrogging those of higher-scoring whites – to ensure that a proper number of minorities be selected for private and public employment; President Bush's Labor Secretary, Lynn Martin, promulgated the "Glass Ceiling Initiative," designed to increase the pressure on businesses to hire and promote minorities and women; and Los Angeles's recently elected Republican mayor, Richard Riordan, has scrupulously observed the new race and gender rules in his appointments ("Mayor's choices for citizen panels include six Latinos, five African-Americans, four Asian-Americans," proclaimed the *Los Angeles Times* in a headline, adding that "exactly half of the twenty-eight appointments are women.")

Library collections, museum holdings, historical records – all are vulnerable to attack. Diversity censuses are planned for the art collection in the U.S. Capitol building, whose failure to display the requisite number of minorities and women has already drawn criticism. Contract and property law must be rewritten to take race into account, argue diversity theorists. The conviction that white judges and juries are unable to mete out equal justice to minorites has spawned an aggressive movement to diversify the bench. Race and ethnicity are central to voting rights, the

recent Supreme Court ruling against racial gerrymandering notwith-
standing.

The business world is awash in diversity; it long since eclipsed the
academy in the production of materials on multiculturalism. CEOs of the
most bloated, top-heavy companies such as Xerox routinely issue sancti-
monious pronouncements in the new jargon of "managing diversity,"
pledging to "manage for change" and install "change agents" throughout the corporation. Increasingly powerful employee caucuses such as
Digital Equipment Corporation's African Heritage Alliance Women's
Constituency police the hiring and promotion of minorities. Ethnic
marketing councils are successfully peddling the idea that only blacks can
sell to blacks, Hispanics to Hispanics, and women to women (ignoring
the necessary corollary that blacks can therefore sell only to blacks,
women only to women, and so on).

The diversity conference circuit is booming. Every week managers
shuttle across the country to learn how to value the different work
"styles" of their employees; back on the job, they attend "sensitivity
training" to further rid themselves of prejudice. The coffers of such publications as *Black Enterprise* are bulging with ads placed by governments
and businesses desperate to fill their quotas, while publications like the
Irish Voice, which serve less favored ethnic groups, are struggling to survive.

Bar associations, universities, and news organizations have pledged to
meet minority hiring quotas. The color-coding of news story and reporter is now common – though, as in the case of ethnic marketing, the
idea is never entertained that you have to be white to cover a "white"
story. *The New York Times* recently committed itself to displaying a
properly diverse mix of models in its real estate advertisements.

Diversity is about more than numbers, however. It is a way of explaining the world. It attributes all the problems experienced by minorities not to a deficit of skills and education nor to a culture that devalues
work, but to racism. Do blacks and Hispanics score poorly on tests? The
tests are biased. Having been admitted to schools with substandard test
scores and grades, do minorities drop out in disproportionate numbers?
The schools don't do enough to celebrate minority culture. Lacking educational credentials, are minorities underrepresented in university teaching and certain professions? Employers are not trying hard enough to recruit them. Having been hired with substandard qualifications, do minorities fail to advance in their jobs? Managers don't "value their differences."

The response of the Community College of Philadelphia to the
problems caused by the abysmal academic preparation of its minority stu-

dents is typical of the upside-down world of diversity. The head of the English department, Alexander G. Russell, told *The Chronicle of Higher Education:*

> The department head deals with a lot of socializing problems. Last year . . . we had a teacher that got beat up in the classroom. We have teachers that are trying to get through material and who are spending time now on conflict resolution and on being clear about setting limits, and on being able to present material in ways that are careful, so as not to antagonize students.

Apparently one of the ways to antagonize students is to expect that work be performed on time. Teachers find that weeks into a course, students may not have obtained the required books and haven't done work assigned at the beginning of the semester. The school's response? Retrain the teachers! The college has begun providing training sessions to "help faculty members better understand the cultural diversity in their midst." The fact that, in the *Chronicle's* delicate phrasing, the students "seem not to appreciate traditional academic values" is of less concern than teaching the professors to appreciate the anti-academic values of the students.

There is a massive disjuncture in this culture between the well-known problem of minorities' low educational achievement and the interpretation of their subsequent performance in the economy. It is as if as soon as minorities enter the job market, their test scores suddenly rise twenty percent and they acquire college degrees. Supporters of affirmative action even argue that minorities hired under affirmative action pressure are *more* qualified than their white counterparts, though where all these superqualified minorities are coming from is never explained.

One of the main functions of the diversity movement is to ensure that the fact of minorities' underachievement in education is never brought to bear to explain their economic distress. It does so by brandishing the charge of racism early and often. In a diversity regime racism is established by numbers alone. To ask what ought to be the next question – "but what is the proportion of available *qualified* minorities?" – is absolutely taboo; even the accused institution will not raise the point in its defense but will penitently promise to make amends. In the view of diversity advocates, "qualifications" is a "code word" for excluding minorities and women. Lawrence Korb of the Brookings Institute recently called for a chairwoman of the Joint Chiefs of Staff, brushing aside concern for "seniority and experience" as the outmoded posturing of "traditionalists." Faced with a threatened lawsuit by black agents, the Federal Bureau of Investigation has changed its policies to ensure a higher rate of promotion for blacks, even though the number of blacks in administrative positions matched or exceeded the number of blacks qualified for those positions.

An institution that hires by the numbers, however, still can't breathe easy. It still has to contend with the "perception" of racism. The prestigious New York law firm of Weil, Gotshal, and Manges commissioned a "culture audit" – a mainstay of the "managing diversity" movement – to determine which, if any, of its policies and practices were discriminatory. The audit uncovered virtually no instances of bias, but the firm went ahead with a major diversity effort anyway, on the advice of its consultants. According to managing partner Ellen O'Doner, co-chair of the firm's diversity committee, "there is a perception [among the firm's black lawyers] that the criteria for advancement are not applied evenly, and one can't tell if that perception is true or false outside of context." The perception among the firm's partners that the firm is a meritocracy was given no weight.

The Subcommittee on Retention of the Committee to Enhance Professional Opportunities for Minorities of the New York City Bar Association surveyed minority lawyers in New York City on their work experiences. The opinions of blacks, on the one hand, and of Asian-Americans and Hispanics, on the other, differed radically. Whereas the vast preponderance of blacks complained of differential treatment, an even greater preponderance – approaching one hundred percent – of Asians and Hispanics said that they were treated equally.

The subcommittee's conclusions were absolutely predictable. While admitting that the "perceptions" of "race-related barriers" on the part of black lawyers "are not based on the animus that we normally associate with racial discrimination" – in other words, that they have no grounding in actual instances of racism – the subcommittee's report warned that such perceptions are "a matter which the firms cannot afford to ignore." It recommended that "the environment in organizations that gives rise to such perceptions . . . be remedied through such techniques as diversity training," even though the report never identified *what* in such "environments" is discriminatory. The subcommittee also recommended that the Bar Association hire a Diversity Director (which the Association promptly did).

"Perceptions" of racism are also rampant in journalism. Former *Washington Post* writer Jill Nelson charges in her book, *Volunteer Slavery,* that *The Post* killed or heavily edited her stories out of racial disrespect, even though by her own admission she was "studiously garbling the English language because [she] thought that 'real' black people didn't speak standard English." The National Association of Black Journalists released a poll this July of its members and their managers on the availability of career-advancing opportunities to blacks. The poll found a huge chasm between the perceptions of the journalists and their largely white managers: the black journalists complained that they were denied opportunities and advancement, while nearly all the managers felt that blacks had an even *better* shot at promotion than nonblacks, an opinion that seems well-grounded, considering the media's aggressive diversity efforts. It does not take much imagination, however, to guess which set of perceptions will form the basis for future diversity policy in the newspaper and broadcast businesses. Said Dorothy Gilliam, a columnist for *The Washington Post* and chairwoman of the survey task force: "Our members are operating in an atmosphere, in an environment, of frustration and fear."

Now it is just possible that these widespread reports of bias are the result of defensive misperception and racial thin skin, thinned by years of hearing that American culture inevitably victimizes minorities. If a black is not promoted, perhaps it is because he is simply not qualified. Given the ubiquitous and costly efforts at minority recruitment and retention throughout the economy, it is remarkable that we continue to credit each and every charge that minorities are not given a fair deal. That no one questions the objectivity of the complainants is all the more ironic, in light of the assault on objectivity and truth by the same forces of multiculturalism which are now charging widespread racism. Postmodern relativism is all very well and good, it seems, as long as it's not *my* perceptions you're relativizing.

However ungrounded, the accusation of racism severely disrupts organizations, as the library of the University of California at Irvine learned to its distress. A gay Chinese-American librarian with known pedophiliac tendencies used to post political clippings on his cubicle, in violation of library policy. Eventually, he was asked to remove them. When he came up for tenure review, he charged the library with racism, based on the clippings incident. He cited as further evidence the fact that several minority librarians had recently quit. Far from being racist, the library had already put a major effort into minority recruitment, hiring librarians who were at best marginally competent, at worst, incompetent and dishonest (one Korean librarian was caught falsifying his cataloguing statistics). Nevertheless, leftists on the faculty turned the case into a major campaign, eventually gaining the attention of the national press, which duly reported on UC Irvine's racism. The University Librarian was ultimately forced to resign, and the chancellor gave the librarian tenure, even though all his previous peer reviews had recommended against it.

Incidents like these explain why so many organizations are preemptively rushing to play by the diversity rules. The spread of diversity is aided as well by the skill with which minorities manage to parlay just about anything that happens into an argument for more diversity. Speaking before the National Association of Black Journalists last July, Lani Guinier attributed her defeat as nominee for the post of Assistant Attorney General for Civil Rights to the fact that "there is simply not enough diversity at the decision-making and gate-keeping levels in either the print or broadcast media." The media's lack of diversity, said Guinier, led it to distort her views and acquiesce in her "silencing."

The culture's obsession with diversity has conferred enormous bargaining power upon minorities. It is hardly surprising that they use it. The president of Students for Black Interest at William Penn College has let it be known that many minority students will leave the school if it doesn't hire more minority faculty, do more to honor Black History Month, and show greater sensitivity to their concerns. Desperate to keep the school's diversity profile intact, William Penn administrators have established several committees to respond to the students' demands.

In March of 1993, Students of Color Building Bridges at the University of Oregon presented to university administrators a petition demanding more minority faculty. If their demands were not met, the petitioners said, they would drop out. That five minority professors had just been hired under an existing "target of opportunity" program, despite university budget cuts, was irrelevant to both the students and the university administrators willing to coddle them: "We will be together on many, if not most of the requests from the students," said Gerald F. Moseley, vice-provost for academic planning and services.

The use of racial extortion becomes more sinister in the building trades. Groups such as "Black Power," "Afro Construction and Demolition," and "Epiphany Enterprises" routinely "help" contractors meet Federal and local laws requiring the hiring of minority workers. Their help often consists of beating owners and foremen, disrupting work, and preventing workers from entering job sites, as well as demanding protection money.

The biggest casualty of the diversity movement is not equal opportunity but the truth. Diversity has foreclosed the possibility of an honest discussion of the cultural problems which are impeding the advance of certain minorities. Any fact which contradicts the diversity-approved explanation of the world is banished as racist stereotyping. In June 1993, National Public Radio devoted an almost unprecedented thirty minutes to a documentary entitled "Ghetto Life 101." Its creator, David Isay, must have thought he was doing everything right. The diversity movement demands that "discourse" be opened to previously silenced "voices," so Isay gave tape recorders to two teenagers in a Chicago housing project and let them record their lives.

The resulting piece provided a compelling glimpse into the inner city. The boys were self-confident narrators and uninhibited interviewers; a jazz background gave "Ghetto Life 101" a cool and sophisticated rhythm. Isay made a fatal error, however: he ignored the emerging rules of journalism. He didn't edit out the segment where the two hosts record themselves breaking car windows, nor where one of the boys' fathers, under prodding from the son, promises unconvincingly to enter an alcohol rehab program, nor where one of their grandmothers tallies up the children and grandchildren she has lost to drugs and violence, nor where one of their sisters brags about knowing who committed several murders.

Retribution was swift. As reported in *The Washington Post*, black staffers at NPR revolted. Reporter Phyllis Crockett charged in a widely circulated memo that "the program repeat[ed] every negative stereotype of poor, inner-city black life . . . a new low in which arrogant whites use unsuspecting blacks for preconceived notions." NPR's minority caucus whined: "We are offended. We feel personally assailed. We feel unwelcome and ignored." Vice president Sandra Ratley complained that "many Americans still believe the stereotypes about the black community: that there is a welfare mentality, a life of drug abuse and alcoholism and avoidance of responsibility."

NPR hastily called an extraordinary five-and-a-half hour meeting, run by two professional diversity trainers, during which blacks argued that the decision to air the show proves that they are excluded from the editorial process. For his part, Isay says that he is now "locked out of doing anything important for a very long time."

Crockett's comment is a fascinating revelation of the diversity mentality. She refuses to hold blacks responsible for their own actions, even though seeing them as NPR's victims in this case requires a considerable twisting of the facts. In charging Isay with "us[ing] unsuspecting blacks," she seems to imply that he set the boys up to break the car windows, or, at the very least, projected so overwhelming an expectation of misbehavior that they were simply compelled to act up. If her argument is that Isay should have edited out the offending segments to protect the boys from themselves, is that not just as paternalistic and patronizing as more traditional racism? As for the entire world portrayed in "Ghetto Life 101," Crockett's statement suggests that if the white media didn't report on it, its problems would cease to exist.

The fact that the "stereotypes" about inner-city drug abuse, alcoholism, avoidance of responsibility, and welfare dependency also happen to be true is no longer relevant to the journalistic mission. That mission is now defined otherwise: to "reflect the strengths of the community," in the words of *Post* editor Ben Bradlee, promising to make amends for an incident of similarly "insensitive" reporting in 1986.

Ironically, the strict taboo on discussing the problems of race creates the appearance of racism where it does not necessarily exist. Until society is willing to acknowledge that the vast proportion of violent crime is committed by young black men, such behavior as crossing the street to avoid a group of raucous young blacks will be attributed to racism, rather than to a rational evaluation of risk. Likewise, the reluctance of communities to accept a homeless shelter or low-income housing is usually due to a well-founded fear of crime and drugs, not to racial animus. But since it is forbidden to note the high incidence of antisocial behavior in certain populations, the resistance is attributed to a dislike of blacks per se.

The prognosis for halting the diversity juggernaut is not good. Political leaders show no more courage than the press in countering racial demagoguery. The situation in Los Angeles is particularly galling. As the trial begins of the four men charged with viciously beating the trucker Reginald Denny during the Rodney King riots last year, black activists are threatening the city with dire consequences should the defendants be found guilty and severely sentenced. News organizations report without comment the activists' charge that the high bail set for the Denny defendants and the low bail set for the four police officers in the King case show the racism of the justice system. Neither the media nor, even more deplorably, a single public figure has pointed out that the Denny defendants' records of serious felony convictions and parole violations more than justify the differences in bail. While political leaders stay safely out of the fray, the maligning of the justice system continues unchecked, feeding racial hostilities and resentments.

Nor is there any chance that the beneficiaries of preferential treatment will suddenly decide that enough is enough and that they have been stigmatized as unable to compete on their merits for too long. Rather, the only hope for breaking out of the diversity madness is that the race, gender, and ethnicity spoils system will self-destruct of its own accord. There are signs that this may already be starting to happen.

In October 1992, blacks and Hispanics in Los Angeles battled over the post of interim superintendent of schools. Antolin Gomez, a local official with the Mexican-American Political Association, merely reiterated diversity gospel when he told *The New York Times:* "I think we can make the assertion that the sensitivity is more heightened if you have a sensitive Latino that represents and is clearly aware of some of the cultural and social and demographic factors which affect the Latino population." Yet Barbara Boudreaux, the only black member of the school board, called such statements racist: "It is insulting to Sid Thompson [the black candidate] to say, 'You're second-in-command but because you are black you cannot assume the Superintendency.' " Sounding more and more like a white patriarchal supporter of classist, sexist, and racist meritocracy by the minute, she added: "We are teaching the students that you can be anything you want to be. . . . But a whole community is saying, 'No, you can't be Superintendent unless you are a member of one ethnic group.' " (It remains doubtful, however, whether Ms. Boudreaux would object if school officials let it be known that they would prefer to hire a black rather than a white. No minorities have been heard to complain in New York City, where school officials are shying away from white candidates for the post of Schools Chancellor.)

The tables are turning in Miami, too. After Ruth Page lost her job to a Cuban, she began to resent the growing Hispanic presence in Miami. She was one of several black residents to speak before the Dade County Commission against the lifting of the requirement that all county business be conducted in English. "They are taking over, and I am a victim of that," said Mrs. Page, after the Commission voted unanimously to rescind the English-only rule.

In New York State, Senator Joseph Galiber has introduced a bill that would require a certain proportion of state contracts to be let to black businesses, defined specifically to exclude businesses owned by Hispanics. The next step will inevitably be a counter-quota bill from the Hispanic caucus to exclude blacks, and then a few more bills from Asians, American Indians, and women, excluding everyone but themselves.

The Education Department's Office for Civil Rights ruled earlier this year that Connecticut had illegally excluded Asian-Americans and American Indians from a program that gives colleges funds to recruit and retain minority students and faculty members. The original beneficiaries deplored the ruling. "It's quite appropriate to focus on blacks and Hispanics. You can just look at all kinds of statistics and you see that they are not there in higher education and there are a lot of Asian-American students up there," said Lori Brown, president of the Black Students Association of the University of Connecticut. The solidarity of "people of color" united against white oppression lasts only so long as there are no competing claims on funding, it seems.

The definition of "diversity" itself is increasingly "contested," as the multiculturalists themselves might say. In June of 1993, Hispanic students marched through the campus of California State Polytechnic University in Pomona holding a coffin that signified the "death of diversity." What had killed it? The university had named an Asian-American, rather than a Hispanic, as vice president for student affairs. In partial atonement, the university is considering a multicultural student center. Meanwhile thirty-five miles to the west, the Asian Pacific Americans for a New Los Angeles accused Mayor Riordan of pursuing "diversity devoid of substance" in his five appointments to the Police Commission: a regional director of the American Jewish Committee, a Hispanic, a black female, a training co-ordinator for the Gay and Lesbian Police Advisory Task Force, and a former Bradley appointee – but no Asians.

Nor is there much inclination to share victim status with nonracial groups. "A lot of blacks are upset that the feminist movement has pimped off the black movement," said Lou Palmer, a black radio show host in Chicago, to *The New York Times*. "Now here comes the gay movement. Blacks resent it very much, because they do not see a parallel, nor do I."

The feminist movement does not necessarily have any warmer feelings toward the black movement. A white female professor of social work successfully sued the University of South Florida for discrimination earlier this year for having hired a similarly qualified black man at a higher salary and rank. A federal jury awarded her $318,212 in back pay and damages.

As President Clinton's unsightly struggles to fulfill his own diversity pledge have shown, the diversity principle wreaks havoc on institutions by blocking their ability to select the best available candidate regardless of race or gender. Fortunately, quotas begin to lose much of their at-traction as soon as someone else asserts them against you. Since Americans are unwilling to rebut head-on the underlying premise of the diversity movement – that America remains a deeply racist country – one can only hope that the victim groups will ultimately reject diversity out of expediency, on the ground that doing away with preferences entirely is better than having to share the spoils.

STEVEN MARCUS

Soft Totalitarianism

It may only be another confirmation of the discouraging state of affairs in society today, but a good part of the phenomena that fall into the category of political correctness was already clearly described in its general outlines more than forty years ago. I am referring of course to George Orwell's classic essay of 1946, "Politics and the English Language," and to his expansion and elaboration of its insights in *1984*, particularly in the Appendix on Newspeak. Although the epoch of Hitler and Stalin has long since passed, and totalitarianism in the forms associated with those two incomparable tyrants no longer prevails as an immediate threat to the world, or to large portions of it, some of the qualities and attributes that characterized the cultural life of the age of totalitarianism linger on and remain with us yet, in modulated, mitigated or attenuated forms, a kind of soft totalitarianism – along with a residual totalitarianoid sensibility. In particular the corrupted language that emanates nowadays from our institutions of culture and intellect expresses at point after point its affiliation with the historic experience of totalitarianism out of which we are still emerging – or from which, one might more austerely suggest, we have not yet fully emerged. Totalitarianism is, after all, the twentieth century's contribution to the forms of extreme orthodoxy. Orthodoxies of one kind or another have enjoyed a long and sustained existence among human societies. Sometimes they act to create order and hold groups of people together. As a rule they also tend to muzzle, stifle or suppress dissent, and create anxiety and fear in those whose thinking deviates from their prescriptions. The situation as it exists today represents a continuation of the state of things represented by Orwell, but by other means and in other dimensions.

The orthodoxies in question are chiefly those that are loosely associated with the liberal left in a variety of areas and discourses and are organized around a variety of causes or projects. One major difference that has occurred since Orwell published his indictments of the political abuses of language and intelligence is that there is at present no single party or group of sub-parties or shadow parties with a unified, centrally-controlled party line and apparatus of propaganda to which believers and adherents can refer their allegiances. Another difference is that the focus of such cultural-political goings-on has, at least in America and some other parts of the West, shifted from the region of politics at large to the more confined though still spacious precincts of our institutions of higher education, our colleges and universities, our learned societies and professional organizations, our philanthropic foundations, museums and other centers of cultural activity. What this transposed location registers, among much else, is the immensely increased importance of higher education in Western societies – an importance that touches almost every locus of human enterprise – scientific, technical, technological, economic, social, cultural. Universities as institutions have become central to the workings of our societies in a wholesale variety of new senses. And as a matter of course, many of the conflicts, inequities, injustices and abuses of those same societies have found new registries and appeared in novel but recognizable forms within these institutions. The ideological orthodoxies referred to by the term political correctness and its variations have largely to do with attitudes and movements that have arisen in opposition to such inequities and injustices and have as their purpose the countering and rectification of their harmful influences. Moreover, the corruptions of both language and thinking that are associated with this group of phenomena have become densely entangled with the organizational structures taken by these virtuous causes themselves. As a result, those causes tend to be reciprocally influenced, not for the better, by the means they are articulated through, by the language in which they are prosecuted and promoted, by the cultural styles of their representations – and as in the past the republic of virtue, even before it is realized, has begun to take visible shape as a congregation of dunces, or something even less savory.

A fundamental assumption of these loosely-associated cohorts is, to cite the ongoing cliché, that "everything is political." In this axiomatic presupposition, they appear to agree with Orwell. "In our age," he wrote, "there is no such thing as 'keeping out of politics.' All issues are political issues." But he then went on to add what few of our contemporaries would, I believe, acknowledge in a similarly convincing self-inclusive and self-incriminating sense: "and politics itself is a mass of lies, evasions, folly, hatred and schizophrenia. When the general atmosphere is bad, language must suffer." Orwell was making his declaration from a restrictive and specific historical perspective; he was not asserting that politics were universally and at all times as debased as he believed, with justification, the politics of his time to be; indeed, he felt trapped in the poisonous political universe of the thirties and forties and longed, often nostalgically, for a world and a time in which political life had a less lethal character to it – his novel of 1939, *Coming Up for Air,* is all about such a daydream. But when our orthodox contemporaries affirm that "everything is political," they are speaking in error and in contradiction of certain of their own philosophical convictions: they are universalizing, absolutizing, and essentializing, to use a few choice fragments of the current jargon. They are, in addition, repeating, in a different region of discourse, an error that certain of their predecessors had made earlier.

One of the historic disabilities of vulgar Marxism was its tendency toward economic reductionism. All human phenomena, including such cultural artifacts as poetry, music and logic, could be "explained" by reference to the economic base, or modes of production and ownership, out of which different societies created and perpetuated themselves. This species of reductive explanation was not to be confused with other kinds of analysis that strove to demonstrate the socially or historically contextualized nature of cultural artifacts, and that insisted upon multiple determination in any explanatory account of social eventuations. Such analyses sought to anatomize simultaneously both the historically grounded circumstances that were almost inevitably refracted in most cultural objects along with the relative autonomy of the so-called superstructure, its loose and incompletely determined nature as well. And it was with the purpose of modulating reductive simplicities and addressing more adequately the complexities of cultural and mental life that such projects as the sociology of knowledge and Gramsci's reflections on hegemony were undertaken. The spirit of these essays in ideological analysis was anti-reductive and anti-totalitarian, even as both worked toward a larger inclusiveness of explanatory purview. Hence the assertion that "everything is political" is at the level of intellectual and cultural pathology the functional equivalent of the return of the repressed; perhaps it would be more salient to remark that it is like a bad penny turning up again.

What moves large numbers – if not all – of those who adhere to soft totalitarian convictions is first a shared sense of victimhood. Such presentment of ill-usage is what tends to join and shape those who share it into a group. The form favored by such groups is extremely likely to be that of a "community," a *Gemeinschaft* no less. Those unfortunate members of our society who have been born with or who have acquired – through whatever agency or combination of natural and human causes – physical handicaps now belong to what they themselves describe as "the disability community." No one can or should blame them for the anger and resentment they bear against nature for their disadvantaged physical state, and against social institutions for treating them as being less than fully endowed in their humanity. At the same time, and in the next breath, that "community" of the disabled rejects the idea of disability itself and demands that it be publicly renamed as the "differently abled," as if the altered nomenclature had some indescribable power to abolish the condition by renaming it. At the end of this line of inelegant variations is the by-now-famous suggestion that very short people are henceforward to be thought of, and referred to, as "vertically challenged" – perhaps "specially non-tall" might have done almost as well. One of the striking things about such examples is the extraordinary insensitivity to language and the common idiom that they reveal; it's almost as if there were a counter-linguistic spirit impelling such locutions and ensuring that they be obtrusive, inept and self-defeating. Another is their immunity to the apprehension that such expressions, in their awkwardness and absurdity, are often open invitations to harsh and virtually irresistible humor and ridicule. Indeed it is the humorlessness, the lack of comic or ironic self-awareness, that is often most arresting about politically correct language, rhetoric and terminology. It shares this incapacity with other historical orthodoxies, one of the compelling characteristics of group thought apparently being that it does not come with a sense of humor as standard equipment.

Even more, orthodoxies tend to be aggrieved by and resentful of humor, jokes and comedy, and regularly respond with clamorous hostility to all three, as if they were exclusively enjoyed at their expense. To be sure, cruel and offensive humor is often used by dominant groups to diminish and render ineligible the claims of those whom they exclude from membership. But jokes and comedy can also be anarchic, aggressive, lawless and individualistic repudiations of the normative assertions made by any group; they can and have been regularly used to resist and expose the pieties that group allegiances are likely to express themselves in. Hence the formidable humorlessness of much politically correct language is in part an understandable counterpart to the aggressive, individualistic resistance of irony, comedy and humor to collective claims.

The reader will also have noticed, as Orwell himself had noted before, that there is a tendency in this kind of language toward euphemism. Insincerity breeds contempt. Vague and blurred language permits one to ignore the gap between "one's real and one's declared aims." It also permits one to express malice in an ostensibly neutral manner. I recently was indirectly a witness to a minor incident that illustrates this last point. It was reported to me that a male colleague had been guilty of making a sexist remark to a younger female colleague and that he had done this while committing substance abuse. What happened was that a senior male had indeed said something both unpleasant and disrespectful to a younger female after he had had too much to drink. What I want to call attention to is the use in this situation of "substance abuse." Scientific in provenance, dispassionate in tone, Latinate in derivation, it is supposed on the surface to supply us with an appropriately impersonal and non-moralistic descriptive context for the behavior in question. But what it does in fact is to assimilate several glasses too many of wine (the substance in question) to lines of cocaine, to the drug trade, Alcoholics Anonymous, potential violence and heaven knows what else. And "substance abuse" becomes itself, in the course of this politically adaptive re-contextualization, a term of abuse.

An analogous fate seems to have overtaken such a word as "diversity," which has mutated from a general term referring to formal ideas about the desirablity of what used to be thought of as pluralisms of goals, ideas and representatives of groups to certain specific and even quantifiable results. In this setting, diversity can come to be compatible with – if not the same thing as – separatism, isolation, and bureaucrati-cally mandated quotas. From the relatively safe and insulated perspective of the American campus, one can see the further playing out on the larger international scene of such ideas in the atrocities that are being committed in the name of "ethnic cleansing." And as part of this latter process, one witnesses the creation of "safe havens," an Orwellian term for extensive concentration camps, which are, to boot, safe to bomb at will. It is difficult not to be reminded of Newspeak and doublethink forty years later. The lines of causal influence run in both directions. Bad, sloppy, careless language is the vehicle of and conduces to careless, foggy, imprecise and manipulated thinking, and both in turn make it easier to do things and support causes that one would otherwise steer clear of, or at least be more cautious in approaching.

The current language of political "struggle" tends to anesthetize the intellect. Out of thousands of examples, here is one chosen almost at random from the writing of a student political leader. "It's about time that we stop apologizing for being hostile, emotional, and militant. It's about time we take sweeping actions to send a message to the racist op-pressors that we are tired of your shit." On the one hand virtually every word or phrase in these two sentences – including shit – is a cliché. Terms such as racism, colonialism, sexism, and equality have tended to lose most of their specific meanings; like fascism in the thirties and forties, they only signify something general that one feels entirely justified in dis-approving of without qualification. On the other hand, such language can be deployed in a tactical sense to useful destructive ends. If in some familiar situation of academic dispute, an ancient fogy of a professor or a dopey administrator rises up and suggests something to the effect that reason and compromise are preferable to intimidation and coercion, such vaguely incendiary expressions as I have quoted can be conveniently brought out to shut him up. Reason and compromise are after all the shit handed out by racist oppressors, and it is we, on the contrary, who are being intimidated and coerced, even as we write and publish these very utterances – indeed such utterances are themselves the proof and warrant of our continued oppression. And there should be nothing surprising in the circumstances that the broad context that originally gave rise to such remarks happened to be a discussion about the curriculum.

Moreover, it is the curriculum that has provided occasions for some of the better illustrations of politicizing language that has been put into anesthetic slumber through overuse, misuse and displacement. Here, for example, is part of a statement outlining the new aims of American studies. "Freed from the defensive constraints of cold war ideology, empowered by our new sensitivity to the distinctiveness of race, class and gender, we are ready to begin to understand difference as a series of power relationships involving domination and subordination, and to use our understanding of power relationships to reconceptualize both our interpretation and our teaching of American culture." Apart from the idea that American studies should henceforth have an overt politically-driven academic agenda, thinking in such a passage is in a state of indefinite repose. "Ideology," "empowered," "sensitivity," "r, c, g," "difference," "power relationships," and "reconceptualize" are all within this context of airless prose as inert as last semester's notes.

Part of the point of such language is that it asserts one's goodness of will, intentions of virtue and benignity, radical courage and solidarity of sentiment with the oppressed, the deprived, the needy and the mistreated. It is very difficult, indeed it would be wicked and perverse, to disparage these motives; they are indeed impeccable. But the results they can lead to are something else. For example, some scholars' *engagés* have undertaken to explore how the English language itself has been the unconscious vehicle for racist and colonialist thinking. "Snow White" as the name of the heroine of a fairy tale is one frequently-cited example of such an unwitting if baleful tendency. I recently ran across another instance brought forward by an anthropologist who is studying American political and cultural colonialism. As evidence of this pervasive social disposition, the anthropologist referred to the candy Mars Bars as a confectionary embodiment of America's indefensible impulse to colonize everything, including extra-terrestrial planetary space. It was not a relevant consideration that: 1) the candy was named and marketed long before space flight had ever occurred; or 2) that the name belongs to the family that owns the candy manufacturing company. In this instance, as in many others throughout our history, silliness and scholarship consort in happy tendentiousness.

As does ignorance consort as well. A colleague recently recounted to me that she had been teaching Keats's "The Eve of St. Agnes" to a class of students who were by and large studying poetry for the first time.

She asked the students what their first responses to this marvelous early nineteenth-century rendering of a romance were, and, after some hesitation, a bright young woman responded, "Date rape." Soft totalitarianism can occur in moments that are almost winning in their poignancy.

I close with these two illustrations that are amusing in their fatuity and triviality. And I do so not because I think that the situation in our universities is a good one or that their condition is not serious. Far from it. But I do not believe either that it is catastrophic or beyond redemption. A good deal of damage has been done, to be sure, to both these institutions and to individual persons as well; and the general intellectual tone has become worse than ever, while standards and judgments of quality, in the humanities and the social sciences, have continued to go more or less out the window. But the long-term prospects may be something else again, and here we have to stand back and regard things in historical perspective. For America as a national society seems in the last generation or two to have arrived at something like a common decision: to use institutions of education – and in particular higher education – as a means for accelerating social change and mobility, redressing injustices, promoting various equalities, and enforcing cultural relativism. In other words, universities have become the contested sites on which certain social ideals are being tested, tried out, or getting a dry run. They are contested sites for several reasons. First, although the decision (or group of decisions) seems to have been made, not everyone agrees with it, nor is there adequately convincing concurrence on the appropriateness of the means that have been enlisted to realize the worthy goals that are at stake. Second, universities by historical tradition and, in some degree, by necessity are not democratic institutions. Scientific problems are not decided by votes; they are often not decided by entirely scientific procedures either, but the social processes that govern the way in which decisions are reached in communities of scientists are not by any stretch of the imagination democratic. And in the social sciences and the humanities, idiosyncratic mixtures of tradition, authority, personal persuasiveness and charisma, along with external social and cultural pressures, appear frequently to act as decisive influences in dealing with both intellectual and scholarly issues.

Institutions of higher education tend, in the main, to be intellectual aristocracies. In their corrupt versions they become ossified and oligarchic. When they work well, they tend to be meritocratic and allow talent to rise to the top, while reproducing at the same time many if not most of the inequities of the social matrix in which the talented unevenly begin as well, and out of which they also unevenly arise. The great European systems of secondary education, for example, were created in the wake of the French Revolution and functioned to enforce the larger

aims of the socially dominant middle and upper-middle classes or bour-
geoisie. Those systems offered to the sons of those classes an education
that would prepare them for leading positions in nineteenth-century society – in the professions, politics, the civil service and other institutions
of social and cultural reproduction – while safely isolating them at the
same time from the different destinies laid out in advance for the majority of those who were stationed or situated beneath them. In America,
our institutions of higher education functioned almost from the outset in
ways that were analogous to continental secondary education – but with
appreciable differences. American class society was always more perme-
able, fluid and loosely articulated than its European counterparts, and as
a result American colleges and universities were earlier and more easily
transformed into institutions that also promoted social and cultural
mobility than was the case in Europe. What we are seeing today, among
many other things, is a further evolution in that tendency, as universities
are becoming one of the most visible locations for the agencies of particular kinds of social change. These changes have largely to do with interpretations and versions of equality, and in the name of equality and
related social values, I have been arguing, quasi- or soft totalitarian ideas,
formulations, persons and arrangements have in recent years made themselves felt as important influences within our colleges and universities.
The connections between the two are neither accidental nor inevitable.
And the outcome of the conflicts that are entailed in the term "political
correctness" and what it refers to is uncertain as well. For the present,
however, one must as an individual continue to resist the decay of
language, the decay in question at this moment having to do with the
discursive occupation of university life by a variety of political and cultural orthodoxies and their thought-stifling idioms. The discourse of political correctness is political in the bad sense, and we could do worse
than to recall Orwell once again. "Political language –," he wrote, "and
with variations this is true of all political parties, from Conservatives to
Anarchists – is designed to make lies sound truthful and murder respectable, and to give an appearance of solidity to pure wind." That
wind continues to blow, and I believe that one still doesn't have to be a
weatherman in order to figure out what one's responsibilities are.

JERRY L. MARTIN

The Postmodern Argument Considered

I. The Fundamental Issue

The debate over political correctness has missed the main point. One side claims that the enforcement of politically correct language, attitudes, and behavior is alarmingly widespread. The other side claims that, at most, there are a few isolated, unverified incidents which have been overplayed in the press. In short, the debate has been about whether PC exists.

What this debate overlooks is that there is a very significant body of opinion in academe which holds that, while the term "political correctness" is an epithet to be avoided, the mission of higher education should indeed be political – that the goal should be not the pursuit of "objective" truth, but nothing less than the fundamental transformation of society. According to this "transformationist" view, education should be, as Miami University professors Henry Giroux and Peter McLaren put it, freed from what Michel Foucault called a "regime of truth" and should become "a form of cultural politics." Teachers should become "engaged and transformative intellectuals" as schools are transformed into "agencies for reconstructing and transforming the dominant status quo culture."

The new view, according to Duke University professor Frank Lentricchia, "seeks not to find the foundation and conditions of truth but to exercise power for the purpose of social change." The professor's task now becomes helping students "spot, confront, and work against the political horrors of one's time. . . ." As Lentricchia puts it, echoing Marx, "the point is not only to interpret texts, but in so interpreting them, change our society." Wesleyan University English professor Richard Ohmann recommends that faculty "teach politically with revolution as our end. . . ."

Not only teaching but the content of the curriculum itself is to be used for political change. Giroux argues for "the development of curricula that embody a form of cultural politics." Writing about women's studies programs, University of Delaware professor Margaret Anderson explains that "curriculum change is understood as part of the political transformation of women's role in society. . . ."

In order to use institutions of higher education to change society, it is, of course, necessary to control them. "The democratic control of these ideological apparatuses," writes literary theorist Terry Eagleton, "along with popular alternatives to them, must be high on the agenda of any future socialist programme."

For the transformationist, rebuffing charges of political correctness is only a tactical maneuver; the strategic design is control over the universities themselves. While "the public and well-financed assault on 'political correctness' in the academy needs to be answered strenuously and in an organized fashion by left intellectuals," argues Columbia University professor Jean E. Howard, "that imperative doesn't lessen the need for continued work on transformation *of the academy itself.*" According to Howard, universities "have been radicalized far too little. To continue that radicalization remains a pressing task. . . ."

It would be a mistake to dismiss the transformationist view lightly, to regard it as either intellectually lightweight or institutionally impotent. It is based on what many regard as the most advanced and sophisticated thinking at elite universities, thinking so dominant that it is declared in a publication of the American Council of Learned Societies to reflect "the consensus of most of the dominant theories" of our time. Going further, a leading literary theorist, J. Hillis Miller, has declared the "universal triumph of theory" – referring not to a single theory but to the cluster of postmodern views that includes deconstructionist, Marxist, feminist, and related theories of literary and cultural interpretation. While it is not clear how many faculty fully avow the transformationist position, the ideas that legitimate it – such as the critique of truth and objectivity and the emphasis on race, class, and gender – are now commonplaces of academic discussion at colleges and universities across the country.

The postmodern argument for the transformationist view is particularly powerful because it directly challenges the traditional university's premise – that the pursuit of truth is a desirable and even possible goal. Once the pursuit of truth is rejected as a goal, "everything is permitted." Once the pursuit of disinterested truth is debunked, appeals to such commonplaces of liberal learning as objectivity, respect for reason, and academic freedom become question-begging.

It is this postmodern argument for the transformationist view that I will consider here. To evaluate the argument, one must first understand what it is, a task made difficult by the absence of a canonical statement. One tends to find separate discussions – here an attack on objectivity, there a discussion of critical pedagogy, perhaps with undeveloped allusions to each other – but no systematic presentation of the argument from beginning to end. But the separate discussions do not form an inchoate mass; they reflect a coherent view that contains an implicit argument. The following is an attempt to articulate that argument, step by step, as a prelude to critical commentary. I have tried to present the argument in the language, and in some cases the very words, of its advocates.

II. The Argument

The Transformationist Thesis: The aim of higher education should be not the pursuit of truth but social transformation.

Step 1: Perspectives. Metaphysical realism naively assumes that there is a single, definitive description of reality which reason has the power to discern and that every text yields a single, definitive reading. But in fact, there are many interpretations of reality, many readings of every text. Each represents only a perspective: "All thought inevitably derives from particular standpoints, perspectives, and interests. . . ."

Step 2: Relativism: No single perspective on reality can claim to be the exclusive truth. Since "there is no external reality subject to partition and definition . . . different viewpoints generate different understandings of events. . . ." An interpretation may claim to be "true," but only relative to its own interpretive framework. There is no way we can step outside our perspectives, our interpretive frames, and see whether they fit an external, independently existing reality. Standards of evidence, rationality, and objectivity are themselves relative to the frameworks. Consequently, the pursuit of "objective" truth is a myth and a delusion.

Step 3: Groups. There is no purely individual act of expression. There is no expression or interpretation without language, and language, like all systems of cultural representation, is social. "The literary act is a social act." Hence, texts, interpretations, and other cultural representations reflect the perspectives not merely of individuals but of groups or "interpretive communities."

Step 4: Identity. A person is not an atomistic, autonomous, essential, noumenal self – free to invent its own identity. The self is "socially constructed," constituted by its membership in society or, more precisely, by its membership in particular groups whose interests may be in conflict with dominant social interests.

Step 5: Interests: "There is no possibility of a wholly disinterested statement" – if there were, we would have no interest in making it. Every judgment or expression reflects the interests not only of individuals but, more crucially, of the social groups or interpretive communities that constitute the society.

Step 6: Power. Whatever else they may be (or pretend to be), texts and ideas are ways of exercising power. In every communication situation, some people have more power than others by virtue of their membership in different groups. The more powerful are able to use such cultural representations as texts and ideas to shape the thinking, feelings, and behavior of the less powerful. Texts, ideas, and other cultural representations are effective in large part because they mask their purposes and seduce their victims.

Step 7: Race, Class, and Gender. The most fundamental interests and power relations are those based on race, class, and gender. The groups suffering the most persistent and intense oppression have been women, minorities, and the poor, both within Western societies and within the reach of the West's global power. The cultural expressions of these groups have been repressed or marginalized by the dominant culture that reflects the interests of Western white male elites.

Step 8: Politics. All cultural expressions and practices reflect, express, and support power relations and are, therefore, political. The question is not whether higher education or some other cultural arena is to be "politicized" – it is political already. The question is whose power is expressed and sustained by a particular institution and whether the current power relationships are to be challenged.

Step 9: Empowerment. The hegemony of one group over another is incompatible with the ideas of equality, liberation, and the full realization of human potential. Hence, Western white male elites should relinquish power over others, and oppressed groups should take power over their own lives.

Step 10: Inclusion. Works reflecting the interests of the dominant class must be unmasked, and their hegemonic biases – patriarchy, racism, and imperialism – revealed. Ideas of what is "central" and "normal" have served the interest of the dominant class, while the traits of oppressed groups have been regarded as "marginal" and "abnormal." These hierarchies and perhaps all hierarchies – perhaps all dualisms – must be challenged. At the same time, work by and for the oppressed must be retrieved and fully appreciated. If these works do not meet traditional academic standards, then the standards should be changed.

Step 11: The Tyranny of Objectivity. Ideals of truth, objectivity, reason, argument, evidence, impartiality, et cetera – elements of a "regime of truth" – are themselves among the instruments of oppression. The "assumed detachment of scientific observers from what they observe," for instance, is "made possible through organized hierarchies of science where, for example, woman work as bottle washers, research assistants, or computer operators." The vaunted superiority of objectivity over subjectivity, of reason over emotion, of mind over body, of universal over particular, reflects hierarchical or "vertical" traits associated with

Western white males and devalues "horizontal" traits associated with women, minorities, non-Western peoples, and the poor.

Step 12: (Re)vision. The "spurious appeal to objectivity, science, truth, universality" must be replaced by "a politics of truth that defines the true as that which liberates and furthers specific processes of liberation." Ideas and interpretations that support hegemonic structures must be replaced by ideas and interpretations that support the interests and increase the power of women, minorities, and the poor. The test of an idea is not whether it meets traditional canons of evidence and argument, but whether it furthers the political interests of the oppressed, whether it is helpful in "generating the history we want."

Step 13: Political Standards. The regime of truth and the tyranny of objectivity must be replaced by norms more sensitive to the perspectives and interests of oppressed groups, that is, by what its critics call "political correctness." What is said, taught, or published – and who is hired – should be judged not by hegemonic standards of merit and objectivity, but by whether it advances or hinders the empowerment and liberation of women, minorities, and the poor. New texts should be selected that will help to empower these groups. Traditional texts should be given interpretations that advance the interests of the oppressed. Matters of historical, economic, or scientific interpretation should be included, excluded, or revised in light of this political goal. "Interpretation that shores up things as they are or prevents social change by encouraging resistance to it, by encouraging the view that change is illusion – because action itself, which would produce change, is too problematically beset by unavoidable historical repetition" – should be excluded from the classroom because of its harmful social effects. This does not mean that an "educational" goal is being replaced by a "political" one. Education, like everything else, is already political. It means that a humane and egalitarian politics is replacing an inhumane and oppressive politics.

Step 14: Higher Education. Therefore, the aim of higher education should be not the pursuit of truth, which is both an illusion and an instrument of oppression, but social transformation – changing ideas, symbols, and institutions from tools of racist, sexist, capitalist, imperialist hegemony to instruments of empowerment for women, minorities, the poor, and the third world. Q.E.D.

Several consequences follow from the transformationist thesis.

Step 15: Critical Pedagogy. If the goal of education were the pursuit of truth, the function of a teacher would be to enable students to see all sides of an issue and to weigh the pros and cons thoughtfully. But this approach to teaching rests on rationalist illusions and supports the status quo by encouraging endless debate. In a transformative university, the aim is not aimless exploration but "changing minds," enabling students to "spot, confront, and work against the political horrors of one's time," helping them become "agents of counterhegemony." One of the main tasks of critical pedagogy is to overcome "patterns of resistance" from students who resist ideas that challenge prevailing norms. Teaching that might to a traditionalist seem manipulative – a violation of a student's intellectual freedom – is actually an empowerment, a liberation.

Step 16: Speech Restrictions. Freedom must now be conceived as empowerment for the oppressed and liberation from the hegemonic illusions of the dominant class. The old notion of academic freedom, including the *lehrfreiheit* of the student, rested on the now discredited ideal of disinterested inquiry. Since social transformation is the proper function of higher education, freedom of discussion is less important than other values, such as overcoming racism, sexism, capitalism, and imperialism. Except as a tactical expedient, it would be inconsistent to allow racist, sexist, and exploitative ideas to be expressed.

Step 17: Public Denial. The transformationist university is by definition in conflict with the surrounding society. However, it depends on that society for both financial support and whatever degree of autonomy it retains. Transformationists would undermine their base of operations if they were always open and candid about their goals and activities. Therefore, in speaking to the public, it will be important to deny that political standards are being enforced and to minimize the extent of curricular and pedagogical change. This may seem deceptive to those who adhere to the ideal of disinterested truth, but for those who understand that the idea of "eternally 'true' theory" must be replaced by "a kind of rhetoric whose value may be measured by its persuasive means and by its ultimate goal," speaking differently to the public than to each other is justifiable.

III. The Argument Considered

Steps 1, 2, and 11: Perspectives, Relativism, and Objectivity. It is not difficult to locate serious arguments about realism, relativism, objectivity, the meaning of truth, and so forth – the history of philosophy from the Greeks to the present abounds in such discussions. But these discussions differ in several ways from the transformationist view. In the past, philosophical critics of such objectivist traditions as realism and rationalism have not tried to derive a new political mission for educational institutions from their critiques. Their philosophical critique has itself been an intellectual project, with intellectual goals and methods, still very much a part of the pursuit of truth.

Serious philosophical critiques of objectivity and realism have themselves been presented with clarity, precision, rigor, and a respect for counterarguments, traits regarded by postmodernists as symptoms of the tyranny of objectivity. One literary theorist, Robert Scholes, has pointed out the postmodernist neglect of the referentialist tradition represented by Gottlob Frege, Bertrand Russell, Peter Strawson, and John Searle – a tradition postmodernists nevertheless claim to have refuted. One finds, instead, ritual invocations of Thomas Kuhn and Richard Rorty, unaccompanied by a close reading of their arguments, much less those of their critics. Nevertheless, Kuhn and Rorty are taken to be conclusive and to license anything that can be called a paradigm shift or a conversation – to license, in fact, a politicization of higher education that neither Kuhn nor Rorty endorses.

Postmodern arguments against objectivity often make the bold and inaccurate assumption that the only forms of objectivism are pristine Cartesian rationalism or empiricist positivism (which, oddly enough, they tend to equate). Since the more extreme forms of Cartesian and positivist thinking are fairly easy to refute (and were indeed refuted long before Jacques Derrida), transformationists end up refuting positions no one holds – heroically jousting at windmills that have already been knocked down – and declaring an easy triumph over Western rationalism without bothering to examine the more credible and sophisticated forms of objectivism. When they do pay enough attention to recent epistemology to note that most philosophers are neither Cartesian rationalists nor positivists, transformationists sometimes leap to the conclusion that these philosophers must agree with their own relativism.

Caricaturing objectivism, transformationists achieve easy triumphs over phantom opponents. Metaphysical realists do not, for example, hold or need to hold that there is a single, definitive description of reality or anything close to it. All they hold or need to hold is that, of the various descriptions of reality, we can say that some are true or more adequate than others, and that reality, and not merely what we say about it, has a role in determining truth and adequacy. Many forms of realism fully acknowledge that mind, language, or conceptual frameworks make a contribution to knowledge. If we did not have the concept of a "key," we could not ask whether one was in the drawer. But having the concept, we can ask, and the answer will be in the drawer, not in our concepts. There are many ways to analyze the relation between what is in our minds and what is in the world, but none of them is as simple-minded as the simplistic realism attacked by transformationists.

Most objectivists hold that we understand the world by applying our concepts to the facts of experience. Objectivists understand that there is considerable latitude within a conceptual framework for arranging facts to fit the framework, for positing epicycles on top of epicycles, as the late followers of Ptolemaic astronomy did, to make the theory consistent with the facts. But objectivists also understand, as transformationists seem not to, that sometimes facts finally overwhelm conceptual frameworks. Otherwise, there would never be the anomalies that, according to Kuhn, lead to conceptual change. Facts may be theory-dependent, but theories are also fact-dependent.

The transformationist form of solipsism — that we are all trapped within our interpretive communities — is in some ways less persuasive than classic solipsism. It is odd to believe that individuals can get outside their own minds but not outside the beliefs of the groups of which they are members: if a person can make one leap, why not the other? Moreover, people seem to be able to challenge their groups' norms, change them, leave one group for another, describe and criticize them with a distance unimaginable if group relativism were right. It has been possible, for example, for people steeped in a culture that regarded African-Americans as less than human, to have experiences of African-Americans that refuted their acculturation. It has been possible for people raised in religious communities to reject religion, and for people raised in secular communities to embrace it. If matters so fundamental as who is a human being and whether there is a God are not determined by cultural membership, what then is left of relativism? The relativist will rush to point out that these experiences themselves (and inferences from them) must be described (and justified) in the language of some group, but so what? The question is whether group membership prescribes ideas and beliefs, and hence circumscribes knowledge and choice, not whether it provides the linguistic apparatus for ideas, belief, knowledge, and choice. Perhaps language is, as Friedrich Waismann said, "open-textured," its rules compatible with open-ended variations; perhaps groups, including whole cultures, are porous, open to new ideas and experiences.

Steps 3 through 6: Groups, Identity, Interests, and Power. The transformationist argument posits that the self is socially constructed through membership in various groups, most notably race, class, and gender. One's identity, interests, and power reflect group memberships. Language, ideas, and values, therefore, reflect the interests of groups and provide effective means by which dominant groups can control and shape the self-understanding of less powerful groups. These connections among personal identity, group membership, interests, power, language, and so forth are sometimes presented a priori, as though they were so interlocking conceptually that they needed no empirical confirmation. Often the connections are simply assumed in interpretations of literary texts, social institutions, and historical events, as if the fact that interesting interpretations could be based on them were sufficient validation — a rather circular proceeding and, in any case, a standard met by every theory with a clever practitioner.

In fact, broken down into individual claims and defined with sufficient precision, some of the transformationist hypotheses should be subject to empirical investigation. Transformationists have, however, given little effort to providing empirical support for the correlations they postulate, and the studies that have been made tend to be too weak in their correlations to support the strong theses advanced by the transformationist argument. For example, various efforts have been made to show that women write, think, talk, value, or behave in distinctive ways. The studies are interesting and suggestive, sometimes confirming what we already thought, sometimes surprising us, but they have never shown that all women write, think, talk, value, or behave differently from men. If some do and some do not, even if most do, such studies provide scant support for transformationist ideas. For example, it has not been possible for even the most discerning readers to deduce the gender of an author from the style alone. Similarly, efforts by Carol Gilligan and others to show that women value differently – value caring more than justice, for example – have been inconclusive. There are abundant examples of women who care passionately about justice – from the "equal pay for equal work" movement to the advocacy of the right to choose and of ownership over one's own body.

Even if most women and only some men value caring more than rights, or act cooperatively rather than competitively, or use conversation to establish relationships rather than to assert positions, do the transformationist theses follow? Feminists themselves are not sure how to interpret the results. Are the "feminine" traits inherent in being female, or are they social products? The former view, which is sometimes called "essentialism," provides clear support to the idea that gender determines identity and interests, but it is difficult to support in the absence of perfect uniformity among women, and it contradicts the transformationist belief in the social construction of the self. But if "feminine" traits are social products, a number of questions arise. Are they constructions by and in the interest of the dominant class, or by and in the interest of women? Are they stereotypes to be fought – "I have a right to be as competitive as I want to be," says the liberal feminist – or traits to be embraced and asserted? "Not if you want to be true to yourself and women everywhere," replies the radical. If the self is socially constructed, and it is only a sexist society that makes men and women different, then why cannot each individual choose his or her own identity?

Sometimes transformationists base the thesis that all ideas are political on the claim that no judgment is totally immune from interest, values, or purposes. But this argument rests on a non sequitur. The idea that judgments involve values and purposes does not imply that they are politically loaded or used to give one group power over another. The values could include, after all, such ideals as objectivity and impartiality.

Empirically, it would appear that people quite often set aside or rise above their interests. People do not appear to hold only those beliefs that support their group's interests. It would take very strong arguments to show that we should discount or disbelieve the empirical evidence. Instead, transformationists provide arguments that either rest on equivocation or validly support only weaker claims. They do, of course, present many detailed interpretations that unmask interests lurking within the most apparently disinterested texts and institutions. Even if one credits these interpretations, it is not clear why they are taken as proof that all beliefs are based on interests rather than as steps toward objectivity. If it is discovered, for example, that the generic use of "man" to stand for all human beings suppresses women, the decision to use "persons" instead seems to be a move toward a disinterested fairness and impartiality. The very ability to unmask interests is a tribute to the possibility of disinterested knowledge.

The concept of hegemony, as it is appropriated by the transformationists, is no clearer. When one culture influences another, the influence is often characterized as hegemony. But it is not plausible to regard all cultural influence as hegemonic, if this means that it is coercive or contrary to the interests of the influenced country. As pizza became popular in this country, perhaps Italy became more powerful — but not at our expense. If power includes the realization of one's values, the spread of Western-style democratic institutions around the world increases the power of the West, but to the benefit, not the detriment, of the new democracies. Denouncing all outside influence that alters indigenous cultures as "cultural hegemony" implies that cultures have nothing to learn from each other. Ironically, it is an extraordinarily reactionary view, a yearning, apparently, for the primordial tribes that dotted the planet five thousand years ago, before any culture bestirred itself to dominate another — the world before cultural hegemony.

Replacing the disinterested pursuit of truth with interest-based rhetoric makes, in classic terms, will rather than reason predominant. Marxist theory, correctly understood, says Lentricchia, is "a form of will to power." Similarly, harking back to the Greek Sophists, Fish has emphasized that the goal of rhetoric is simply to prevail, by whatever means are at one's disposal. On this view, argument is a test of wills conducted with verbal weapons, not an exchange of ideas in the pursuit of truth. If there is such a thing as truth, then the person who is open to persuasion, who can give up beliefs that are not well-founded, who is therefore open to the truth, is better off than the willful person who insists on "winning" every argument, a closed soul who can learn nothing. If there is no such thing as truth, then there is nothing but winning – and maybe not even that, since presumably there would also be no truth to the question of who won.

Step 7: Race, Class, and Gender: Traditional social reformers tried to create a society in which each individual would be able to fulfill his or her potential. But the group-interest thesis requires that social goals be framed in terms of the power of groups, not the aspirations of individuals. Marx singled out class as the critical category and provided a theory of history to justify this choice. Recent thinkers emphasize race and gender as well. The emphasis on race, class, and gender has less to do with a general theory of social and historical dynamics than with a theory of oppression. The argument for focusing on race, class, and gender is not so much that they are the moving forces of history as that they identify the most oppressed groups. Occasionally someone mentions that people have also suffered because of their religion or other factors, but, oddly enough, even so persistently persecuted a group as Jews receives scant attention in current debates. No one seems to be proposing that more Jewish texts and topics be added to the curriculum – Maimonides and Spinoza are regarded as just more dead, white, European males. The problem is, of course, that, despite a history of persecution and discrimination, American Jews are rather successful. Sometimes there is hesitation over Asian-Americans, some of whom have been successful, while others at this point are less so. There even seems to be a bit of irritation when such groups succeed, refusing merely to be victims, since this success does not fit with the image of a closed, oppressive capitalist society. The emphasis is always on groups that have been oppressed but have not, so far at least, succeeded. Since some members of various groups – some Asian-Americans, some Latinos – have been more oppressed or, conversely, more successful than others, the groupings to be favored have to be fine-tuned. Gradations have been established among various Asians and Hispanics, depending on racial background, national origin, and social class. By these criteria, it would be more important for the curriculum to include works by Carlos Fuentes than Miguel de Cervantes, but even more important to include works by a working-class Chicana.

The logic of this position is puzzling. If it is important to focus attention on the precise subgroup that has suffered, then why not go all the way to the individual level? Two individuals may be identical in their group membership, and yet one may have suffered more hardships or handicaps than the other. If hardships and handicaps are the key to consideration, why not focus on the particular individuals who have suffered the most? Even if it were true that individual identity were formed primarily out of group affiliations, it would not follow that one should treat individuals in terms of their group memberships rather than in terms of their own particular traits and histories. If it is valuable to read the writings of an oppressed person, then one should read the writings of an individual who was in fact oppressed, not the work of an individual who happens to be a member of a group, many or most of whose members were oppressed. Of course, then some members of the white-male-European canon (the slave Epictetus, for example) would count.

Even more doubtful than the focus on the group is the idea that some oppressed people "speak for the oppressed," while others do not. The minority writer who denounces America as hopelessly racist may be seen as speaking for the oppressed, while the minority writer who sees America as an increasingly open society may be seen as a tool of the dominant class. In spite of the talk of "other voices," the only voices that count are those who share the general sociopolitical outlook of the transformationists. Besides the problems this view poses for academic freedom and intellectual diversity, it poses a logical problem for the transformationist position. What is the point of all the talk about relativism and group interests if it turns out to be perfectly possible to identify the correct political views regardless of one's race, class, and gender? There is an implicit universalism here that the postmodernist is supposed to reject.

Steps 8, 9, 10, and 12: Politics, Empowerment, Inclusion, and (Re)vision. Consistent or not, there is an implicit universalism at the heart of the transformationist view as it plays out on American campuses. All the talk of hegemony and domination, inclusion and empowerment, rests on strong normative commitments, a belief in radical egalitarianism and the transformation of people into "better people." Given these strong normative commitments, one might expect to see more discussion of the rich literature on such normative political topics as the different meanings of equality, the ways in which strong values such as freedom and equality can conflict, the epistemological grounding of rights and goods, and so forth. While postmodernists pride themselves on the sophistication of their critical analyses, their normative claims seem to be based on little more than a passion for equality, an anger at what they see as oppression, the shock at "the political horrors of one's time" and the feeling of being "alienated and dispossessed" reported by Lentricchia.

When questions about the proper conception of freedom or equality are raised, they are often recast as questions of strategy. What conception of freedom empowers women? What conception of equality undermines capitalism? These discussions do not answer the kinds of objections outsiders would raise, and presumably are not meant to do so. Individuals who see themselves primarily as members of oppressed groups, and who believe that distinctive insights and perhaps even an exclusive truth follow from that membership, do not necessarily feel the need to answer the objections of outsiders. History is, alas, littered with the remains of groups – some of which have done much harm – that felt no need to justify their beliefs and actions to others. Such an attitude closes rather than opens discussion, protects rather than inhibits irrationality, and encourages the pursuit of power rather than the pursuit of mutual understanding. Epistemologically, no one group has sufficient grounds to claim a privileged status for its beliefs. Institutionally, higher education cannot perform its function – to expand human understanding – if it surrenders to such claims.

Steps 13 through 17: Political Standards and Critical Pedagogy. The mission of a university dedicated to the pursuit of truth is to teach students the modes and methods of inquiry, the major alternative views in each field, and ways to articulate and assess arguments on each side. The university teacher, declares the American Association of University Professors' 1915 Statement of Principles, should

> set forth justly, without suppression or innuendo, the divergent opinions of other investigators; he should cause his students to become familiar with the best published expressions of the great historic types of doctrine upon the questions at issue; and he should, above all, remember that his business is not to provide his students with ready-made conclusions but to train them to think for themselves, and to provide them access to those materials which they need if they are to think intelligently.

The ethic of teaching that follows from these principles supports the academic freedom of students as well as professors and restricts the right of teachers to use their power over students, which is psychological as well as practical, to push their own agendas.

By contrast, the mission of the transformative university is to produce students who are agents of social transformation. This mission assumes that professors have the right to use the classroom to advance their own political agendas. Teachers should be "transformative intellectuals," says Henry Giroux, "not merely concerned with forms of empowerment that promote individual achievement and traditional forms of academic success" but also with "social engagement and transformation" and with "educating students to take risks and to struggle within ongoing relations of power."

But what right do teachers have, one may ask, to push their own

political agendas in the classroom? To justify such a role requires, according to Giroux, a "theory of ethics that provides the referent for teachers
to act as engaged and connected intellectuals." Giroux bases this new
ethics of teaching on the concept of "emancipatory authority," the idea
that "teachers are bearers of critical knowledge, rules, and values" which
allow them "to judge, critique, and reject" prevailing social authorities.
"In my view," he says, "the most important referent for this particular
view of authority rests in a commitment that addresses the many instances
of suffering that are both a growing and threatening part of everyday life
in America and abroad."

In any case, political commitment is the touchstone; and hence the
goal of critical pedagogy is not open-ended inquiry but the political
transformation of the students. This goal presents a pedagogical challenge, since many students do not share the political views of their
transformationist professors. This disagreement is not, according to
transformationists, a healthy sign, a tribute to the diversity of free minds,
a basis for thoughtful dialogue and debate. Instead, it is a problem to be
overcome. In fact this problem – "the problem of resistance," as it is
called – is a major theme in transformationist writings on pedagogy. Jim
Merod writes that "the first resistance any teacher confronts is the student's defense against the threat of change" and places this resistance
within the context of "the collective nature of defense structures . . . the
cultural and ideological matrix that frames social action." "When the
culture at large or the neighborhood that has powerfully informed the
precritical intellect becomes an opponent for the somewhat stumped
teacher," writes Merod, "such opposition constitutes a defense that
dampens the possibilities of bringing distrustful students to the threshold
of critical imagination."

To their credit, some teachers who share transformationist goals
worry about the latent authoritarianism within politicized teaching.
While advocating an "anti-hegemonic teaching" that "addresses students
as socially and historically inscribed subjects who can be agents of social
transformation," University of Connecticut professor Maria-Regina
Kecht argues that "instructional methodology should not subordinate
the students" but should allow students to "represent their own worlds
and perspectives." Similarly, Carnegie Mellon University professor David
R. Shumway holds that "although teaching theory means teaching
Marxism, feminism, and other politically motivated discourses, it also
means teaching students not to accept uncritically what their teachers tell
them."

The transformationist proposes to mold students into, among other
things, radical egalitarians; but to do so would give teachers authority
over students that is incompatible with radical egalitarianism. The dicta-

torship of the proletariat may have been replaced by the dictatorship of the professoriate, but the dilemma remains the same – how to achieve anti-authoritarian ends by authoritarian means.

In spite of its language of "critical thinking" and "liberation," critical pedagogy limits rather than opens inquiry. It assumes the finality of a single set of political commitments, an assumption that is epistemologically unfounded and untenable. Critical pedagogy also fails ethically because it treats other human beings as less than free and rational elements to be respected. At best, it is paternalistic; at its worst, disingenuous and manipulative.

IV. Conclusion: The Transformationist Vision and Its Consequences

Although the postmodern critique of objectivity has been put in the service of leftist causes, it seems more akin to fascism in its roots. How could the postmodernist resist the following logic:

> In Germany relativism is an exceedingly daring and subversive theoretical construction. . . . In Italy, relativism is simply a fact. . . . Everything I have said and done in these last years is relativism by intuition. . . . If relativism signifies contempt for fixed categories and men who claim to be the bearers of an objective, immortal truth . . . then there is nothing more relativistic than Fascist attitudes and activity. . . . From the fact that all ideologies are of equal value, that all ideologies are mere fictions, the modern relativist infers that everybody has the right to create for himself his own ideology and to attempt to enforce it with all the energy of which he is capable.

The quotation is from Benito Mussolini and expresses a central idea of the postmodernists – that, since contending beliefs represent contending interests and there is no rational way to adjudicate between them, the ultimate arbiter is power. For postmodernists, it is primarily verbal power, control over words and images, but power nonetheless.

As Mussolini understood, ideas have consequences. If the great intellectual achievements of civilization are taught solely as instruments of oppression or are simply thrown out of the curriculum to make room for more "empowering" materials, they will be lost. Older transformationists who themselves received a traditional education think that this is a misplaced fear. They continue to teach – and often to love teaching – Shakespeare even if their love is expressed in clever unmaskings of his patriarchal imperialism. They assume their students will also continue to read Shakespeare and to share their joy. But young African-Americans, for example, may not see the point in reading those they have been taught to see as their oppressors. What will the older professor say to persuade them? That they need to know the tradition the better to resist it? Will that be a compelling reason to young people who have already been "empowered"?

The most serious problem is that the postmodern argument for making the university an agent of social transformation protects itself from criticism, not only theoretically, but institutionally as well. The early steps of the postmodern argument may be questionable, but only grant them, and the remaining steps — including political correctness, critical pedagogy, speech codes, and denial — follow. Rejecting the principles and procedures of rationality, the view cannot be subjected to rational (as distinct from political) criticism. If the test of a theory is its effectiveness in producing desirable social change, then any critique will be condemned as reactionary. Any counterargument will be seen as oppressive. It is already considered "antifeminist harassment" for male students to pick at flaws in feminist arguments. The door is closed to further debate; the new orthodoxy cannot be questioned. You may freely embrace the transformationist argument, but, having once embraced it, you are never again free to question it. Allow this argument to shape the university, and no one will be free to question it.

Advocates of using the university for social transformation will be unmoved by these considerations. Yet what if they are wrong? Given the limitations of perspective they have themselves emphasized, they may have misread history and misargued epistemology. Racism, sexism, and economic inequality are complex phenomena. It is easy to condemn them but difficult to analyze them correctly, and more difficult still to determine the best solutions. Knowing that the analyses and prescriptions which represent today's most advanced thinking may be tomorrow's debunked myth, would it be wise to stop questioning, to give up the search for truth, to banish competing views from the curriculum, to close off further inquiry, and to substitute for these activities the training of students to become agents of a political ideology? Could a rational person freely choose such a course?

DAPHNE MERKIN

Notes of a Lonely White Woman

Once upon a time, there was a white upper–middle-class woman (although to hear her tell it she felt if not poor, then at least strapped for money most of the time), who was heterosexual (although she has recently been made to understand that such proclivities are no more fixed than the evening tide) and Jewish (an ethnic minority historically associated with victimization and literary talent, now held to be under suspicion on both these scores). This woman was also a mother (paid lip service to as a socially useful occupation, but mostly seen as a demo-graphic opportunity for exploitation by new magazines aimed at parents of "advanced maternal age" and by ever-proliferating children's stores) and a writer. She went ambling through the world, lonely as a Wordsworthian cloud, in search of company to pass the hours when she was not either staring at a blank piece of paper until the drops of blood formed on her forehead (an appealingly dramatic definition of her cho-sen vocation which she has pasted up on her computer screen), or wor-rying whether her child was developmentally abreast – if not ahead – of her peers.

She happened to come upon a group of women sitting under a tree, their heads bent together in discussion. She approached them shyly, as befitted a newcomer. One of them, evidently the leader, turned to her and asked her whether she had ever explored her bisexuality. Being an honest sort, she shook her head. The leader stared at her sternly. "Don't you read *New York* magazine?" Eager to belong, she answered truthfully in the affirmative. (Although she subscribed to a number of more de-manding and less trendy magazines, *New York* was the one she took to her bed when it arrived, happy to graze upon its smoothly-ingestible smorgasbord of gossip, reviews, listings, and soft "hard" articles.) Didn't she know, then, that lesbianism was chic, the leader asked her. She al-lowed that she did, but no one could hear her answer above the din. The leader's voice had risen to a shout: "AND WHAT ABOUT YOUR SELF-ESTEEM, WHAT ARE YOU PLANNING TO DO ABOUT THAT?"

I will here without further ado abandon my lonely white woman to her symbolic predicament – which is in some way the predicament of being a complex person in an age of cultural revanchism – and turn to the underlying problem behind this predicament, which is the problem of "political correctness."

I must say right off that although I see "political correctness" as a continuing and pervasive problem, both in and out of the academy, to expand upon the dilemma in a forum such as this one strikes me as the intellectual equivalent of bringing coals to Newcastle. What I mean by this is that a large part of the world goes about its business without any awareness that the term has come into being, or if they have heard of the term, they remain uncertain as to what it signifies. (Just as the term "multiculturalism" is commonly misunderstood to stand for an old-fashioned "melting-pot" approach to different cultures, rather than the newfangled compensatory approach which looks upon all cultures as either privileged – and therefore inherently bad – or marginalized – and therefore inherently valuable.) This part of the world is privy to political correctness, if at all, in its most watered-down, generalized form – that is, as a form of keeping up, culturally speaking, with the Joneses.

Thus, in June of this year (1993) *The New York Times* reported that a teacher's decision to show an anti-abortion film to seventh-grade students in Westchester County outraged parents and ignited a larger community debate about how "politically sensitive" issues should be addressed in the public schools. And in the July 1993 issue of *Vogue,* mention was made of a prominent New York socialite who was spotted wearing "the world's first politically corrrect charm bracelet (featuring the acronym C for Choice; H for Housing; A for Animal Rights; R for Racial Harmony; and M for Money to Fight AIDS). It was also this summer that I received a note from an editor at *The New Yorker* telling me an essay I had submitted was too "ethnocentric" – the translation being that it was too "Jewish." What stopped me short was that I couldn't imagine the word being applied by anyone but a liberally-inclined assimilated Jewish editor to anything but an essay on a Jewish theme. If it's Jewish, I thought to myself, it's the wrong kind of ethnocentrism. Next time around I'd try writing as a black Muslim and see who'd dare call me *ethnocentric. . . .*

Clearly, then, there is a whole hierarchy of pieties and subterfuges that accompanies the phenomenon, and one locates oneself according to which level of "correctness" one's antennae have picked up on. One doesn't, in other words, call blacks "Negroes," unless one wants to demonstrate a state of utter indifference to the post-sixties *Zeitgeist.* One doesn't call blacks "blacks" either, but rather "African-Americans," unless one wants to exhibit a somewhat somnolent attitude to the more recent developments in the nomenclature of penitence. (*The New York Times,* it's interesting to note, can't make up its mind in the course of one and the same article whether to employ the former or the latter term, as though a designation alone could redress a piece of history.)

The part of the world that *has* heard of "PCism" and its attendant disturbances is either at pains to distance itself from the host of implicit and explicit opinions that go along with being a convert to what isn't so much a movement as a singular, heavily media-influenced shift in ordinary modes of cognition (for example, "I know this is very un-PC of me, but I really think most women still want to get married by the time they're twenty-five"); or they're caught up firmly in its grip and can't imagine who would choose the darkness of the pre-PC epoch over the enlightenment of multiculturalism and gender studies.

To ascertain how thin PCism really is, one has only to look at the thinness of the criticism of it. (Camille Paglia, for instance, has gotten as far as she has with her thuggish mode of anti-feminism because the stage is otherwise empty.) Political correctness has, with a few rare exceptional instances, confounded any critique of itself because it has so successfully carried off the intellectual spoils of a global consumer democracy – with that system's implied promise of equal choices for all and its denial of the continuing realities of power, violence, and class. Jacques Attali, in his provocative jeremiad, *Millennium: Winners and Losers in the Coming World Order,* touches upon some of the unresolved imperatives underlying a market society such as ours, which includes a basic refusal to deal with the politically *in*correct fact that there will always be haves and have-nots: "To be sure," he writes, "a central conundrum remains: how to balance economic growth with social justice."

The real trouble with "political correctness" as it is played out in the media is that it so often appears to be a done deal – the triumph of cultural osmosis over *realpolitik*. What one knows and feels to be the truth about contemporary life – for example, that AIDS is not only a tragic plague but also a darling of the press, attended to with an insistence other ravaging diseases (such as breast cancer or schizophrenia) have failed to garner for themselves – is not only resisted as a notion but defined by the continual assertion (most recently made by a writer in an interview in *The New York Times,* several days after his sensationalistic piece about having contracted AIDS appeared in *The New Yorker*) that AIDS is ignored by the reigning powers-that-be.

I can think of no other disease the symbol of which – the telegenic looped red ribbon – is worn tirelessly, pinned to lapels and collars, at occasions and events which have no connection whatsoever to the subject of AIDS. Hollywood has embraced it as a platform *nonpareil,* but so have less likely tribunes. "AIDS awareness" has overtaken the arts to a degree that verges on the automatic. Last year, as a judge of the

National Book Critics Circle, I was handed a pre-pinned red ribbon to wear on stage along with the other judges, minutes before the awards ceremony began. It simply hadn't occurred to the person who had arranged for this homage to inquire beforehand whether there were any of us who were disinclined to wear the ribbon.

Of course, just as AIDS is a PC illness if ever there was one, so the pro-choice movement in all its uncalibrated stridency is a perfect PC cause. When I suggested to the features editor of one of the more literate women's magazines, that it would be interesting to write a piece from the other side − from the point of view of a woman inside the right-to-life movement − I was told that the magazine had a policy of not acknowledging such views. The credentials of both the pro-choice cause and the AIDS cause are impeccable, since both imply a subversion of the conventional assumptions of the body politic without directly attacking those assumptions. Both touch, as well, on the all-important issues of class, race, and gender − that trio of analytic cudgels used, in a more academic context, to smash the daylights out of a canon perceived as being composed of too many benighted late nineteenth-century and twentieth-century *Übermenschen*.

What is unfortunate is that the quality of irreproachable moral superiority which is one of PC's more insidious characteristics has effectively muffled a frank atmosphere of debate and silenced those who have qualms about its operating principles. To even begin to question the premises of either of these holy causes is to risk being branded a shrill and heartless troglodyte. To suggest, for instance, that in America, at least, AIDS continues to be a very specifically induced, localized disease largely affecting homosexuals and intravenous-drug users and has *not* passed into the heterosexual population in the manner initially predicted and might, therefore, not be the paradigmatic casualty of our times; or to suggest that the right to abortion on demand has had little effect on inner-city mothers who, ignoring the hard-won option of terminating unwanted pregnancies, continue to bear children at a breathtaking rate without the means to care for said children, is to come up against a horrified reaction to one's "homophobic" or "racist" views.

This brings me, curiously enough, to the not unconnected matter of why I fled the academy. I attended Columbia University as a graduate student in English in the late seventies, just when political correctness − not to be given its *soi-disant* identity for another decade − was beginning to gain a toehold. One might have imagined the university to be, a decade after the turmoil and disenchantment of the sixties, if not quite a haven of higher learning, certainly restored to its original disinterested purpose of educating. But if nature abhors a vacuum, nature particularly abhors a vacuum when the playing field is smaller rather than larger. I sensed the glimmerings of a new style of repressive order in very specific ways: In the first day of a seminar on the British moderns – Samuel Butler, Virginia Woolf, E. M. Forster, and so on – my hip, cowboy-booted professor approached the writers under discussion with all the guilt-ridden hostility of a card-carrying Weatherman. How, he wanted to know, did these writers produced by the British class system account for or deal with the fact of European hegemony – the global dominance of Empire, with George the Sixth straddling the top and the Third World down at the bottom? Although this was not the first time I had heard the Third World referred to in this way or the free world referred to as "the 'so-called free' world," it was certainly close to it. (If this strains the imagination, remember that this was still in the seventies, before "texts" took over where "novels" had once stood. Too, I had graduated from Barnard College which, with a few exceptions, had continued to teach English literature not as an offshoot of a larger contextual ideology but as a matter of readers and writers.) Even without further exposure, I knew I was not interested in "learning" how to read with the aid of this pious template that was being clamped down on a subtle and highly individualistic literature, squeezing the juice out of it.

There were other experiences: In another seminar, led by a dubious but *au courant* Britisher, I read *S/Z* by Roland Barthes and so entered into the lost horizon of deconstructionism. Although I found Barthes's writing entertaining and provocative, I immediately found myself wondering how it offered a deeper elucidation than other, more traditional approaches. (The truth be told, I found myself musing on the pity of it that Barthes wasn't born into a Talmudic family, where his close, irony-filled readings could be applied to less flimsy narratives.) I glimpsed the future – a future filled with dense semiotic murmurings, clogged with atonal words like "marginalized" and "valorized" – and I ran.

I ran, as it happened, straight into the arms of book publishing, which was itself about to be taken over by a fit of political correctness. (The furor caused by the publication of Kingsley Amis's misogynist novel, *Jake's Thing,* was just one example.) But since book publishing is a bottom-line enterprise where the academy is not, PCism is more a matter of cocktail-party patter than anything else. If a book looks like it'll sell, in other words, it makes not a whit of different whether it's by John Kenneth Galbraith or Rush Limbaugh. (Of course, it could be argued that, a few egregious instances of campus censorship of First Amendment rights aside, the triumph of political correctness is, in the end, largely a cocktail-party triumph: a mode of social discourse which ensures that the espouser of its views – however visibly privileged – is taken to be a thoughtful, well-meaning creature, fully attuned to the baneful ways of the democratic society he or she inhabits.)

To sum it up as I see it: Political correctness is a form of specious moral one-upmanship, an unholy stew composed of some leftovers from the egalitarian sixties mixed together with an expedient, yuppie-style approach to age-old questions of probity. It posits a false evening-out of the human topography, as though everyone could be pulled back to the starting gate where some referee would be there to see that no one had a leg up over the other competitors. The bitter truth is that there are, inevitably, head starts in real life, just as the bittersweet truth is that privilege isn't always privilege (being born into money and status doesn't ensure happiness, much less success). I find myself thinking often these days of a deeply cynical adage that used to be quoted to me with great relish by my publisher, Bill Jovanovich, a self-made, politically uncorrect man if there ever was one: *Life's a bitch. And then you die.* It strikes me as a more useful aphorism – in its toughness, if nothing else – than what I construe to be the politically correct version: *Life's an apology. And then you go work out.*

So, should we sit *shiva,* or is there any hope? One can place one's faith in the very fickleness of the American psychic landscape – that vast acreage filled with enough ontological anxiety to insure that within a crowded span of less than a decade there first appear phenomena and then, inevitably, counter-phenomena. For example, the Abused Inner Child syndrome (in which everyone from Roseanne Barr on down discovers that they were sexually abused or emotionally damaged as children) has been followed by the counter-syndrome of False Memory Syndrome (in which supposed adult survivors of sexual abuse discover that they have been misled by overzealous therapists into "remembering" incidents which they have repressed – not out of pain but because the incidents never happened in the first place.)

Media consultant David Garth, who began as a liberal and helped engineer John Lindsay's two mayoral victories, signed on with Rudy Giuliani, as he told *New York* magazine, in spite of an initial perception that Giuliani was "way right of center." "When I got to know him," Garth said, "I saw he was a decent guy, moderate and very smart, much quicker on his feet than people give him credit for. His major sin seems to be that he isn't politically correct – *and I've gotten a little sick of political correctness.*"

Many little sicknesses just might make an epidemic, if you see what I mean. Just as there was once a pre-PC era, so there will be a post-PC period, with new orthodoxies of its own, no doubt. I'm sure the student radicals of the sixties never envisioned the day when Jerry Rubin would start a dating service, or that Abbie Hoffman would spend his last years hocking fake Rolexess.

As for that lonely white woman out there looking for company: Perhaps she should start an Anti-Self-esteem Movement. Anyone care to join?

MARK MIRSKY

False Gods

Have I been a victim of "political correctness" for a good twenty years now? Like other sneaking diseases, it worked unnamed, undiagnosed, through the body politic for many of those years. I learned of the term only last November. It was in the wake of a conference on Céline. Returning home to the City College campus with a new definition of myself, I realized what had been going on for many years in the English Department. Even dedicated liberals like my colleague Leonard Kriegel had finally risen in a burst of frustration and complained about the same old list of recommended books, the politically correct blending of African-American protest poets from the sixties, Puerto Ricans, token Chinese-Americans, et cetera.

That latest of politically correct terms, "African-American," stuck awkwardly in my throat the first time I used it. Resentfully, I mastered it, feeling that I was being orally abused by the rhetoricians of liberation. In my life, I have already gone from "colored" to "negro" to "black," and now a new word was being forced upon me, while I had to teach Dubois's and Johnson's work apologetically, because they had not anticipated that the old language which described the African-American would be found wanting, even insulting. There was an agenda hidden in the term with which I could sympathize – the idea of disappearing into the American melting pot, leaving Africa behind, had been abandoned. Yet although I share the sentiment of wanting to keep ethnic identity alive, I have had no desire to be known as a Byelorussian-Jewish-trans-European West Semitic American. I didn't want the title "American Jew." I prefer to be an American and a Jew, to disappear at will into either identity and to mix them up. Something vaguely laughable seemed to hover over the German Jews' euphemism at the turn of the century, "American Hebrews." I might almost have suspected the same of "African-American," except that it was asserted in the very breath and by those who warned that America was to embrace another dose of "affirmative action," a term which meant that the faculty was to once again suspend judgment and make choices on the basis of color and gender. "Affirmative action" in hiring decisions meant that all our appointments of black faculty were suspect as acts of kindness rather than as acts of impartiality. The demoralizing effects of this, both on several brilliant black members of our English faculty and on many of the white faculty cannot be calculated. I can no longer swallow the old chestnut, "If there are two candidates, equally qualified. . . ." Human beings are unique, like their fingerprints, and they are never "equally qualified." No – we are back in the language of "separate but equal," which meant school facilities that were rarely equal but certainly separate.

"Do you see multiculturalism as politically or intellectually motivated?" The answer to this is the key to "political correctness." At the university, watching hiring practices, it is clear that the struggle to teach certain subjects is at one with the attempt to increase minority representation on the faculties. No one can untangle the movement's political and intellectual motivations. Since no intelligent American wants to see discrimination in terms of the old political categories – preferential treatment for men over women, for sons and daughters of the American Revolution, Protestants preferred – it becomes very difficult to answer the questions, "How strong is this movement?" and "What can – or should – be done to oppose it?" To demand a truly political curriculum, in literature for instance, is to mount a roller coaster. Are we to measure the relative strengths of Haitian, Jamaican, West African, and Chinese student populations, campus by campus, to determine a valid humanities reading list? Are we to count women against men at the beginning of a semester and revise our reading lists accordingly? "Why don't you mention more women?" an aggrieved feminist asked me in the middle of a graduate seminar in the writing of fiction. I began to reel off those I had, whose influence I felt: Isak Dinesen, Cynthia Ozick, Grace Paley, Virginia Woolf . . . but the student was not assuaged. I realize now what was wrong – my attitude. This is one of the aspects of "political correctness" that is most worrisome. Students imbued with an idea of what is "politically correct" come to class not to learn from the instructor, or discuss, or argue, but to have confirmed an attitude they already hold.

In writing courses, students, especially if they are humorless, who discover that the teacher does not share their assumptions are prone to defend themselves against criticism of their prose by asserting that they are not being understood. In courses where literature makes up most of the curriculum, students who have never been adequately prepared to think about the classics of English and Western literature are sorely tempted to bring the discussion around to texts that are closer to their own experience, especially ones they have read already. To recognize in the texts of another culture one's own experience is what education at a great university is all about. I was raised to believe that.

There were few if any books about the Jewish world I grew up in, when I studied at Boston Latin Public School, Harvard College, and Stanford University. It was not altogether "correct," and so I do retain a sneaking sympathy for "multiculturalism." When there were few African-American students at City College, I was assigning pages from Zora Neale Hurston's *Mules and Men* and photocopying pages of American Indian poetry that had been collected and translated at the beginning of this century. The new multiculturalism – will it teach the Yiddish poems written in America about the "African-Americans" whom the émigres from Vilna and Warsaw watched with fascination on the subways? I long to sneak a few subversive texts into an American litera-ture or civilization course. What I have observed at City College, how-ever, is that most of the Jewish faculty is far too "assimilated" to find the cause of teaching Jewish texts in the literature courses appealing. (Only the Holocaust is a subject which is politically attractive.) They sympa-thize with "multiculturalism" but with little devotion to the culture they knew once upon a time. For many academics who have lost interest in their own scholarship, the promise of a new reading list that will bring a political awakening, a renewal, to the department is irresistible.

The lapse in standards embraced by the universities at the beginning of the 1970s has made it more difficult, not less so, to address real prob-lems in the education of minorities in the United States. We have had not just "affirmative action" in employment but also "affirmative educa-tion," a euphemism for passing problems along. Standards at City College in the 1960s were too rigid, and there was no question in my mind that strong steps had to be taken to enroll more minority students. This is not the place to discuss open admissions at length. It has to be apparent to most intelligent citizens, however, that when you are trying to bring more students up to a certain level, it makes no sense to lower that level, claiming to have accomplished the wonderful when a signifi-cant number are able to hurdle a depressed bar. An educational bureau-cracy downtown watching numbers and teachers with their eyes on in-dividual students and classes have different perspectives. Several times in my capacity as a professor of English, I have been asked while marking placement examinations to assign a minimum grade to a student who has simply left a blue book blank or inscribed a single sentence, touching in its honesty, "Me no speak English." It may well be that this student is literate in another language. (There is a graduate-level mathematics semi-nar at Harvard, I am told, which is held entirely in Chinese.) I question, however, whether without special dispensation one can assign a class in remediation to such a student at a college. Generations of immigrants, my father among them, enrolled in elementary school, although they were well beyond the age of the rest of the class, in order to gain the proficiency in English and in American history to study at a college. It may well be that the elementary and high schools of American cities were a more serious place then, because of that enrollment. Have we badly confused social and educational goals in not insisting that most remedial work be carried out before college? Looking at the blank blue book which is certainly a sign of despair, I am troubled. In the freshman English courses I regularly see students who have been passed along by other instructors though they lack basic skills. I don't want to participate in such a cruel hoax.

The faith in the role of the university to heal society which is the basic tenet of "political correctness" is something I share. What I am suspicious of, however, is the belief that it can be done today and tomorrow. This is why the struggle over the traditions the university teaches is so bitter. If it were only a question of literary and historical texts, the texts themselves would be at the center of the discussion. Under the guise of the canon, it is the role of the university which is being argued. What is frightening is that in their search for tax funds, university administrations have been willing to represent themselves to the public as evangelical bodies ready to save society if they are adequately funded. Everyone who actually teaches knows how slow education is, and how uncertain, how dependent on the attitude of the student.

This is the real political situation, and the question of the correct texts and courses follows from it. Here we arrive at the cases of Michael Levin and Leonard Jeffries. Real politics, as I learned on the knee of my father, who was a state legislator, turns out to be a circus in which the public, guided by the media, turns to the clowns who have the wit or luck to parody the issues. No one on the campus easily discusses Professor Jeffries, because we are most of us, as my former student and colleague Michelle Wallace has pointed out, intimidated. "Just knowing he's down the hall makes discussion of race and ethnicity loaded," she told an interviewer for *The New Yorker*. We have all seen the professor walking down the corridors with what seems to be a praetorian guard, and some of us wonder why this is happpening on an academic campus. We read in the *Harvard Crimson* interview that threats were made to the interviewer and shuddered.

Yet like many other professors at City College, I would consider it dangerous if Professor Jeffries lost his tenure or position as a teacher because of unpopular, even outrageous views. I don't require Professor Jeffries or Professor Levin to muzzle their very wounding and often unfounded remarks. The court cases had nothing to do with this issue. Why should Professor Levin have sought to challenge the college administration's decision to give students, aware of his oft-expressed view that "poor educational and economic attainment by blacks in society is due to a lower average intelligence, not to race discrimination" and upset by this rhetoric (as I am), a chance to enroll in another section? A particular teaching schedule as opposed to a demonstrably inappropriate one is not a constitutional right. The college was not punishing Professor Levin, who has a reputation among some minority students as a good classroom teacher despite his provocative public statements, but rather giving students an alternative. I was quite shocked however when the late Irving Howe, once my professor, expressed outrage at the Levin case, but fell into a deep swoon of silence when I tried to press him on that of Professor Jeffries, Chairman of the African American Studies Department. Among other sweeping assertions in a speech at Albany that led to his dismissal as chairman, Professor Jeffries claimed, "Russian Jewry had a particular control over the movies, and [with] their financial partners, the Mafia, put together a system of destruction of black people."

A chairmanship at City College entitles its holder to make college-wide decisions as a member of the Personnel and Budget Committees, rule on division tenure recommendations (in Jeffries's case, the Social Sciences Division), and automatically seats the holder on the Faculty Council. The chairman sets policy within a department and must be responsible not only to the department but to the administration. A chairman is entitled to free speech, of course, but he or she cannot be a loose cannon, and the college rules, allowing the President to dismiss a faculty-elected chairman, recognize this. The meddling of a federal court in issues of college policy is a kind of specious doublethink. Tenure was not questioned, salary was not docked, nor were punitive teaching schedules imposed by the college. Professor Levin's course is a required one for every student at the college. During some semesters, Levin taught the sole section on a particular day and hour. Professor Jeffries's department teaches courses that are optional requirements of education majors at City College. One of my minority students came to me in the course of a past semester, deeply upset by remarks about race made by an instructor under Professor Jeffries's jurisdiction. It is a strange notion of academic freedom that excludes a student's right of choice when faced with instructors whose views are deliberately abrasive either to minorites or majorities.

There is some painful irony here. The administration at City College, in trying to be both correct and decent, was rapped on the knuckles. Professor Jeffries and Levin were judged "politically correct." That message may have amused the media, but it sent a wave of dismay through many of the teaching and secretarial staff to whom the college's sense of decorum is important. The difficult issue of how independent a department is of the central administration, of the goals of the college at large, was in question in the case of Professor Jeffries. We all know that departments are not independent of the college deans and officers, yet no

one on the faculty would wish their departments to simply be sub-
servient. Departments, however, which have become so "political" that
their members no longer share the same standards of impartial judgment,
of concern for facts that can be demonstrated, as one hopes most rep-
utable public and even private colleges assume, cannot simply function as
private enterprises.

I was told that in both the Levin and the Jeffries cases, the lawyers in
the State Attorney General's office arguing for the college administration did not adequately present either its views or the facts. One hopes
that it is only an instance then of an incompetent defense. The decisions,
however, were ominous, for they signaled that the judicial system is susceptible to the dread symptom of "political correctness," the virus of
"victimology." Despite opinions which were deliberately provocative,
both men were confirmed in their role as victims. A kind of malpractice
glee seemed to have seized the judicial system – everyone is a victim. The
courts awarded a large cash penalty to Professor Jeffries, who had not
gone into painful retreat upon his dismissal as chairman but embarked,
like Professor Levin, on the lecture circuit, where both profited from the
publicity and considerably supplemented their salaries.

When Professor Jeffries's views about a world split between "sun
people" and "ice people" were trumpeted in the media, no one questioned how he could have been put on curriculum committees of the
State of New York. His attitude had been well known to *The New
York Times* and to state officials for many years, but there was no review
of his appointment and no public demand for his review. (At the time of
his appointment, I was informed, there *was* some questioning of his
qualifications, by some alumni and trustees.) The attitude that race or
race and gender are the facts determining the direction of an individual's
life seems to me as questionable as choosing sexual preference or nationality as one's overriding identity. In the rhetoric of such advocacy, I feel
as if the intuition that has matured in American democracy, that the individual is distinct from background, color, creed, and gender, has been
subsumed. Yet it is exactly the constitutional defense of the individual
and the right of free speech that brought Professors Levin and Jeffries
their court victories.

In their speeches and reviews, there are heaps of victims on their side,
with a few desertions, dangerous or dumb, to the other side. Lost as well
in their manifestoes is the idea of self-criticism, humor, the agonized
questioning of one's own assumptions, all of which distinguish literature,
the profounder reaches of religious thought, psychoanalysis, and other
forms of intellectual speculation. Such self-scrutiny, based on a notion of
the individual as distinct from a society of truth-bearers (or a society of

intelligence or guilt-bearers), is a form of a too-often degraded political virtue, humility. Being humble and claiming to be a victim, though often confused, are two very different points of view.

Political correctness is finally a judgment of political discretion or, the real root of politics, of what is expedient. It has been politically expedient, or good politics, to define the African-American as a victim. That the African has been a victim, and a victim of political process, as the European Jew has been a victim, is true. Can you correct through politics? Of course you can — that is what politics is all about — but that doesn't necessarily make politics correct. We can all recognize that efforts to correct a politics that discriminates represent the slow sea change of constitutional movement toward the common good. To create a politics that constantly judges what is correct, or rather expedient, and creates categories of discrimination, is the very opposite. It poses a disastrous challenge to the idea of fairness. Political correctness and its fungus "victimology" heralds a twentieth-century world in which not health but disease, past and naturally present, is what nations aspire to. The correlative in the university literature course is the teaching of the novel, the short story, the poem as the confession of a victim or the chart of victimization. Literature taught from this perspective alone begins to shade into an ingenious form of propaganda.

If political correctness was only a religion of expediency, it would not be so dangerous, but like all false gods it has an uglier face, for what the decent, smiling mask conceals is its aspect as fashion. There is something noble about political expediency, for it recognizes that sometimes compromises with cherished principle have to be made for the sake of a difficult present situation. I saw such expediency practiced all the time in my father's career — such compromises are the stuff of politics. If my father ruined his political career by refusing to be expedient at many moments, fighting on for lost causes, stubbornly voting against what he considered corrupt giveaways, still he understood its importance and did not necessarily denigrate it. We have been witness here in New York to a fashion show in which a candidate with strong political credentials, Elizabeth Holtzman, was judged by the media to be the less glamorous of the two female office seekers in the last Senate campaign. Her hard-hitting criticism of Geraldine Ferraro was declared politically incorrect. It wasn't her criticism, however, but her presence in the race that irritated the opinion-makers. Holtzman was warned to stand aside from the political process, and when she didn't, she was blamed for the defeat of the other woman. When the male candidate proved to be an incompetent campaigner and was defeated, as Elizabeth (I freely admit she is a personal friend) had predicted, she was blamed yet again. Now she has been the subject of vitriolic attacks at dinner tables of normally intelligent people in Manhattan, to whom political correctness is not just a religion but the very fabric of their lives.

We arrive at the oxymoron. For the sake of correctness, or fashion, political correctness asks that politics, that is, the politics of judgment, cease. Yet when I question whether issues of race, gender, or nationality are primary in literature, when I scorn the notion that literature is best dissected in English departments by political considerations, the hornets begin to buzz. When I suggest that a certain epic is badly translated, or minor, or that since the Western tradition has in fact shaped the language we speak, English, we should give primary consideration to teaching Homer, the Bible, Dante, and Shakespeare in our humanities courses and be careful about too many side treks into the world of multiculturalism, I am met by a stubborn suspicion that I am anti-minority, Euro-centered, clearly out of fashion. I see the various groups assemble in department meetings by race and gender and wonder where I fit in among these gaggles. Political correctness is a church-going. Since the Bible, however, is the text of the congregation formerly in the present worshipers' pews, it in particular is in a sorry state. The Bible, that central literary text of so many centuries of literary men and women, and in particular of English-speaking men, women, and children, is clearly out of fashion in this secular Calvinism, relegated to a week of study in world humanities courses — and here where indeed the study of its "multicultural" milieu, its Hebrew, Greek, and Aramaic linguistic background or its commentaries as developed by the rabbis and church fathers might be relevant, there is rarely either time or will to do so.

It is always painful to be out of fashion. You feel stupid. Looking back, however, over the last twenty years to reading lists which bowed to expedient fashion, to the lowered standards, to the way students who should never have been admitted to a college until they mastered the rudiments of English were recruited, I feel anger. I fear the politically correct on the campuses I have attended or where I have taught, Harvard, Stanford, City College, because I look to these institutions for challenge, stimulation, and the preservation of a very difficult literary inheritance, sanctioned by a judgment that is ruthlessly fair, free from the politics of expedience and fashion. I look at the distortion of literature not just today but in the past, by authors temporarily in the grip of political correctness, even masters like Isaac Babel, and I am dismayed. I think of the havoc political correctness played in New York political life, in American politics, hobbling the Democratic party in particular. (I do not even allude to its distortions in the world of nonprofit foundations and arts councils.) It does not try to address what is real, but to disguise reality, to offer false hopes and romantic ideals of men's and women's capacity for instant conversion and indefinite charity.

It is not in its aspect of expediency, or fashion, that political correctness is most dangerous but in these charlatan dreams into which it lures us, flattering self-pity, encouraging a notion of moral superiority, promising the imminent Messianic age. It is the brutal, ugly inquisitor of this decade, of the end of a century, and its dulcet voice, announcing that it has come to save us, must not blind us to the rage which stokes its fires.

WILLIAM PHILLIPS

Against Political Correctness:
Eleven Points

1. The Issues

The first thing that strikes one in reading about the controversy over political correctness – or ideological cleansing, as it might properly be called – is that the issues are not accurately stated, at least not by the PC side. In fact, the PCers try to make it appear that they are simply bringing the so-called canon up to date. Despite the usual dismissal of Western traditions as a concoction of dead, white European males, they pretend that they are only adding representations of women and contemporary minority groups, such as blacks, gays, and lesbians. The truth is that the main body of the PCers are for throwing out most of what they mistakenly refer to as the canon.

The positions are usefully summed up by John Searle. In fact, he presents the arguments for PC in the best possible light, and he includes those with less extreme views. It becomes clear from the summary by Searle of the opposing camps that on one side are the traditionalists who give primacy to the legacy of Western traditions and history, though they would also include a study of other cultures, while the PCers want to do away with or deconstruct the past and concentrate on women, minority cultures, gay and lesbian movements, and third-world history. In addition, they distort and exaggerate the contribution of this history.

2. Conservatism and the Middle Ground

The PCers characterize those who do not go along with them as conservatives, while some academics propose a so-called middle ground. However, both these ploys are disingenuous. Left extremists usually try to discredit their critics by labeling them conservatives or reactionaries. Thus, the Stalinists called the anti-Stalinists imperialists, reactionaries, and enemies of progress. The truth is there is no distinct conservative position on traditional culture and education. The far right occasionally exploits the situation for its own ends, but even they do not insist on a fixed canon. The neoconservatives, who do not all take the same positions, also do not talk about a fixed canon. Indeed, nobody does.

As for a middle ground, it simply does not exist. One either supports the teaching of Western traditions and values, or dismisses them as the product of dead, white males. And the fact is that most practicing writers and critics who do not mouth the abstract theories widespread in the academy take for granted that there is a usable Western tradition which they draw on and perpetuate. Writers realize that they continue the Western literary and intellectual legacy – with modifications and additions, to be sure. Such academics as Gerald Graff pretend to present a middle ground by proposing to teach the conflict. However, the conflict is not a substitute for Western civilization, which is precisely what political correctness does not propose to teach. The suggestion is much like teaching the conflict between justice and injustice, murder and the preservation of life, Communism and anti-Communism.

There are also some academic commentators, such as David Bromwich and the art critic Robert Hughes, who create a false antithesis between the left and the right. They try to balance a criticism of the politically correct left by also criticizing Ronald Reagan and William Bennett. The trouble with this approach, however, is that Reagan and Bennett are not in the same arena as the PCers. And what Bromwich and Hughes actually are doing is covering their left flank, to ward off the standard criticism that opponents of political correctness are conservatives – which, of course, is the deadliest sin. Henry Louis Gates, Jr. also tries to cultivate the middle ground. He says he is against both extremes, which is a safe position, since everyone is against extremes, except extremists, who sometimes also pretend they're not at either end of the spectrum.

3. PC

What is political correctness? It is a loose but useful term, denoting a wide movement with many facets and differences, but essentially a new new left configuration. It includes extreme and radical feminist theories, gay and lesbian liberation studies and activities, ideas stemming from the deconstructionists, neo-Marxists, and remnants of old, revolutionary postures. It is not basically Marxist or revolutionary, but it is to a large extent anti-American, in some quarters anti-capitalist, pro-third world, pro-minority, and anti-Western cultural and political interests.

There is certainly no reason why such views should not be freely expressed. But the movement has gone far beyond the rights of intellectual advocacy. Unfortunately, it has seized academic power and has come to dominate large sections of university life and to intimidate the rest of the faculty and the administrators. The movement also has sought to silence academics and students who disagree with its premises and tactics. Instead of simply arguing their case, the politically correct academics have distorted and smeared the opposition.

What to do about this ideological cleansing is difficult to say – I'm afraid I can suggest nothing beyond constant intellectual and political argument against political correctness by those who have not lost their faith in independent thought and in the values of Western civilization. Unfortunately, students are in a weaker position, since they cannot cope with the superior knowledge and skills of their politically correct teachers.

It might be noted that no serious person denies the unsavory elements in the history of Western civilization. But what the PCers do is to equate Western civilization with its faults, failing to concede or to recognize its achievements. They seem to deny that what we are today is the culmination of our achievements in the past – unless of course we assume that ours is an evil civilization.

4. Multiculturalism

Multiculturalism is the battle cry of the politically correct and those under its influence. But this too is an argument in bad faith. For no serious person denies that America is made up of people who have come from different cultures. The issue is whether America is to be united or divided by its cultures, as Arthur Schlesinger, Jr. argues persuasively in his recent book, *The Disuniting of America*. In fact, the issue is further clouded by the PCers who, behind a mask of championing the cultures of different groups, are actually pushing the interests of blacks and putting down the legacies of the dominant cultures of the West. They also, to repeat, are promoting a largely inflated African heritage for blacks as a source for the knowledge and science of the West. If they were to succeed, Western culture would be wiped out, or at least demoted to the status of an evil past.

It might be further noted that there is very little if any competition to the mainstream of Western culture from most of the cultures and nationalities of those who have emigrated to America. There are no demands made, for instance, by the Polish, or Italian, or Danish, or Brazilian, or Czech, or Russian, or Jewish, or Asian people – among many others – to have their cultures given equal, if not greater, representation in American education.

5. Deconstruction, Relativism, etc.

Some observers maintain that deconstruction and kindred doctrines are on the wane in the academy. This may be true, but their influence persists, partly in the aura of such figures as Derrida and Foucault in the ideological atmosphere of the politically correct movement. The traditions of Western literature and thought are being systematically deconstructed to deny their achievements or intellectual authority. Works from the past are whittled down to expose their bias against women, blacks, and non-Western peoples. Shakespeare was an imperialist and colonialist, Columbus an imperialist and colonizer, Plato and Aristotle the scions of a slave society, et cetera.

The politically correct movement is also imbued with the idea of relativism, with the notion of an absolute relativity. The idea is rampant that no work can be considered better than another, or that there are no truths we can accept. Of course, the number of absolutes – such as that murder is evil, for example – is limited. But there are some truths and many facts, and some ideas are more valid than others. And if literary standards and distinctions are abolished, we're lost in an ideological nihilism that borders on chaos. However, this nihilism does not seem to prevent the politically correct from promoting certain ideas and works over others – works that fit the prescriptions of the various components of the politically correct movement. It also allows for the dismissal of any criteria of judgment and standards associated with Western civilization and tradition.

There is a good deal of confusion about the source of literary standards – which is further confused by political correctness. Many PCers blatantly assert that traditional literary standards reflect the power and political interests of various groups. There are also some politically correct academics, such as Barbara Herrnstein Smith, who seem to believe that academics invent literary standards in conformity with their own ideas and causes, and therefore create the curriculum.

The truth is, however, that standards in literature, as in the other arts, are set by professionals in the field. This should not be surprising, since standards are set by professionals in all fields – in medicine, sports, law, even carpentry. Whether, for example, one basketball or football player is better than another is determined not by academics or amateurs but by professional players and coaches.

6. Open Debate

Part of the problem, to repeat, is that the PCers argue in bad faith by concealing their true agenda and by distorting the positions of their critics. In addition, they use punitive tactics against their critics by threatening their status and even their jobs. They try to isolate them from their students and from the rest of the faculty, by calling them reactionaries, racists, and homophobes. In their assault on the so-called traditionalists, as Alan Wolfe pointed out, they have the assistance of administrators, who are either too cowardly to resist the pressures of the PCers or who have come to agree with them. The examples are numerous and often hair-raising.

7. Students

Aside from the harm of political correctness to the clarity of thought, its main victim is the helpless student. Political correctness would not only deprive students from learning something of the heritage of Western civilization, it also tries to brainwash students with a substitute culture of minorities and with the politics of popular culture. As I have said, it also teaches students that truths and judgments are relative and therefore cannot be applied to moral or intellectual questions. It indoctrinates students with the idea that standards are code words for racial and gender interests and that they serve only to perpetuate white, male power. The educational effects are disastrous. For without the deconstructed outlook of political correctness, students have enough trouble with whatever traditional knowledge is offered them; now they have a rationale for not learning even a minimal distillation of Western civilization.

8. Egalitarianism

It would be a mistake, however, to attribute all the ills of education to political correctness. Political correctness is the false educational remedy that not only acts to miseducate students but also has the effect of obscuring some of the fundamental causes of the educational crisis in America. The fact is that a wave of anti-intellectual and anti-educational attitudes has swept over the country. The belief that a properly educated person makes for a civilized citizen has almost disappeared. We cannot conceal the fact that standards have fallen, that the primary value for many students is in getting a degree, not in learning. This situation has been documented over and over again by educators who do not mouth the clichés of educational jargon. It has been demonstrated endlessly by Albert Shanker, one of the few commentators to take the issues head-on. Unfortunately, this dismal situation has been obscured not only by advocates of political correctness but also by those myopic politicians dazzled by the power of money who advocate more and more spending. But spending, it should be clear by now, is not the solution to what is basically a cultural malaise. And, unfortunately, there are no easy solutions to this widespread cultural phenomenon. The only answer, I'm afraid, is for clear thinking by intellectuals and educators to mount a steady campaign for the importance of a traditional education in maintaining a civilized society. Of course, the PCers are of no help in this matter. Their putdown of so-called elitism and of intellectual traditions supports the native lowbrowism and middlebrowism – and the myth if not the reality of egalitarianism.

9. The University

As Alan Wolfe notes, the character of the American university has undergone many changes. Until recently, it has been assumed that the purpose of the university is to transmit knowledge to students. It has been free of the trendiness and gimmickry of multiculturalism. But it has not been the educational utopia of some nostalgic commentators. In literary studies, until the arrival of the New Criticism, it was full of old-fashioned, Germanic scholarship. It did leave room for genuine research and thinking, and for independent ideas. It did not have an ideological power group such as the PCers today. It was possible for good students to get a classical education. One of the by-products of multicultural contemporaneity is the elimination of courses with general historical and intellectual content in favor of studies in movies, feminism, gay liberation, pop culture, and various other causes and trendy subjects. But in addition to the deteriorating effects of such politically correct curricula, in general, there has been a drift to more popular subjects which the PCers have exploited for their own ends.

One of the side effects of political correctness is to obscure the basic conversion of many universities into conveyors of mass culture. And this is a cultural phenomenon that most educators and intellectuals have not faced. Perhaps this shift has been unavoidable in the wake of mass education. So far as I know, America is the only country where egalitarianism has gone so far as to assume that everyone has the right, regardless of qualifications, to go to college. Even in the former Communist countries, it was taken for granted that only qualified students had this right. Other students went to vocational schools. I don't suppose the clock can be turned back. But some bold steps would have to be taken to restore the intellectual level of the university. Nor can the infusion of money do anything but conceal the problem.

10. Theory

PC is heavily weighted with literary theory and the entire movement by a foundation of general theory – or perhaps it should be called ideology. It is interesting to note that both the literary and the general theory have their source in the line that runs from Saussure through Levi-Strauss, Lacan, Derrida, and Foucault. As Brian Vickers points out in his excellent book, *Appropriating Shakespeare,* the thread consists essentially of isolating language, separating it from its object, detaching the signifier from the signified. The process was started, though only partially, by Saussure, but subsequently continued, in a distorted form, by the other French luminaries. The result was to make language autonomous, and to deprive it of meaning and interpretive power. The American literary theorists imported this concept of language and its corollaries: the autonomy of the text and the multiplicity of meaning. Furthermore, to this intellectual baggage was added, from Derrida and Foucault, the Marxian and Nietzschean rejection of the past, and of the principle of objectivity. Vickers further points out that the systems of the American theorists, like those of the French, are self-referential and self-contained. Thus they cannot be checked against either reality or with other ideas. These concepts died a natural death in France, yet they found a new life in the American academy.

11. The Culture

As I have suggested – and the point has been elaborated by Edith Kurzweil and Mark Lilla – political correctness would not have spread so quickly and widely in the academy if it were not also supported by more primitive but basically similar trends in the culture as a whole in this country. The native anti-intellectualism, the disdain for "elitism" and high culture, the egalitarian myth, the liberal guilt over the heritage of black slavery, the indifference to cultural standards, the immersion in popular culture, the widespread notions about the relativity of truth, morality, and aesthetic criteria – all these cultural currents create a popular parallel in the larger culture to the academic political correctness. It is hard to say whether the political correctness of the academy is the cause or the symptom of the malaise. Perhaps the academy and the popular culture influence and fertilize each other. In any event, the popular culture did not need Derrida, and the academy did not need Madonna.

In this respect, political correctness is an American phenomenon and one indigenous both to academic and popular culture in this country. But, at the same time, it is in this respect difficult to eradicate. The hope is that a false ideology will run its course and that those writers and intellectuals with a sense of their craft and their traditions will have an effect on the rest of the culture. For the opposition to PC, in addition to independent academics, exists largely in the serious culture of writers and practicing critics.

RONALD RADOSH

McCarthyism of the Left

Can anyone doubt at this late date that both political correctness and multiculturalism are a real threat to the integrity of our culture? Certainly, a countereffort has been made by its adherents to present themselves as a group with a reasonable agenda – attempting only to once and for all have some attention paid to women, blacks, gays, and other oppressed minorities whose contributions have been ignored for decades. Actually, for the past twenty years responsible historians have been engaged in rectifying the old scholarship, as anyone who reads professional journals knows. But that is not what the PC debate is really about. Let me just mention a few highly publicized incidents occurring in 1993, which allow us to perceive the real issues.

As readers know, the jury verdict in the Leonard Jeffries trial found the City University of New York to have violated Jeffries's free speech when it removed him from the chairmanship in the Department of Black Studies at The City College of New York. The response of City University was more instructive. Its administrators sought to appeal the verdict, without owning up to the fact that when Jeffries was originally hired, all standards applied to others in the system had been waived. Jeffries had been given tenure and a chairmanship immediately after receiving his doctoral degree, had not been required to show any scholarly growth, and was never admonished for his consistent loony ranting – until *The New York Post* exposed him and his position became difficult for the university.

Having exposed its desire to run a school by placating a militant minority, City University then proceeded to appoint as president of City College of New York a junior administrator from the state university college system, who announced as she took office that scholarship and standards would be denigrated and new value put on "community activism," since high standards adversely affected the black minority.

At the University of Pennsylvania, a Jewish student was brought up on charges of racial "harassment," because he had told noisy black female students who were carrying on in front of his dorm window at 2 A. M. to be quiet and had referred to them as "water buffalo." As the world learned, the student, of Israeli origin, had used a term which, roughly translated, means "rowdy, rude, and noisy." The university first sought to have the student plead guilty to the charge and force him to attend sensitivity training seminars, all of which led his advisor, Professor Alan Kors, to observe that universities are "becoming increasingly surreal." Under the guise of protecting diversity on the campus, the notion of free speech was squandered. And at the same university, when a conservative student writer wrote a column in the student paper attacking affirmative action, black students responded by stealing and destroying all copies of the paper's edition. Instead of protesting this blatant infringement on free speech, President Sheldon Hackney, the NEH director designate, commented that "two important university values now stand in conflict," freedom of the press and the need to make minority students "comfortable." Hackney argued that while free expression was a "supreme common value," a university must also be "a diverse and welcoming community." As columnist Richard Cohen pointed out, Hackney took no action against students who seized the paper, and Hackney's explanations actually patronized the black students "as people and failed them as their teacher." Such failure, it seems, is becoming more and more common as PC and multicultural concerns take over the campus.

The evidence is strong that in elementary and secondary education, the push for so-called multiculturalism comes from African-American political elites, employed as a convenient mechanism for gaining political power and as an emotional scapegoat for the poor state of the black inner city student body. In Baltimore County, for example, the Board of Education paid Professor Molefi Asante of Temple University, one of our leading Afrocentrists, to help develop a compulsory Afrocentric curriculum for Maryland – albeit one that is improperly dubbed a multicultural curriculum. What, one wonders, are they going to teach high school students? That ancient Egypt was a black African culture which shaped Western civilization? Is it true? Who knows? The assistant superintendent of education for the county, Evelyn Chatmont, explained: "We know for a fact," she told the press, "that so much of history has been distorted, that it's very, very difficult to determine what is true." The answer? Simple. "Our responsibility is to present it all, and let the children sort it out."

Having just hired Dr. Asante to develop their Afrocentric curriculum, at great cost to the local taxpayers, the Board of Education perhaps did not stop to consider that sixth through ninth graders have little background by which to discern whether what they are being taught is true, or whether it is regarded as a hoax by the vast majority of practicing scholars. In his new best-selling book, *Culture of Complaint: The Fraying of America,* Robert Hughes puts it as bluntly as possible: "To plow through the literature of Afrocentrism is to enter a world of claims . . . so absurd that they lie behind satire, like those made for Soviet science in Stalin's time." Of course, Hughes is of white Australian descent, which by definition forbids that he be allowed to evaluate the merits of Afrocentrism.

The Baltimore story, however sad, seems sane compared to the recent scandal surrounding the District of Columbia's attempt to join the crowd in the march to Afrocentrism. The D. C. Board of Education began a pilot progam for one hundred-thirty children of the Webb Elementary School, in which the new Afrocentric curriculum would be tested. They hired Abena Walker, a woman who had created her own "university" and who promptly awarded herself a Master's Degree to give herself credentials. The Superintendent of Schools approved the program, on the basis of a skimpy study outline, and never examined the worthiness of Ms. Walker's "Pan-African University," of whom she is perhaps the only student, professor, and president.

Her outline promises "special programs in the arts, the martial arts, and African languages," as well as "genuine love, concern for and identification with students." In other words, build up self-esteem through Afrocentrism – supposedly a good substitute for a real curriculum of learning. But of course, self-esteem – if indeed it is created via Afrocentrism – bears little relationship to academic achievement in math and English, or anything else. As usual, it was left to skeptical Washington columnists, particularly William Raspberry and Richard Cohen, to respectively raise the question few dared to ask. As Cohen put it, "their self-esteem . . . will be no compensation for not being competitive." Jobs will not be available to them, "if they come out of school pumped up with racial chauvinism but dismal basic skills." But in today's world, it does seem that ideology regularly triumphs over education.

Some have proclaimed a new consensus. Diane Ravitch argues that the real issue on the campus and the classroom is "not whether there will be multiculturalism, but what kind of multiculturalism there will be." She defines two kinds of advocates: pluralists, who know that our common culture has been shaped by the interaction of different cultural elements; and particularists, who seek to use history and literature in a politicized fashion to create self-esteem for oppressed minorities, or to develop a new mythology to replace the one-sided approach to history and literature of the early twentieth century. I fear that Ms. Ravitch's distinction between good and bad multiculturalists, however well-meaning, comes too late as a corrective and has not had the effect she meant it to have.

Recently, an effort has been made, by the likes of Robert Hughes, Gerald Graff, Henry Louis Gates, Jr., and others, to depict themselves as moderates caught between two extremes – the nasty right whose members cannot accept the reality of an ever-changing canon and equally malleable standards of judging what should belong to it, and the demonological left, which insists on treating all literature and history as part of the struggle to change the world. This dichotomy has been thoughtfully and fully analyzed by Carol Iannone (*Commentary,* June 1993), and she is careful to observe that the dichotomy drawn is a false one. These scholars, as Iannone writes, "concede some of the excesses of the radicals, but in doing so they yield not an inch of PC territory," choosing instead to present "a new and improved version of the PC project, a kind of PC with a human face." Seeming to reject PC, in reality these individuals, who have defined the issue as one of a left–right split, cannot help but put themselves, when push comes to shove, on the left. This is accomplished by the clever technique of taking swipes at the right and the neoconservatives, while proceeding to make precisely the same points these so-called neocons have been making for some years. They have adopted their argument while condemning the prior messenger at the same time.

Recently, I have had the opportunity to engage in a series of debates with Paul Lauter, one of the leaders of the newly formed Teachers for a Democratic Culture, and one of those whose efforts are engaged in trying to put a human face on the PC monster. Lauter claims to be above the debate and portrays himself as a scholar involved in broadening the curriculum to include the previously nonexistent voices of women, blacks, and so on. But when challenged, Lauter refused to even criticize, not to speak of condemn, Afrocentrism, which, he has argued, is a complex and compelling response to racism, made up of some thoughtful scholarship and some bad scholarship, just as in any other scholarly field. Moreover, when asked what kind of exercise could be engaged in to produce a favorable multicultural effort among faculty, he responded that one idea would be to do as he and his colleagues had done: form study groups to ponder the new "queer theory," which he sees as the cutting edge of scholarship. One wonders precisely what "queer theory" might be. Whatever it is, it is definitely PC. And, again, Teachers for a Democratic Society and Lauter stand on the right side of the left's cultural battle.

For many members of the former Marxist left, the death of Communism has been replaced equally fervidly with advocacy of the new PC. One has only to read the scary reports appearing in each issue of *Heterodoxy* to realize the extent of the madness. What can one make of the professor at the University of Wisconsin at Milwaukee, who has written in one of her books that "pederasty is undoubtedly a useful

paradigm for classic European pedagogy," since a "greater man pene-
trates a lesser man with his knowledge," while the empty student is a
"receptacle for the phallus." This same good professor, at a conference,
announced that the meeting was about "graduate students' sexual preferences, and my sexual preference is graduate students."

At Wellesley College, one has the case of Tony Martin, Professor of
Africana Studies, who uses the Nation of Islam's anti-Semitic book, *The
Secret Relationship Between Blacks and Jews,* as a text and whose defense of
his choice is to condemn his critics as racist and hide behind his First
Amendment rights to choose his own course material. What, one wonders, would happen on this or any other campus, if a Jewish professor assigned a text of the Ku Klux Klan as course material and used the same
reasoning in his own defense? To ask the question is to provide the answer. He would be condemned, forced to rescind the assignment, or removed from teaching responsibilities, not to say removed from his job.
Martin, we have learned, chastises Jews not only as being responsible for
the slave trade, but for organizing "the international prostitution of
(mainly) Jewish women, by Jewish entrepreneurs," and for participating
in "the extermination of the Native Americans." Who cannot be concerned, when this is the kind of academic offering being presented in our
finest colleges?

This is hardly, Alfred Kazin has written wisely, a "tempest in a
teapot." In the name of class-gender-race equality, teachers and students
all over America are now being trained in such intolerance to defame
and exclude those who do not follow the party line. Kazin judges that
by now "the cultural damage is irrevocable," and that teachers should
nourish a desire in minority students to know the world outside of
themselves "instead of flattering them that many classics can be discarded
for books about their own experience."

Unfortunately, Kazin stands rather alone. The noted feminist historian Alice Kessler-Harris, the new president of the Association of
American Studies, has recently argued that the fight over multiculturalism
is a "tug of war over who gets to create the public culture." Rejecting a
"false search for unity," Kessler-Harris says the nation's culture will become stronger if multiculturalism is adopted. Is she not, I wonder, vali-
dating what Robert Conquest has observed and shrewdly criticized, that
"everything is a struggle for power, or being empowered, or hegemony,
or oppression"? That, he notes, is mere "repetition of Lenin's destructive
doctrine." This is not surprising, given that so many former socialists have
moved to this new agenda for their political struggles in the nineties.
One must also note how close Kessler-Harris seems to be to Patrick
Buchanan, whose call during the last Republican Convention for a war

over the culture echoes her own, except that Buchanan wants to exclude groups he does not like, particularly gays and women. Kessler-Harris's view seems to be close to becoming the new perceived wisdom. She argues that one can incorporate gender, class, and race into the study of our culture and, in so doing, help change the nature of the American identity; that the "multicultural enterprise," as she calls it, will strengthen the democratic ethos and help create a transformation of the culture in which we all participate.

The specifics, unfortunately, do not give us grounds for optimism. In his book *Politics by Other Means: Higher Education and Group Thinking,* David Bromwich relates what happened to Professors Jeffrey Wallin and Norman Holland at Hampshire College two years ago. The professors' contracts were renewed by committees of their own disciplines. The president of the college, however, resubmitted their appointments to a committee developing a third-world studies curriculum. This committee voted to reverse the decision to renew their contracts. When the duo took their case to the college faculty committee on academic freedom, it voted to support their appointment. The president then created a new third committee, in order to gain a second negative vote. What was the great offense of the two professors, Bromwich asks, "that they taught poorly, or lacked the necessary intimate knowledge of their subjects?" No, it seems that Professor Holland is a Panamanian American who, despite his Hispanic roots, taught European literature and refused to adopt the PC politics of victimization. He had sinned, Bromwich writes, "by opening himself to the charge of *Eurocentrism.*" Holland's adversaries accused him and Wallin of failing to "mount a 'Third World' challenge to the canon." In particular, Bromwich notes, Holland did not "characterize European literature as a virus, against which students were to be inoculated in suitably small doses and with elaborate warnings." In a different epoch, such judgment would be condemned for what it is – McCarthyism. Of course, to use that term would be to acknowledge that there is a McCarthyism of the left, yet to any politically correct professor, this is a virtual non sequitur.

What can we expect? This past year the Nobel Peace Prize was awarded to Rigoberta Menchu, a Guatemalan woman who is pro-guerrilla and favors neither peace, reconciliation, nor intellect. Her own much-heralded book, added a few years back to the greatly-debated Stanford curriculum, was ghostwritten by a French Marxist feminist. Perhaps the award was given in error to Menchu: After all, Dr. Abaiel Guzman, the now-imprisoned head of the Peruvian Shining Path, was unavailable to travel to Stockholm to get the prize. Am I too facetious? Perhaps, but judging by the recent full-page signed petition on Guzman's behalf that appeared in *The Village Voice,* some of our New York far left intellectuals, such as Stanley Aronowitz of the City University of New York and Bertell Ollman of New York University (along with the great cultural leader Sinead O'Connor, who gained some more attention recently by ripping up a photo of the Pope on "Saturday Night Live"), think that Dr. Guzman is in prison for the simple fact of his being the acclaimed leader of the Peruvian people and that he is falsely being called a terrorist by the ruling classes.

To resist these trends, we must stand firm against the culture of victimization. And we must oppose the nonsense which says, for example, that only blacks can write the history of slavery or evaluate cultural projects. Spike Lee announced that when his film *Malcolm X* came out, he would give interviews only to African-American critics, since only they could understand the meaning of *Malcolm X.* What will happen if a black critic decides he does not like the film? Of course, Lee will accuse him of "thinking white." It is a no-win proposition. Last year, former Modern Language Association President Houston Baker, its first black president, declared that reading and writing are "technologies of control" and that literacy perpetuates "Western hegemonic arrangements of knowledge." Baker believes there is no reason to mourn the passing of "the old order of literacy." If students can be freed from "white male" core reading lists, he says, then "the powerful syncretic, corporally minimalistic urgings of African-American rap music signal this legitimate defense of a new humanity and a new humanities." I cannot decide which is sadder: the head of our nation's literature professors attacking reading, or barely literate students, especially those from minority communities, being told at our nation's colleges that their indifference to reading is admirable and that all they have to do is listen to rap music and watch MTV videos, thereby supposedly creating a new democratic culture.

What is so unfortunate is the capitulation to this madness. Nathan Glazer writes that since the majority of inner-city students are black and Latino and since there is a political dominance of black and Latino administrators along with weak teachers of history, "demographic and political pressures change the history that is to be taught." Yet what does it say about our system of public education, if the result is that white suburban schools reject Afrocentrism while inner-city schools teach it as the truth? The Sobol Report suggested that such differences will be attributed to "multiple perspectives." The evidence indicates, I think, that sections of the black intellectual community will explain this outcome as the product of white conspiracies, asserting that the white elite does not want African-American youth to learn about its roots. Indeed, in a recent issue of *Phi Delta Kappan,* Kimberly Vann and Jawanzi Kunjufui bemoan the fact that students are given *Julius Caesar* and *A Tale of Two Cities* to read (would that it were so) and not given Maulana Karenga's *Introduction to Black Studies*. The very analogy between two major classics of our humanities tradition and the writings of a California-based thug and convicted felon is so absurd that one hesitates to take it seriously, except for the fact that the claim was published in a most distinguished educational publication. What Vann and Kunjufui ask for is clearly not education but a politicized curriculum meant to instill pride in ghetto residents − out of a false belief that mythological history, such as Karenga's Kwaanza holiday − will provide the inspiration to lift up the black underclass. Juxtaposing multiculturalism and Afrocentrism as one and the same, they write that "all students would benefit from an Afrocentrist, multicultural curriculum." They are wrong. Few students, least of all the very African-American youths they hope to reach, would benefit.

The academy seems more and more mired in madness. The Modern Language Association's recent convention featured sessions on "Outing Goethe . . . Homosexuality and Heterotextuality," whatever the latter is. Papers were presented on such topics as "Cruisin' for a Bruisin': Hollwood's Deadly Lesbian Dolls" and "Henry James and Queer Performativity." The historical profession is only slightly less guilty. The most recent issue of *The Journal of American History* features as its lead article, "America's Boy Friend Who Can't Get a Date: Gender, Race and the Cultural Work of the Jack Benny Program, 1932-1946." Having read the article, I cannot decide whether the late comedian would be flattered to have learned that he was engaging in "cultural work," or to find that the author had posthumously outed Benny − by claiming that his program provided a "homoerotic subtext" that was "depicted safely." And to think that when I was growing up, I thought I was enjoying a half-hour of comedy. Now I am informed that by my act of listening, I was "trying to make sense of a world in economic and social disorder," or engaging in valuable cultural work. And hence, the Marxian project never dies; it just lives on in academia.

I must leave it to others to suggest how to teach traditions. But as usual, the best antidote to PC is solid and meaningful work of a non-PC character. PC academics talk only to themselves, while the broad book-buying public, that same public which has made bestsellers of both Arthur Schlesinger, Jr.'s book *The Disuniting of America* and Robert Hughes's book on PC and multiculturalism, will respond intelligently. In the end, the PC academics will find themselves more and more isolated. May that time be closer than we now think possible.

DIANE RAVITCH

The War on Standards

We can't blame the fall of standards in American education on political correctness; depending on your perspective, you can trace the decline of standards to the 1930s or the 1960s. And possibly, if it is fair to speak of "PC Diaper Babies," the war on standards is a generational phenomenon.

It was in the 1930s that many of the tenets of progressive education were institutionalized in the public schools. The literature of the profession, the reports by city and state superintendents and pedagogical experts, contains numerous references to the pernicious effects of competition for grades and distinction; to the need to eliminate spelling and grammar as artificial activities that have no value; to the value of abolishing college entrance requirements and allowing free choice for students; to the virtue of replacing subject matter with topics relevant to teenagers. Some, but not much, of this baggage was thrown out in the post-Sputnik era, that brief explosion of public concern about standards and academic performance. Then when the 1960s brought a revival of the attack on objective standards, the educational profession – at least that part that had any institutional memory – knew that it was again able to reassert its egalitarian, anti-meritocratic values.

The campus rebellions of the 1960s, intended to protest the war in Vietnam, often turned into protests against the standards in higher education. Under pressure from student (and faculty) activists, colleges and universities diluted or abandoned their entrance requirements; weakened their graduation requirements; retreated from their curricular requirements so that students could have more freedom to choose their courses. Few universities emerged with their curricular requirements intact. In consequence, the number of highly selective institutions declined, as did the number of selective institutions. The former (institutions such as Harvard, Yale, Amherst, Brown) make up less than ten percent of all institutions of higher education and could be highly selective because they had eight to ten applicants for each place in the freshman class; the latter could call themselves "selective" only because students had to present some qualifying credential, like a high school diploma. By the mid-1970s, American high school students knew that they could go to college if they wished, regardless of their academic performance in high school, if they could pay the usually minimal fees or qualify for federal student aid (which was based on need, not on academic ability) – regardless of their academic performance in high school.

The effect on high schools was predictable. Incentives for academic excellence were removed for all but the most able students, those who aspired to apply to the top colleges. For everyone else, there was no longer any reason to study foreign languages, because most public and private universities no longer required them for admission. The number of students enrolled in foreign languages declined, and many high schools stopped offering foreign languages. Similarly, the demand for advanced courses in mathematics and science fell, since no one "needed" them for college admission except for the few who planned to apply to institutions like Stanford or Princeton or MIT. The withdrawal of support for the high school curriculum by the colleges was a devastating blow for those who believed in standards. After all, if the course wasn't needed to get into college, why take it and why offer it?

Since the primary college admission test – the SAT – is not directly connected to what students study in high school, the curriculum was set adrift by the abandonment of college entry requirements. The student who takes the SAT needs to know mathematics, but nothing else learned in high school counts on the test. It is a test of "ability" or "aptitude," not achievement in high school. There was, then, no support for science, history, literature, or foreign languages in the curriculum, no incentive to study beyond the most basic courses, and no incentive to do homework or excel. Students often ask, "Will it be on the test? Do I need to know this?" The answer to almost everything in the traditional curriculum was, "No. Take whatever you want."

The removal of incentives, rewards, or sanctions for academic performance happened not by accident in the 1960s and early 1970s but because it expressed a purposeful, earnest desire to eliminate competition and any barriers to college entry. Competition implied winners and losers; that was bad, losing made people feel bad. No one should ever feel bad. The literature of the 1960s, eagerly consumed by aspiring teachers, emphasized the oppressive nature of traditional schools. Books like *Summerhill* became bestsellers, and for a time it seemed that American students could become educated like Rousseau's Emile, free from constraints and unwanted directives. The open-classroom movement briefly (and expensively) swept the country; the walls went down, and students went "into the community" to learn about real life.

In 1975, *The New York Times* noted that SAT scores had peaked in 1963-64 and had then fallen steadily and precipitously. The decline had been greatest at the top of the ability distribution; fewer students were receiving high scores. The College Board, which sponsors the SAT, convened a study panel, which examined all the possible reasons for the score decline. Some part of the decline resulted from the changing population of test-takers. But even after the composition of the test-takers stabilized in the early 1970s, the scores continued to fall. After looking at such things as the effects of nuclear testing, birth order, junk food, and other exogenous factors, the panel concluded that students were reading less than they had in the past and writing less than they had in the past; that homework had been substantially reduced; that textbooks had been dumbed down; and that solid academic courses had been replaced by a proliferation of fluffy electives in non-academic areas.

The panel implied, but did not say outright, perhaps for fear of giving offense, that the reforms of the 1960s produced a sharp decline in academic achievement and in academic standards. Then as now, there was reluctance to say anything critical about the 1960s, which is now seen in retrospect as a fabulous era, remembered for its idealism, its passion, its sense of liberation and community. What the College Board's review panel found, sadly, is that students are economic animals; they respond to expectations, to requirements, and to rewards. Remove those, and most students do not study, do not do their homework, do not take advanced courses, do not read more than they have to, do not write much, and – compared to students who do all of those things – do not perform well on academic tests.

Well, that was one way of understanding what happened in the 1960s, but there were other ways to make sense of it. One distinguished educator wrote an article asserting that we should welcome a decline in test scores because it reflected the increased number of minority students who were applying for college; the more the scores fell, he reasoned, the more successful we were as a society! This argument presumed that it was somehow axiomatic that minority students could not be educated to higher levels of achievement and that their participation in the test-taking pool would necessarily – and happily – drag down the overall average scores. His argument also ignored the fact that the number of high-scoring students had declined precipitously, both in absolute numbers and in proportion, even though the number of students taking the SAT was stable. Was this too a cause for joy? He didn't say.

Another response to the falling scores was to say that the test was irrelevant and also culturally biased, so it didn't matter what the scores were. Objective tests became a punching bag during the 1960s, and took a pummeling from critics from which they never fully recovered. There was reason enough to dislike multiple-choice tests, even if one is not on the left or politically correct; Jacques Barzun was one of the fiercest critics, because of the mechanical, anti-intellectual presentation of knowledge that is central to the multiple-choice test. The critics on the left shared Barzun's complaint but went further: the tests were no good because there were widely disparate outcomes for whites and blacks, and for boys and girls. It became a cardinal principle that any test that produced disparate outcomes for different groups was *ipso facto* biased. Even when the bias was not apparent, the very fact of different outcomes was proof of bias.

Since the tests, it was claimed, were unfair to minorities, those in pursuit of not just equal educational opportunities, but equal educational outcomes for all groups proposed two complementary tacks. One was affirmative action in admissions and hiring; the other was test-norming for different groups. Both would produce the exactly equal results for all groups that never had been produced by any form of objective testing.

It is worth looking closer at the issue of objectivity. One of the tenets of political correctness is that objectivity is impossible, and that any system or selection process or test will always be biased to favor those who are in power. Characteristic of political correctness is the assumption that any difference in performance demonstrates bias in the measure. By now, we have heard so many attacks on objective measurements that it is no longer novel when claims of bias are raised. Given the fact that there has been real discrimination in our history, it is reasonable to suspect lingering bias whenever charges are lodged in the press. Whenever the pass rates for groups differ, we can expect to hear claims of test bias, regardless of the test.

Take the issue of gender bias. It is well known that boys get higher scores than girls on tests of mathematics and science; it is not so well known that girls get higher scores on tests of reading and writing. Numerous studies contend that the SAT is biased against girls because their scores are not as high as those of boys; the gap is greater in mathematics and relatively small on the verbal section (where girls' scores were higher than boys' until 1972). Researchers claim that the content of the math questions favors boys. They say that references to sports, the military, or finance give unfair advantage to boys, while girls do better on questions that refer to cooking, clothing, and jewelry. It should be embarrassing to researchers to reinforce gender stereotypes. Why shouldn't girls be expected to figure out the win-loss record of a basketball team (it might even be a *girls'* basketball team)? How will women succeed in today's workplace if they can solve only problems that are connected to the kitchen or their wardrobe? Ironically, many of the math questions on which girls do poorly have no words at all, but are number problems. According to the researchers, the problems are biased anyway because girls can't solve them as often as boys. Even if all the word questions were eliminated, boys would still get higher scores than girls. I do

not know why this is so. It may have to do with cultural attitudes that
are shared by students, parents, teachers, and the larger society about
what kinds of school subjects are for boys and what kinds are for girls. It
may be that boys take more math courses than girls (they do). But
whatever the cause, the test reflects the problem, it doesn't cause it.

The larger issue behind the PC perspective is that objective measures
are not possible. Objective tests are never objective. Universal ideas are
never universal. The "canon" is an artificial construct invented to favor
dead white males and to disfavor everyone else. Decisions about which
authors are "best" are always arbitrary and are always determined by the
race, ethnicity, gender, and biases of those who make up the list. All decisions, all choices, all competitions are engineered to favor some group,
depending on who is in power. The idea of merit is a social construct,
invented by the powerful to protect people like themselves.

Since any means of allocating places or promotions is inherently biased, practitioners of PC seek out processes that produce equal outcomes
for all groups. Whereas "fair" used to mean that the test given was the
same for everyone, "fair" now means that the same proportion of all
groups will succeed on any test. The original version of President
Clinton's education reform legislation ("Goals 2000") contained language about new occupational skill standards, written by the
Department of Labor, that would have required the use of "certification
techniques that are designed to avoid disparate impacts (which . . . means
substantially different rates of certification) against individuals based on
race, gender, age, ethnicity, disability or national origin." When this language was exposed to the light of day by the press, it was quickly re-
drafted. But the original intent was clear: to promote norming by race,
gender, age, ethnicity, disability, and national origin. This would have
made a mockery of the bill's effort to establish standards, because the
process of "norming" by group is at odds with the fundamental concept
of standards that are the same for everyone. The public understands fairness in its commonsense definition, that is, that everyone is judged in the
same way by the same criteria. The public, in other words, believes in the
possibility of objective standards. It is somewhat startling to realize that
no one who drafted or read the Clinton bill found the concept bizarre
until it was subject to critical comments in the press.

Given this background, it is hard to imagine that our society will
ever be able to establish real academic standards. Incredibly enough,
however, there is now a movement to develop national standards for
American schools. It has bipartisan support, to an extent, but it faces
formidable obstacles. (The Democratic left fears that standards will lead
to tests, and that tests will have disparate consequences for minorities; the
Republican right fears that the left will capture the process and produce

a national curriculum that will impose leftist ideology.)

The movement has many parents, but it probably got its start with the publication of *A Nation at Risk* by the National Commission on Excellence in Education in 1983. That report warned of a "rising tide of mediocrity" in the schools, which would lead to a lowered standard of living. The report was as stunning an indictment of the American education system as can be imagined, and it had a dramatic effect. Scores of task forces and commissions were created to react to its recommendations, and many states increased their graduation requirements for high school students.

The most emphatic response to the report occurred in the southern states, where the Southern Regional Education Board began pressing for higher standards and for tests to measure progress. SREB states, including Tennessee (whose governor was Lamar Alexander), South Carolina (whose governor was Richard Riley), and Arkansas (whose governor was Bill Clinton), agreed to raise academic standards and even campaigned for state-by-state comparisons in the National Assessment of Educational Progress, the national test regularly administered to large samples of students in order to report on the progress of American education.

In 1989, President Bush convened the nation's governors in Charlottesville, Virginia, and they jointly agreed to set goals for the nation's schools for the year 2000. When the goals were announced in early 1990, they included a pledge that American students would be first in the world in mathematics and science by the year 2000, and that American students would be able to demonstrate competency in challenging subject matter, including mathematics, science, history, geography, and English. An organization called the National Education Goals Panel was created to monitor progress towards the goals; the panel consists of governors, members of Congress, and representatives of the administration.

While Lamar Alexander was Secretary, the U.S. Department of Education made grants to professional and scholarly groups to develop voluntary national standards in science, history, the arts, civics, geography, English, and foreign languages. The grant recipients agreed to define what American children should know and be able to do in various fields of study, that is, *content* standards. (I was assistant secretary for the Office of Educational Research and Improvement, which made the grants.) The Democratic majority on the powerful House Education and Labor Committee was less than happy and periodically threatened to suspend our funds and to prohibit the standard-setting activities we funded, but we pushed ahead.

The standards for mathematics had already been published by the

National Council of Teachers of Mathematics. Their success provided a model. Because the new national standards for mathematics were so widely accepted by the nation's math teachers, they were enormously influential. More than forty states adopted them as the basis for teacher training; they were endorsed even by schools of education, which are usually averse to standards. Published in 1989, the NCTM standards affected not only teacher preparation but textbooks, tests, and classroom instruction. It seemed clear that education reform could begin only with an agreement about what children should learn, and what they learned should be at least as demanding as what their peers were learning in other industrialized countries.

The Clinton administration's education reform legislation embraced the importance of standards. Clinton and Riley had been active in the Southern Regional Education Board, and Clinton had played a leading role in the framing of the national education goals. We might now be well on our way to establishing voluntary national standards for education, an historic first, but for two elements that Congress – namely, the House Committee on Education and Labor – imposed on the Clinton bill. First, there would be no national testing, and any state test that won the approval of the federal government could have no consequences attached to it for at least five years. That is, tests could not be used to determine whether students would be promoted or graduated. The legislation creates a body that will function like a national school board, called the National Education Standards and Improvement Council (the year before, in the Bush legislation, the same body was called the National Education Standards and Assessment Council, but in 1993 Congress deleted the word "assessment" to express its hostility to testing). All of the twenty members of this new body will be appointed by the President, and all are likely to be professional educators. Any state that submits its testing system to this agency for certification can no longer use that test for purposes of graduation, promotion, or program placement. In other words, once certified, the test is rendered useless.

Second, Congress insisted that "opportunity-to-learn" standards must be as important as content standards. "Opportunity-to-learn" standards refer to resources. The bill will create a new federal commission to define what these standards are, and they may likely include the preparation of the teachers (teacher educators will no doubt insist that every teacher have the requisite pedagogical courses); class size; policy for grouping by ability; equality of resources with other districts in the state; and almost anything that the members of the commission decide is necessary to create the right "opportunity to learn." If the commission is captured by representatives of education interest groups, a common phenomenon in Washington, it will present every school with a very expensive list of

"must-haves." The commission could become a source of expensive un-
funded mandates, as well as a means to impose national policies on issues
that are controversial in local districts. The opportunity-to-learn commission will wield a great deal of power, even though there is no federal
money to back up its recommendations. Although Secretary Riley always
takes pains to point out that the opportunity-to-learn standards will be
voluntary, it is predictable that lawsuits will quickly be filed to compel
districts to comply with the new federal standards, at their own expense.
The result will be a federal agency with the power to set "standards" for
spending and pedagogy but with no increase in the current federal contribution of about seven percent of the costs of schooling.

The good news is that it is possible for the first time in many years
to speak about the value of standards. For the moment, everyone is
jumping on the standards bandwagon. However, at the first mention of
tests, the bandwagon comes to a grinding halt, and most of the passen-
gers flee. Those who flee tend to be educationists, for whom testing is
equated with bias and unequal outcomes; by contrast, when the Gallup
Poll asked whether there should be a national test, the public responds
with overwhelming enthusiasm. The public apparently has no problem
with real standards and real consequences. Parents seem to know that
students are not motivated to study when what they study doesn't count
for anything. We are one of the few nations in the world that tests students on their "ability" or their "aptitude," rather than on what they
have learned in school.

What gives me hope is that parents, business people, politicians, and
many educators know that our schools and our students are handicapped
by low standards. Nothing has brought this awareness home as dramatically as the poor performance of American students on international
comparisons of mathematics and science. Despite efforts to discredit the
international tests and to discredit any other tests that aspire to objectivity or permit comparisons, there is genuine support for setting standards
and developing tests based on them. In the early stages of this movement,
I predict, there will be broad support for setting national standards, so
long as they remain fairly vague and nonprescriptive. But as soon as any
attempt is made to establish tests tied to the new standards, watch for
opposition. And as soon as any suggestion is made that student performance on tests should affect entry to college or employment, the heavy
artillery will be rolled out. We are in one of those rare historical moments where there is a chance to do things differently; there will be
many voices raised to make sure that it doesn't happen.

ARTHUR SCHLESINGER, JR.

Multiculturalism v.
The Bill of Rights

The Bill of Rights is once more in peril, especially its cornerstone, the First Amendment. Traditionally the First Amendment has been the object of attack by the right. In the good old days, it was conservatives and hyperpatriots who were the militant advocates of repression and censorship. But today, in a bizarre switch of roles, attacks on the First Amendment are coming from the left. Even more ironically, the demand for repression and censorship is centered in our universities – the places above all where unlimited freedom of expression had previously been deemed sacred. And those who lead the assault on the First Amendment do so in the name of the multicultural society.

Now multiculturalism is an ambiguous term. Insofar as it means the recognition of other cultures, other continents, other colors, other creeds, its impact on American education has been highly beneficial. Insofar as it asks us to see history from a variety of perspectives – the arrival of Columbus, for example, from the viewpoint of those who met him as well as from the viewpoint of those who sent him – it greatly enriches our historical understanding.

But one must distinguish multiculturalism as an influence from multiculturalism as an ideology and a mystique. The ideologues of multiculturalism go farther than simply calling attention to neglected groups and themes. They would reject the historical purposes of assimilation and integration. They see America not as a nation of individuals making their own free choices but as a nation of ethnic groups each more or less permanent and ineradicable in their nature. They would have our educational system reinforce, promote and perpetuate separate ethnic communities and do so at the expense of a common culture and a common national identity. If the First Amendment is an obstacle, they would qualify and restrict the First Amendment.

The contemporary meaning of the First Amendment can be summed up in a few familiar phases. "The question in every case," said Justice Holmes, "is whether the words are used in such circumstances and are of such a nature as to create a clear and present danger that they will bring about the substantive evils that Congress has a right to prevent." "No danger flowing from speech," said Justice Brandeis, "can be deemed clear and present, unless the incidence of evil apprehended is so imminent that it may befall before there is an opportunity for full discussion. If there be time to expose through discussion the falsehood and fallacies, to avert the evil by processes of education, the remedy to be applied is more speech, not enforced silence." Freedom, Justice Holmes emphasized, means not just "free thought for those who agree with us" – what great virtue resides in that? – "but freedom for the thought that we hate."

Freedom for the thought that we hate: this is the proposition that is now under attack from the multicultural perspective. Through most of this century the thought that we hated has been totalitarian political thought: fascism, Nazism, communism. That was the age of the warfare of ideologies. Many argued that free speech should not be used to undermine free speech; that liberty should not be available to those who would use liberty to destroy liberty. Under pressure, first of the hot war and then of cold war, the Supreme Court gave ground from time to time in its construing First Amendment protection of hateful ideological utterance. But in the main the Bill of Rights survived hot and cold wars intact.

Thus in the midst of the Second World War, at a time of the highest patriotic fervor, with the life of the nation truly at risk, the Court threw out as a violation of the First Amendment a West Virginia statute requiring school children to salute and pledge allegiance to the American flag. "If there be any fixed star in our constitutional constellation," wrote Justice Jackson, "it is that no official, high or petty, can prescribe what is orthodox in politics, nationalism, religion, or other matters of opinion." This decision against compulsory flag salutes and pledges of allegiance was handed down when young American were fighting and dying on many fronts for flag and country. But the American people, in 1943, far from denouncing the Court, applauded the decision as a pretty good statement of what we were fighting for.

In the later years of the Cold War, the Court in *Brandberg* v. *Ohio* (1969) reaffirmed and reformulated Holmes's clear and present danger test. In the *Skokie* case (1978) the Court upheld the right of neo-Nazis to march down the streets of an Illinois town inhabited by Holocaust survivors and their families. Hurt feelings were not considered enough to justify reduction of constitutional protection. As Justice Brennan wrote in *Texas* v. *Johnson* (1989), "If there is a bedrock principle underlying the First Amendment, it is that the Government may not prohibit the expression of an idea simply because society finds the idea itself offensive and disagreeable."

Today, in the name of the multicultural society men and women of good will, animated by the highest motives, are leading an assault on the Holmes-Brandeis-Jackson-Brennan conception of the Bill of Rights.

We ordinarily regard the Constitution as a document written for individuals and the Bill of Rights as the guarantee of specific protections for individuals. The multicultural ideologues approach the Constitution from a different perspective. They regard it is a document written for groups and therefore would curtail individual rights in order to protect group rights. Thus Professor Kathryn Abrams of Cornell Law School deplores "the constitutional habit of considering rights-bearers as unaffiliated individuals." She argues that "expression is overprotected" in the United States and that "we need limits on free expression in intellectual life" in order to enhance "respect for and recognition of politically marginalized groups."

This novel theory of the Constitution as the bulwark not of individual but of group rights undermines the traditional idea of civil liberties. But the new theory is driven by potent group emotions – the emotions of Holocaust survivors in Skokie, the emotions of women long subjected to harassment and abuse, the emotions of all oppressed and harried minorities. As Henry Louis Gates, Jr., the W. E. B. DuBois Professor of the Humanities at Harvard, notes, "Civil liberties are regarded by many as a chief obstacle to civil rights. . . . The byword among many black activists and black intellectuals is no longer the political imperative to protect free speech; it is the moral imperative to suppress 'hate speech'."

The very phrase "hate speech" is new. It does not appear as a concept or even as an index entry in Leonard Levy's invaluable *Encyclopedia of the American Constitution,* published in 1986, or in Kermit E. Hall's *Oxford Companion to the Supreme Court,* published in 1992. Nor does the related phrase "political correctness" make it as a concept or index entry in either of these useful works. According to a *New York Times* computer search, there were one hundred three newspaper references to "political correctness" in 1988; ten thousand in 1993.

We must not be too quick to dismiss the case for the suppression of hate speech. As the warfare of ideologies emphasized for many the vulnerability of free society to fascist and communist propaganda and led to demands that society protect itself by restricting speech, so the warfare of ethnicities emphasizes the vulnerability of free society to racial conflict and leads to comparable demands for self-protection. Democratic governments, with memories of the holocaust and apprehensions about growing ethnic hostilities, are naturally and honorably concerned with arresting the spread of ethnic and racial hatreds.

The United Nations has been in the forefront of the drive to declare, in the words of the International Convention on the Elimination of All Forms of Racial Discrimination (1966), "all dissemination of ideas based on racial superiority or hatred . . . as an offense punishable by law." The United States has signed this document, but the Senate has thus far refused to ratify it on the ground that it is not compatible with the First Amendment.

One can understand why Germany, in the light of its own experience, would ban neo-Nazi groups and Holocaust deniers as a clear and present danger to society. But Western democracies with secure democratic traditions have passed laws punishing – to use the language of the British Racial Relations Act of 1965 – the circulation of materials aimed at fomenting "hatred against any section of the public in Great Britain distinguished by color, race, ethnic or national origins," including the use of "threatening, abusive, or insulting" words. Section 319 of Canada's Criminal Code is similarly designed to prohibit hate propaganda against racial and religious minorities. Charles Pasqua, the French Minister of the Interior, is preparing legislation that would define racist groups as criminal conspiracies and punish individuals who incite racial discrimination, hatred or violence.

The adoption of such laws by other democracies strengthens the case of those who would censor hate speech in the United States. Nor is there any mystery about why the agitation for censorship finds a special location in our universities. The problem of hate speech acquires peculiar poignancy in educational settings.

It is no fun running a university these days. White students can be cruel in their exclusion of minorities, their wanton harassment, their heavy-handed pranks, their vile and wounding cracks. Minority students, for the understandable reasons, are often vulnerable and frightened. Racial jokes, slurs, epithets hurled by majority bullies pose difficult questions for educational administrators. Consider how a shy and scared black kid at the University of Michigan must have felt when posters appeared around the campus parodying the slogan of the United Negro College Fund: A MIND IS A TERRIBLE THING TO WASTE – ESPECIALLY ON A NIGGER.

After a while, university administrators begin to ask themselves: which is more important – protecting hate speech or stopping racial persecution? Does not the tolerance of racism prevent minority students from joining the life of the university on equal terms? Does not the Bill of Rights protect equality as well as liberty? Does not hate speech destroy equality and thereby nullify the very premises of education? "The right of free expression," says the Stanford University Discrimination Harassment Provision, "can conflict with the right to be free of invidious discrimination" – so it is proper to ban words "commonly understood to convey direct and visceral hatred or contempt for human beings on the basis of their sex, race, color, handicap, religion, sexual orientation, or national and ethnic origin." Nor is there any loss thereby, because the opinions banned are in their nature without any redeeming social value.

One has a certain sympathy for beleaguered administrators who, doing their best to keep the peace and give minority students a chance, try to crack down on bigoted speech. More than three hundred institutions have speech codes. Those adopted by the University of Michigan and the University of Wisconsin have been invalidated by the courts as manifestly unconstitutional. Others, more narrowly drawn, make ingenious claims to constitutionality – some resting on the argument that the purpose of the First Amendment is to ensure worthwhile debate and on a "two-tier" distinction between "high-value" and "low-value" speech; some on the proposition that the constitutional guarantees of liberty and equality are on a collusion course and that liberty should not be furthered at the expense of equality: the First Amendment right to speak should not be preferred to an implied Fourteenth Amendment right to obtain an equal education. Some proponents like Catherine McKinnon even argue that the state has a constitutional duty to prohibit expression that promotes inequality; still others invoke the "fighting words" doctrine in *Chaplinsky* v *New Hampshire* (1942), though the Supreme Court has found little sustenance in that doctrine when employed in anything more than a restatement of clear and present danger.

As a non-lawyer, I am not rash enough to pass on the constitutional merits of the various arguments for the abridgment of the First Amendment. Free speech is not an absolute; no judgment can escape the balancing of competing values. We regulate speech every day through statutes punishing libel, slander, false advertising, perjury, pornography, criminal solicitation, and so on. But in a free democracy the presumption must always lie in favor of speech unless an overwhelming practical case can be made for censorship. And as an historian I may perhaps be permitted comment on the practical impact of both racist speech and anti-racist legislation.

Multicultural ideologues regard the impact of racist speech as grievous enough to justify repression, even though censorship of racist expression could well create precedents for future censorship of other sorts of expression. It is even suggested that the creation of such precedents does not matter since free speech is no help to minorities anyway. "African-Americans and other people of color," Professor Charles Lawrence of the Stanford Law School tells us, "are skeptical about the argument that even the most injurious speech must remain unregulated because, in an unregulated marketplace of ideas, the best ones will rise to the top and gain acceptance. Experience tells us quite the opposite. People of color have seen too many demagogues elected by appealing to America's racism."

One wonders where Professor Lawrence has been over the last half century; for experience tells us on the contrary that, in the unregulated marketplace of ideas, the idea of white supremacy has vanished and the idea of racial equality has finally been accepted in principle if not, alas, in practice. There are few stronger arguments for the unregulated market-place of ideas than the revolution in race relations over the last half century. Read Gunnar Myrdal's *An American Dilemma* (1944), and compare it to the situation today. When I was young, senators and congressmen would orate about the virtue and necessity of "white supremacy"; but in the last forty years has anyone uttered that phrase on Capitol Hill? I would never have believed it half a century ago if someone told me that in my lifetime, with black Americans making up only twelve percent of the population, a black general would be chairman of the Joint Chiefs of Staff; that black Justices would sit on the Supreme Court,; that there would be a black governor of Virginia and black mayors in Atlanta, Birmingham, New Orleans and other southern cities, as well as in New York, Chicago, Philadelphia, Los Angeles, Kansas City, Detroit, and Seattle. It was precisely the First Amendment, Professor Gates reminds us, that "licensed the protests, the rallies, the organization and the agitation that galvanized the nation."

The struggle for racial justice is far from over; there are still miles to go before we sleep. But changes have been made. One doubts that these changes would have come faster if we had followed Professor Lawrence and prohibited racist speech. What that would have done is to transfer the debate from civil rights to civil liberties and elevate neo-Confederates into great champions of the First Amendment.

No one needs an untrammeled First Amendment more than those who seek to change the status quo. Radicals are always in the minority, and minorities gain the most from the protections of the Bill of Rights. Free speech may be offensive, odious, repulsive, an instrument of domination and oppression, but historically it has been far more significant as a means – no, *the* means – of liberation. As Norman Corwin, the author half a century ago of that once-celebrated radio program on the Bill of Rights called "We Hold These Truths," put it, "The Bill of Rights doesn't offer freedom *from* speech. To silence an idea because it might offend a minority doesn't protect that minority. It deprives it of the tool it needs most – the right to talk back."

A more positive argument for censorship is that educational institutions must take a stand against bigotry. But surely there are many ways short of censorship with which an educational institution can condemn bigotry. Censorship breeds its own evils. In some institutions radicals can lay down a party line, denounce deviationists as politically incorrect, and even drive them from the lecture platform. The rise of left-wing thought police reminds one of the right-wing students who in Joe McCarthy's day used to haunt the classrooms of liberal professors (like me), hoping to catch and report whiffs of Marxism emanating from the podium. Of all institutions, universities surely should have the least truck with thought police.

This obsession with "insensitivity" — saying something that might hurt somebody's feelings — reinforces the assault on the First Amendment. Multicultural ideologues emphasize the harm that uncensored speech is believed to do to defenseless individuals. Unquestionably slurs and insults can be injurious, but is the injury words inflict on sensibilities sufficiently weighty and enduring to justify so drastic a remedy as limitations on free speech?

Beware the insensitivity standard! Ray Bradbury foresaw all this more than forty years ago in *Fahrenheit 451* — the demand of minorities to burn the books that might make them unhappy. "Colored people don't like *Little Black Sambo*. Burn it. White people don't feel good about *Uncle Tom's Cabin*. Burn it. . . . Don't step on the toes of the dog lovers, cat lovers, doctors, lawyers, merchants, chiefs, Mormons, Baptists, Unitarians, second-generation Chinese, Swedes, Italians, Germans, Texans, Brooklynites, Irish men, people from Oregon or Mexico." But what was dystopian fantasy for Ray Bradbury forty years ago is moving into actuality today.

If we start down the insensitivity road, we will end up endorsing Ayatollah Khomeini and his crusade against *The Satanic Verses*. Does the fact that *The Satanic Verses* hurts the feelings of devout Muslims really justify the murder of Salman Rushdie? Bernard Shaw said, "All great truths begin in blasphemy." The hurt-feelings standard, if imposed in the past, would have silenced Mark Twain, Ambrose Bierce, Mr. Dooley, H. L. Menken, and so many others whose scorching wit has enlivened and illuminated American life.

And how practically effective have anti-racist statutes been in stopping the dissemination of racist ideas? Germany because of its special history may well require special measures, but in neither Britain nor Canada has legislation diminished racism nor discouraged the merchants of hate; indeed, both countries, despite their anti-racist legislation, have seen a dismaying increase in racial incidents.

The Millwall ward in the East London borough of Tower Hamlets recently elected a councilman representing the neo-fascist British National Party, and the British Commission on Racial Equality reports that an "increasing number of people" say they have "experienced racism – either directly when they have been on the receiving end of verbal abuse, or more subtly, when they have been turned down for a job." In Canada feminists, wielding the legal theories of Catherine McKinnon, rejoiced when the Canadian Supreme Court in *Regina* v. *Butler* (1992) affirmed the power of the state to ban literary or visual expression that "degrades" and "dehumanizes" women. But the main consequence has been the seizure by the Canadian Customs of books ordered by feminist and lesbian bookstores. Neither the British nor the Canadian experience demonstrates that censorship is more effective than free discussion in bringing about a tolerant and harmonious society. Driving thoughts underground may only cause them to explode later.

When hate speech leads to physical assault and violence, that is another matter and one requiring prompt and sharp counteraction. But there are plenty of statutes to deal with violent crime, and it may well be a good idea to provide for the enhancement of punishment when hate is demonstrably the motive, the constitutionality of which the Supreme Court upheld in *Wisconsin* v. *Mitchell* (1993).

Since the advocacy of censorship in the name of multiculturalism is couched in the vocabulary of "power" and "hegemony" and it assumes that all ideas are designed to enable one group to dominate another, one may be permitted to subject multicultural advocacy itself to the same analysis. Obviously, "political correctness" is a strategy of intimidation in the struggle for intellectual and educational power. As Professor Linda S. Greene of the University of Wisconsin Law School candidly confesses, the object is to talk "about what speech we want to empower people to engage in . . . about what we want people to be able to say at the university." But the First Amendment denies that anybody should have the power to decide what people are able to say.

It is ironic that the celebration of diversity concludes in a demand for conformity. In the long run there is surely no more self-defeating proposition for reformers and radicals than the creation of precedents for the curtailment of debate and expression. "It is by the enjoyment of a dangerous freedom," as Tocqueville wrote a century and a half ago, "that Americans learn the art of rendering the dangers of freedom less formidable."

The idea of bringing harmony to the American multicultural society through censorship is an evasion of the real problem. Speech reflects social inequities and disparities and injustices; it does not cause them. If we are serious about bringing minorities into full membership in our society, our society must provide jobs, schools, health care and housing; it must provide equal opportunity in employment and education. The answer lies along these lines. It does not lie in the amputation of the Bill of Rights.

And, above all, the members of the white majority must open their minds and hearts. The burden to unify the country does not fall primarily on the minorities. Those who want to join America must be received and welcomed by those who think they own America. Assimilation and integration constitute a two-way street. Instead of slamming doors against minorities and burning crosses on their lawns, thereby driving them into defensive and defiant separatism, the majority must begin treating them as they would their own. Racism is the problem: political correctness, the assault on the Bill of Rights, is only an ill-judged, wrong-headed and dangerous response.

The American population is today more heterogeneous than ever. But this very heterogeneity makes the quest for unifying ideals and a common culture all the more urgent. Racial harmony is not an impossible dream. America, as Scott Fitzgerald said, is "a willingness of the heart." We have it within our power to make this a fair and a just land for all our people.

Recall some words of Mahatma Gandhi — words that used to be inscribed on public posters throughout India, a country far more fiercely divided than our own by ethnic and racial and religious and linguistic antagonisms. "We must cease," Gandhi said, "to be exclusive Hindus, or Muslims or Sikhs, Parsis, Christians or Jews. Whilst we may staunchly adhere to our respective faiths, we must be Indians first and Indians last." It is because India has abandoned these teachings of Gandhi that it is so violently and tragically divided today.

But in the spirit of Gandhi, while we heterogeneous Americans may staunchly adhere to our diverse traditions, let us never forget that in the end we are members one of another — Americans first and Americans last — bound together by a constitution that guarantees our liberties. In a world savagely rent by ethnic and racial fanaticism, it is all the more essential that the United States continue as an example of how a highly differentiated society holds itself together and preserves its freedom.

JOHN R. SEARLE

Is There a Crisis in American Higher Education?

There is supposed to be a major debate – or even a set of debates – going on at present concerning a crisis in the universities, specifically a crisis in the teaching of the humanities. This debate is supposed to be in large part about whether a certain traditional conception of liberal education should be replaced by something sometimes called "multiculturalism." These disputes have even reached the mass media, and several best-selling books are devoted to discussing them and related issues. Though the arguments are ostensibly about Western civilization itself, they are couched in a strange jargon that includes not only "multiculturalism" but also "the canon," "political correctness," "ethnicity," "affirmative action," and even more rebarbative expressions such as "hegemony," "empowerment," "poststructuralism," "deconstruction," and "patriarchalism." I myself have contributed to this "debate" in an article I wrote for *The New York Review of Books*. I find the debate at best puzzling and at worst disappointing, not to say depressing.

Among its disquieting features are at least the following. First, it is conducted at a rather low level. It tends to be shrill and vindictive, and the level of argumentation is not entirely appropriate to the presentation of a philosophy of education. The best-selling books – and here I am thinking of the books by Allan Bloom, Roger Kimball, and Dinesh D'Sousa – are without exception defenses of a traditional conception of higher education, but they are weak in articulating exactly what that tradition is and how it might address itself to the specific features of our present historical situation. On the other side, opposing the tradition, are authors from a variety of points of view: Marxists, feminists, deconstructionists, and people active in "ethnic studies" and "gay studies," as well as many 1960s-style student radicals who are now middle-aged university professors. Most of these opponents of the tradition, in spite of their diversity, are of the left-wing political persuasion, and they tend to write in tones of moral outrage – the outrage of those who are exposing vast and nameless oppressive conspiracies – that we have come to expect from the academic left since the 1960s. I would not like to think that this is the best that American academics can produce by way of a debate about the nature of higher education: On the one side, for the most part, journalists and politicians; on the other, resentful radicals. I am also distressed at the implication that one is somehow forced to choose sides in this debate, that the choice is, so to speak, between the Great Books of Western Civilization conception of higher education on one side, and the Studies of the Victims of Western Imperialist Oppression on the other.

A second disturbing feature is that the issues being argued about, for the most part, are not the major problems in American higher education. I teach several courses a year, and these issues are not really live issues in my teaching. I discuss philosophical problems, without any regard to the issues in the "great debate." And leaving aside questions of curriculum, we have many more serious problems than multiculturalism. We have that permanent problem in American higher education: There is not enough money. Furthermore, students come in unprepared, with poor English and math skills, little information, and no work habits. Another basic problem is that many of our Ph.D.'s are having a hard time getting jobs. In the state of California there is a special problem that hardly anyone has even remarked on: In several of the university cities, new faculty members cannot afford to buy houses. Another problem seldom remarked on is that many universities in the United States practice certain forms of racial discrimination against white males. This is overt in the case of undergraduate admissions. It is present, though less explicitly so, in the hiring of faculty members, but there is no question that white males are discriminated against. I regard this as unacceptable, and I believe the day will come when we will be deeply ashamed of having allowed it to occur, as we are now ashamed of previous forms of discrimination. However, here I am going to address myself mostly to the issues in "the great debate," though I will have something to say about some of these other issues in conclusion.

I noted that the debate was disappointing, but I believe it can be made more interesting if we approach it from a theoretical point of view. By challenging the assumptions behind the traditional conception of a liberal education, the academic left forces us to reexamine those assumptions. Even the most conservative among us will be forced to articulate them, to try to justify them, and perhaps even to alter them. Since I do not know of a neutral vocabulary, I will describe the debate as between the "defenders" and the "challengers" of the tradition. I realize that there is a great deal of variety on each side and more than one debate going on, but I am going to try to expose some common core assumptions of each side, assumptions seldom stated explicitly but which form the unstated premises behind the enthymemes that each side tends to use. Let us start by stating naively the traditionalists' view of higher education and, equally naively, the most obvious of the challengers' objections to it. This will, I hope, enable us to get into the deeper features of the debate.

Here is the traditionalists' view: There is a certain tradition in American higher education, especially in the teaching of the humanities. The idea behind this tradition is that there is a body of works of philosophy, literature, history, and art that goes from the Greeks right up to the present day, and though it is not a unified tradition, there are certain family resemblances among the leading works in it, and for want of a better name, we call it the Western intellectual tradition. It extends in philosophy from Socrates to Wittgenstein or, if you like, from the pre-Socratics to Quine, in literature from the Greek poets and playwrights right up to, for example, James Joyce and Ernest Hemingway. The idea is that if you are going to be an educated person in the United States, you must have some familiarity with some of the chief works in this tradition because it defines our particular culture. You do not know who you are, in a sense, unless you have some familiarity with these works, because America is a product of this tradition, and the United States Constitution in particular is a product of a certain philosophical element in this tradition, the European Enlightenment. And then, too, we think that many works in this tradition, some of those by Shakespeare and Plato for example, are really so good that they are of *universal* human interest.

So much for the naive statement of the traditionalist view. There is an objection put by the challengers, and the objection, to put it in its crudest form, is as follows: If you look closely at the reading lists of this "Great Tradition," you will discover that the books are almost all by white males from Europe and North America. There are vast areas of the earth and great civilizations whose achievements are totally unrepresented in this conception of "liberal education." Furthermore, within the population of the United States as it is presently constituted, there are lots of ethnic minorities, as well as the largest minority of all, women, whose special needs, interests, traditions, and achievements are underrepresented or in some cases not represented at all in this tradition.

What is the response of the traditionalists to this objection? At this point, the debate already begins to get murky, because it is hard to find traditionalist authors who address the objection directly, so I am going to interject myself and present what I think the traditionalists should say, given their other assumptions. The traditionalist should just acccept this objection as a valid criticism and amend the "canon" accordingly. If great works by Asian authors, for example, have been excluded from the "canon" of great works of literature, then by all means let us expand the so-called canon to include them. Closer to home, if great women writers have been excluded, often because they are women, then let us expand membership in the list to include them as well. According to the traditionalist theory, one of the advantages of higher education is that it enables us to see our own civilization and mode of sensibility as one possible form of life among others. And one of the virtues of the tradition is the enormous variety within it. In fact, there never was a "canon." There was a set of constantly revised judgments about which books deserve close study, which deserve to be regarded as "classics." So, based on the traditionalists' own conception, there should be no objection to enlarging the list to include classics from sources outside the Western tradition and from neglected elements within it.

As I have presented it, the challengers are making a common sense objection, to which the traditionalists have a common sense answer. So it looks as if we have an obvious solution to an interesting problem and can all go home. What is there left to argue about? But it is at this point that the debate becomes interesting. What I have discovered in reading books and articles about this debate is that the objection to the so-called canon — that it is unrepresentative, that it is too exclusive — cannot be met by opening membership to include works by previously excluded elements of the population, since some people would accept such reform as adequate, but many will not. Why not? In order to answer that question I am going to try to state the usually unstated presuppositions made by both the traditionalists and the challengers. I realize, to repeat, that there is a great deal of variety on both sides, but I believe that each side holds certain assumptions, and it is important to try to make them explicit. In the debates one sees, the fundamental issues often are not coming out into the open, and as a result the debaters are talking past each other, seldom making contact. One side accuses the other of racism, imperialism, sexism, elitism, and of being hegemonic and patriarchal. The other side accuses the first of trying to destroy intellectual standards and of politicizing the university. So what is actually going on? What is in dispute?

I will try to state the assumptions behind the tradition as a set of propositions, confining myself to half a dozen for the sake of brevity. The first assumption is that the criteria for inclusion in the list of "the classics" is supposed to be a combination of intellectual merit and historical importance. Some authors, Shakespeare for example, are included because of the quality of their work; others, Marx for example, are included because they have been historically so influential. Some, Plato for instance, are both of high quality and historically influential.

A second assumption made by the traditionalists is that there are intersubjective standards of rationality, intelligence, truth, validity, and general intellectual merit. In our list of required readings we include Plato but not randomly selected comic strips, because we think there is an important distinction in quality between the two, and *we think we can justify the claim that there is a distinction*. The standards are not algorithmic. Making judgments of quality is not like measuring velocities, but it is not arbitrary either.

A third assumption behind the tradition is that one of the things we are trying to do is to enable our students to overcome the mediocrity, provincialism, or other limitations of whatever background from which they may have come. The idea is that your life is likely to be in large measure a product of a lot of historical accidents: the town you were born in, the community you grew up in, the sort of values you learned in high school. One of the aims of a liberal education is to liberate our students from the contingencies of their backgrounds. We invite the student into the membership of a much larger intellectual community. This third feature of the traditional educational theory, then, is what one might call an invitation to transcendence. The professor asks his or her students to read books that are designed to challenge any complacencies that the students may have brought to the university when they first arrived there.

A fourth assumption made by the traditionalists, which is related to the third, is that in the Western tradition, there is a peculiar combination of what one might call extreme universalism and extreme individualism. Again, this tends to be tacit and is seldom made explicit. The idea is that the most precious thing in the universe is the human individual, but that the human individual is precious as part of the universal human civilization. The idea is that one achieves one's maximum intellectual *individual* potential by coming to see oneself as part of a *universal* human species with a universal human culture.

A fifth feature of this tacit theory behind educational traditionalism is that a primary function of liberal education is criticism of oneself and one's community. According to this conception, the unexamined life is not worth living, and the examined life is life criticized. I do not know of any intellectual tradition that is as savagely self-critical as the Western tradition. Its hero is Socrates, and of course we all know what happened to him. "I would rather die by the present argument than live by any other," he said. This is the model we hold up to our students: the lone individual, standing out against the hypocrisy, stupidity, and dishonesty of the larger community. And that tradition goes right through to the nineteenth and twentieth centuries, through Freud, Nietzsche, Marx, and Bertrand Russell, to mention just a few. The tradition is that of the extremely critical intellectual commentator attacking the pieties and inadequacies, the inconsistencies and hypocrisies of the surrounding community.

I will mention a sixth and final feature. Objectivity and truth are possible because there is an independently existing reality to which our true utterances correspond. This view, called realism, has often been challenged by various forms of idealism and relativism within Western philosophy, but it has remained the dominant metaphysical view in our culture. Our natural science, for example, is based on it. A persistent topic of debate is: How far does it extend? Is there, for example, an independently existing set of moral values that we can discover, or are we, for example, just expressing our subjective feelings and attitudes when we make moral judgments? I am tempted to continue this list, but I hope that what I have said so far will give you a feel for the underlying assumptions of the traditionalist theory of liberal education.

I am now going to try to do the same for the challengers, but this is harder to do without distortion, simply because there is more variety among the critics of the tradition than there is in the tradition itself. Nonetheless, I am going to do my best to try to state a widely held set of core assumptions made by the challengers. Perhaps very few people, maybe no one, believes all of the assumptions I will try to make explicit, but they are those I have found commonly made in the debates. The first assumption made by the challengers is that the subgroup into which you were born – your ethnic, racial, class, and gender background – matters enormously; it is important for education. In the extreme version of this assumption, you are essentially defined by your ethnic, racial, class, and gender background. That is the most important thing in your life. The dean of an American state university told me, "The most important thing in my life is being a woman and advancing the cause of women." Any number of people think that the most important thing in their lives is their blackness or their Hispanic identity, et cetera. This is something new in American higher education. Of course, there have always been people who were defined or who preferred to be defined by their ethnic group or by other such affiliations, but it has not been part of the theory of what the university was trying to do that we should *encourage* self-definition by ethnicity, race, gender, or class. On the contrary, as I noted in my list of the traditionalist assumptions, we were trying to encourage students to rise above the accidents of such features. But to a sizable number of American academics, it has now become acceptable to think that the most important thing in one's life is precisely these features. Notice the contrast between the traditionalists and the challengers on this issue. For the traditionalists, what matters is the individual within the universal. For the challengers, the universal is an illusion, and the individual has an identity only as a member of some subgroup.

A second feature of this alternative view is the belief that, to state it crudely, all cultures are equal. Not only are they morally equal, as human beings are morally equal, but all cultures are intellectually equal as well. According to this view, the idea that we have more to learn from the representatives of one race, gender, class, or ethnic group than we do from the representatives of others is simply racism and old-fashioned imperalism. It is simply a residue of Eurocentric imperalism to suppose, as the traditionalists have been supposing, that certain works of European white males are somehow superior to the products of other cultures, classes, genders, and ethnic groups. Belief in the superiority of the Western canon is a priori objectionable because all authors are essentially representatives of their culture, and all cultures are intellectually equal.

In this alternative view, a third feature is that when it comes to selecting what you should read, representativeness is obviously crucial. In a multiculturalist educational democracy, every culture must be represented. The difficulty with the prevailing system is that most groups are under-represented, and certain groups are not represented at all. The proposal of opening up doors just to let a few superstars in is no good, because that still leaves you, in plain and simple terms, with too many dead, white, European males. Even if you include every great woman novelist that you want to include – every Jane Austen, George Eliot, and Virginia Woolf – you are still going to have too many dead, white, European males on your list. It is part of the elitism, the hegemonism, and the patriarchalism of the existing ideology that it tries to perpetuate the same patterns of repression even while pretending to be opening up. Worse yet, the lack of diversity in the curriculum is matched by an equal lack of *diversity in the faculty*. It's no use getting rid of the hegemony of *dead* white males in the curriculum if the faculty that teaches the multi-cultural curriculum is still mostly *living* white males. Representativeness is crucial not only in the curriculum but even more so in the composition of the faculty.

I want to pause here to contrast these three assumptions of the challengers with those of the traditionalists. The traditionalists think they are selecting both reading lists and faculty members on grounds of quality and not on grounds of representation. They think they select Plato and Shakespeare, for example, because they produced works of genius, not because they are specimens or representatives of some group. The challengers think this is self-deception at best, oppression at worst. They think that since the canon consists mostly of white European males, the authors must have been selected *because* they are white European males. And they think that because most of the professors are white males, this fact by itself is proof that there is something wrong with the composition of the faculty.

You can see the distinction between the challengers and the traditionalists if you imagine a counterfactual situation. Suppose it was discovered by an amazing piece of historical research that the works commonly attributed to Plato and Aristotle were not written by Greek males but by two Chinese women who were cast ashore on the coast of Attica when a Chinese junk shipwrecked off the Pireaus in the late fifth century B.C. What difference would this make to our assessment of the works of Plato and Aristotle? From the traditionalist point of view, none whatever. It would be just an interesting historical fact. From the challengers' point of view, I think it would make a tremendous difference. Ms. Plato and Ms. Aristotle would now acquire a new authenticity as genuine representatives of a previously underrepresented minority, and the most appropriate faculty to teach their works would then be Chinese women. Implicit in the traditionalist assumptions I stated is the view that the faculty member does not have to exemplify the texts he or she teaches. They assume that the works of Marx can be taught by someone who is not a Marxist, just as Aquinas can be taught by someone who is not a Catholic, and Plato by someone who is not a Platonist. But the challengers assume, for example, that women's studies should be taught by feminist women, Chicano studies by Chicanos committed to a certain set of values, and so on.

These three points, that you are defined by your culture, that all cultures are created equal, and that representation is the criterion for selection both of the books to be read and the faculty to teach them, are related to a fourth assumption: The primary purpose of education in the humanities is political transformation. I have read any number of authors who claim this, and I have had arguments with several people, some of them in positions of authority in universities, who tell me that the purpose of education, in the humanities at least, is political transformation.

For example, another dean at a big state university, herself a former Berkeley radical, has written that her academic life is just an extension of her political activities. In its most extreme version, the claim is not just that the purpose of education in the humanities *ought* to be political, but rather that all education always has been political and always will necessarily be political, so it might as well be beneficially political. The idea that the traditionalists with their "liberal education" are somehow teaching some politically neutral philosophical tradition is entirely a self-deceptive masquerade. According to this view, it is absurd to accuse the challengers of politicizing the university; it already is politicized. Education is political down to the ground. And, so the story goes, the difference between the challengers, as against the traditional approach, is that the traditional approach tries to disguise the fact that it is essentially engaged in the political indoctrination of generations of young people so that they will continue to accept a system of hegemonic, patriarchal imperialism. The challengers, on the other hand, think of themselves as accepting the inevitably political nature of the university, and they want to use it so that they and their students can be liberated into a genuine multicultural democracy. When they say that the purpose of the university is political, this is not some new proposal that they are making. They think of themselves as just facing up to the facts as they always have been.

Once you understand that the challengers regard the university as essentially political, then several puzzling features of the present debate become less puzzling. Why has radical politics migrated into academic departments of literature? In my intellectual childhood, there were plenty of radical activists about, but they tended to operate in a public political arena, or, to the extent they tended to be in universities at all, they were usually in departments of political science, sociology, and economics. Now, as far as I can tell, the leading intellectual centers of radical political activity in the United States are departments of English, French, and comparative literature. We are, for example, in the odd situation where America's two "leading Marxists" are both professors of English. How did this come about? What would Marx think if he knew that his main impact was on literary criticism? Well, part of the reason for the migration of radical politics into literature departments is that Marxism in particular and left-wing radicalism in general have been discredited as theories of politics, society, and historical change. If ever a philosophical theory was refuted by events, it was the Marxist theory of the inevitable collapse of the capitalist economies and their revolutionary overthrow by the working class, to be followed by the rise of a classless society. Instead, it is the Marxist economies that have collapsed and the Marxist governments that have been overthrown. So, having been refuted as theories of society, these views retreated into departments of literature, where to some extent they still flourish as tools of "interpretation."

There is a more important reason, however. During the 1960s a fairly sizable number of leftist intellectuals became convinced that the best arena of social change was culture, that high culture in general and university departments of literature in particular could become important weapons in the struggle to overcome racism, imperialism, et cetera. We are now witnessing some of the consequences of this migration. As someone — I think it was Irving Howe — remarked, it is characteristic of this generation of radicals that they don't want to take over the country, they want to take over the English department. But, I would add, they think taking over the English department is the first step toward taking over the country.

So far, then, I have tried to isolate four presuppositions of the challengers: that ethnicity is important; that cultures are intellectually equal; that representativeness is crucial in the curriculum and in faculty composition; and that an important function of the humanities is political and social change. Now let me identify a fifth: There are no such things as objective standards. As one pamphlet published by the American Council of Learned Societies put it, "As the most powerful modern philosophies and theories have been demonstrating, claims of disinterest, objectivity, and universality are not to be trusted, and themselves tend to reflect local historical conditions." According to the ACLS pamphlet, such claims usually involve some power grab on the part of the person who is claiming to be objective. This presupposition, that there are no objective or intersubjective standards to which one can appeal in making judgments of quality, is a natural underpinning of the first four. The idea that there might be some objective standards of what is good and what is bad, that you might be able to show that Shakespeare is better than Mickey Mouse, for example, threatens the concept that all cultures are equal and that representativeness must be the criterion for inclusion in the curriculum. The whole idea of objectivity, truth, rationality, intelligence, as they are traditionally construed, and distinctions of intellectual quality, are all seen as part of the same system of repressive devices.

This leads to the sixth presupposition, which is the hardest of all to state, because it is an inchoate attitude rather than a precise thesis. Roughly speaking, it involves a marriage of left-wing politics with certain antirationalist strands derived from recent philosophy. The idea is that we should stop thinking there is an objective reality that exists independently of our representations of it; we should stop thinking that propositions are true when they correspondend to that reality; and we should stop thinking of language as a set of devices for conveying meanings from speakers to hearers. In short, the sixth presupposition is a rejection of realism and truth in favor of some version of relativism, the idea that all of reality is ultimately textual. This is a remarkable guise for left-wing views to take, because until recently extreme left-wing views claimed to have a scientific basis. The current challengers are suspicious of science and equally suspicious of the whole apparatus of rationality, objective truth, and metaphysical realism, which go along with the scientific attitude.

A seventh presupposition is this: Western civilization is historically oppressive. Domestically, its history is one of oppressing women, slaves, and serfs. Internationally, its history is one of colonialism and imperialism. It is no accident that the works in the Western tradition are by white males, because the tradition is dominated by a caste consisting of white males. In this tradition, white males are the group in power.

I have tried to make explicit some of the unstated assumptions of both sides, because I think that otherwise it is impossible to explain why the contestants don't seem to make any contact with each other. They seem to be talking about two different sets of issues. I believe that is because they proceed from different sets of assumptions and objectives. If I have succeeded here in articulating the two sets of assumptions, that should be enough. However, the philosopher in me insists on making a few comments about each side and stating a few assumptions of my own. I think the basic philosophical underpinnings of the challengers are weak. Let us start with the rejection of metaphysical realism. This view is derived from deconstructionist philosophers as well as from an interpretation of the works of Thomas Kuhn and Richard Rorty. The idea, roughly speaking, is that Kuhn is supposed to have shown that science does not give us an account of an independently existing reality. Rather, scientists are an irrational bunch who run from one paradigm to another, for reasons with no real connection to finding objective truths. What Kuhn did for science, Rorty supposedly also did for philosophy. Philosophers don't provide accounts that mirror how the world is, because the whole idea of language as mirroring or corresponding to reality is flawed from the beginning. (The works of Kuhn and Rorty, by the way, are more admired in academic departments of literature than they are in departments in the sciences and philosophy.) Whether or not this is the correct interpretation of the works of Kuhn, Rorty, and the deconstructionists, the effect of these works has been to introduce into various humanities departments versions of relativism, anti-objectivism, and skepticism about science and the correspondence theory of truth.

Because of the limitation of space, I am going to be rather swift in my refutation of this view. The only defense that one can give of metaphysical realism is a transcendental argument in one of Kant's many senses of that term. We assume that something is the case and show how that metaphysical realism is a condition of possibility of its being the case. If both we and our adversaries share the assumption that something is the case and that which we assume presupposes realism, then the transcendental argument is a refutation of our adversaries' view. It seems to me obvious in this case that we as well as the antirealists assume we are communicating with each other in a public language. When the antirealists present us with an argument, they claim to do so in a language that is publicly intelligible. But, I wish to argue, public intelligibility presupposes the existence of a publicly accessible world. Metaphysical realism is not a thesis; rather, it is the condition of the possibility of having theses which are publicly intelligible. Whenever we use a language that purports to have public objects of reference, we commit ourselves to realism. The commitment is not a specific theory as to *how* the world is, but rather that there is a way the world is. Thus, it is self-refuting for someone to claim in a public language that metaphysical realism is false, because a public language presupposes a public world, and that presupposition is metaphysical realism.

Though I will not develop it here, it seems that a similar argument applies to objective standards of rationality. Again, to put it very crudely, one can't make sense out of presenting a thesis, or having a belief, or defending a view without presupposing certain standards of rationality. The very notions of mental and linguistic representation already contain certain logical principles built into them. For those who think that I am exaggerating the extent to which the traditional values are challenged, I suggest they read the ACLS pamphlet from which I quoted above.

Another fallacious move made by the challengers is to infer, from the fact that the university's educational efforts invariably have political consequences, that therefore the primary objective of the university and the primary criteria for assessing its success or failure should be political. The conclusion does not follow from the premise. Obviously, everything has political consequences, whether it's art, music, literature, sex, or gastronomy. For example, right now you could be campaigning for the next presidential election, and therefore this article has political consequences, because it prevents you from engaging in political activities in which you might otherwise be engaging. In this sense, *everything* is political. But from the fact that everything is political in this sense, it doesn't follow that our academic *objectives* are political, nor does it follow that the criteria for assessing our successes and failures are political. The argument, in short, does not justify the current attempts to use the classroom and the curriculum as tools of political transformation.

A further fallacy concerns the notion of empowerment. The most general form of this fallacy is the supposition that power is a property of groups rather than of individuals and organizations. A moment's reflection will reveal that this is not true. Most positions of power in the United States are occupied by middle-aged white males, but it does not follow that power accrues to middle-aged white males as a group. Most white males, middle-aged or otherwise, are as powerless as anyone else. In these discussions, there is a fallacy that goes as follows: People assume because most people in positions of power are white males that therefore most white males are in a position of power. I hope the fallacy is obvious.

Finally, in my list of criticisms of the challengers, I want to point out that we should not be embarrassed by the fact that a disproportionately large percentage of the major cultural achievements in our society have been made by white males. This is an interesting historical fact that requires analysis and explanation. But it doesn't in any way discredit the works of, for example, Descartes or Shakespeare that they happen to have been white males, any more than it discredits the work of Newton and Darwin that they were both English. Representativeness as such is not the primary aim in the study of the humanities. Rather, representativeness comes in as a desirable goal when there is a question of articulating the different varieties of human experience. And our aim in seeking works that articulate this variety is always to find works of high quality. The problem with the predominance of white males is not that there is any doubt about the quality of the work, but that we have been excessively provincial, that great works in other cultures may have been neglected, and that, even within Western civilization, there have been groups, most notably women, whose works have been discriminated against.

My criticism of the traditionalists is somewhat different from my criticism of the challengers because I do not, as a matter of fact, find much that is objectionable in the assumptions behind the traditionalist philosophy of education. The difficulty is how those assumptions are being implemented in contemporary American universities. There are many forms of decay and indeed corruption that have become entrenched in the actual practice of American universities, especially where undergraduate education is concerned. The most obvious sign of decay is that we

have simply lost enthusiasm for the traditional philosophy of a liberal education. As our disciplines have become more specialized, as we have lost
faith in the ideal of an integrated undergraduate education, we simply
provide the student with the familiar cafeteria of courses and hope things
turn out for the best. The problem with the traditionalists' ideology is
not that it is false but that it has run out of gas. It is somewhat hypo-
critical to defend a traditional liberal education with a well-rounded
reading list that goes from Plato to James Joyce, if one is unwilling actually to attempt to educate undergraduates in this tradition. I do not,
frankly, think that the challengers have superior ideas. Rather, they have
something which may be more important to influencing the way things
are actually done. They have more energy and enthusiasm, not to say fanaticism and intolerance. In the long run, these may be more effective in
changing universities than rigorous arguments can be.

All institutions naturally suffer from a tendency to decay and corruption. The only way to combat this is to have certain constraints on the
institutions. In the case of business in a capitalist society, the constraint is
obvious: you have to make a profit to survive. In the case of elected officials in a democratic society, the constraint again is obvious. You have
to face periodic elections. But there are lots of institutions that really
shouldn't be governed by profit or electoral constraints, because if they
were, they couldn't possibly survive. Yet they are essential to society.
Here I am thinking of such institutions as public libraries, public parks,
and museums. They could not survive on the basis alone of making a
profit or pleasing constituencies. It seems to me that universities are
clearly in this category, too. If it is just a question of earning a profit or
gaining votes, they can't make it, so there has to be some other set of
constraints. Quality, within the standards of a discipline, sets its own
constraints. The problem arises when the discipline's objectives and standards decay or collapse.

When institutional corruptions set in, when institutions lose a sense
of their mission, there are several forms of decadence. One is that they
become patronage institutions, ways of getting jobs for friends, relatives,
and other approved groups. I believe that certain forms of affirmative-action hiring programs fall in this category. In cases where you think that
the results of your selection process really matter – if, for example, you
are selecting a brain surgeon to operate on your brain or a quarterback
to lead your team – you will select entirely on grounds of quality. Only
if you think the results do not much matter, will you allow considerations other than quality to enter into the selection process. A second
sign of institutional loss of self-confidence appears when institutions ac-

quire a mission other than their official one, such as perhaps a moral one. (Something like this is taking place in some churches. When clerics no longer believe in God, they sometimes turn their churches into institutions for social benefit.) Another sign of decadence occurs when the official custodians of the institution are unable to repel assaults on it from within and without. Some of these signs of decadence are visible in certain humanities departments today. For example, having lost their sense of humanistic mission, various faculty members in the study of literature have acquired a political mission which they regard as morally preemptory, and even those who do not share this mission are rather feeble in resisting the politicization of their disciplines.

For reasons that I do not fully understand, a fairly sizable number of professors in literature departments have lost interest in the study of literature as it has been traditionally construed. Of two major lectures I heard in the past year by famous professors of English, one was entirely about Freud, the other about the power of the president of the United States to initiate nuclear war. No one seems to find this odd. But it is typical of the way in which a great deal of the contemporary study of literature is not so much about literature as it is about other issues. My guess is — and it is only a guess — that it may have been a mistake to think there is an academic subject of literary *criticism* in addition to such old-fashioned subjects as literary history, philology, and stylistics. Another piece of anecdotal evidence is this: My interests take me to conferences on a variety of different subjects, including neurobiology, artificial intelligence, psychology, linguistics, and a number of others, and I am frequently struck by the differences in intellectual level and discursive style among different academic disciplines. I believe that as far as general intellectual level is concerned, the field of "literary theory" is probably the lowest I have experienced. The carnival-like atmosphere of the annual meetings of the Modern Language Association contrasts sharply with, for instance, the atmosphere of conferences on neurobiology. My impression of neurobiology conferences is that the participants are deeply committed to neurobiological research and think that what they do is important. My guess is that many of the participants at the MLA have lost interest in doing what they are officially supposed to be doing, so they are doing something else, such as advancing political causes. My impression is that they do not believe the scholarly study of modern languages and their literatures is worth devoting their lives to, so they devote themselves to what seem more worthwhile activities.

Where undergraduate education is concerned, we do not have a coherent vision of what we are trying to do. We have lost confidence in

the traditional ideal of an integrated, well-balanced education for undergraduates, but we have not replaced it with a coherent alternative.
We really are in doubt as to what constitutes success and failure in undergraduate education. We educate high school students for college, and
we educate undergraduate students in their respective majors for the
graduate and professional schools, but we do not have an adequate theory of what constitutes success in general education for undergraduates.
Though we pay lip service to the traditional ideals of quality and excellence as exemplified by the Western intellectual tradition, many of us
would rather not spend much time teaching courses which convey that
tradition to undergraduates. In certain humanities disciplines, especially
those concerned with the study of literature, there is a crisis of self-definition. In such a situation of institutional loss of self-confidence, a determined minority can have an influence vastly out of proportion to its
numbers or the strength of its arguments.

The most offensive trait of American academics as a class is their
timidity. In many cases, even those who have tenure are unwilling to
take controversial stands (for fear of being hated by their colleagues and
students, I suppose). In this situation, at a time when the mission of
higher education is in doubt, we have to keep reminding our students,
their parents, and the public generally of a few truths about our mission,
even when these truths are unpopular. I would like to conclude by stating a few of my own assumptions.

If the system of higher education – as opposed to high schools, trade
schools, and community colleges – is to serve a democratic society, it
must by its very nature be elitist. Good universities are elitist in the same
sense that good professional football teams are elitist. They try to get the
best coaches and players and make them do the best they can. We try to
get the most brilliant faculty and the most able students and make them
all work as hard as they can. Higher education is elitist because its essence
is the relentless quest for intellectual quality. Without a commitment to
quality, we merely become trade schools or social welfare agencies. Our
efforts are based on assumptions such as that some books are better than
others; some people are more intelligent than others; some theories are
true and others false; some ideas are original and others derivative.
Furthermore, we are convinced that with some effort and training, we
and our students can be taught to ascertain the presence of these features.

Because its mission is the relentless search for quality, such otherwise
socially desirable traits as representativeness are really of secondary importance to universities. It would not, for example, be a valid criticism of
the world's best math department that its faculty is not representative of

the population as a whole. The best argument for faculty diversity is as follows: Assume that academic talent is randomly distributed across the gene pool. Then, if you are recruiting talent from only a subsection of that pool, you are losing access to a large number of talented people. By expanding your talent search, you increase the probability of a higher quality faculty. The argument for diversity is that simple. But notice that implicit in the argument is the claim that achieving diversity just for the sake of achieving diversity is not an objective of a university, any more than it is of a football club or a team of brain surgeons. If our objective is to improve the intellectual quality of the university, we will make our talent searches as broad as possible, but hiring people because of their race or ethnicity is just as irrelevant as hiring people because they are left-handed or suffer from premature baldness. Worse yet, there is no way to discriminate in favor of the members of some groups without discrimi-nority, the minority person is given preference. The basic change is that originally race, sex, and ethnicity were grounds *for encouraging someone to compete;* now they are among *the criteria for judging the competition.* There is a traditional term for such policies; they are called racial and sexual discrimination.   It is not the aim of education to make the student feel good about himself or herself. On the contrary, if anything, a good education should lead to a permanent sense of dissatisfaction. Complacency is the very opposite of the intellectual life. The dirty secret of intellectual life is that first-rate work requires an enormous amount of effort, anxiety, and even desperation. The quests for knowledge and truth, as well as depth, insight, and originality, are not effortless, and they certainly are not comfortable.

DAVID SIDORSKY

Multiculturalism and the University

The key to understanding the great debate over multiculturalism in the American university is that it is taking place on two different levels. Only on one level is it a debate about curriculum. For the curricular debate which appears to be about inclusiveness and pluralism carries within it a decision about the nature of the university. Multicultural claims for inclusiveness raise anew the question of *why* a book is required reading in a prescribed curriculum. The answer involves the issue of *how* any text is to be taught in the university classroom.

The terms of the debate thus shift away from the question of including one or another book from more pluralistic cultural sources to the legitimacy of using texts as instruments for consciousness-raising, cultural sensitization, or political initiation. The issue is then not the desirability of some curricular changes but the nature and desirability of the ongoing transformation of the university. Only if the debate about multiculturalism is identified as confrontation about the politicization of the university, rather than as disagreement about the breadth of reading lists, can the polarization that it has generated be understood.

The Issue of Curricular Expansion

The current movement for multiculturalism, if viewed solely as an effort toward curricular reform, would be another of a continuing series of demands for a more inclusive and pluralist university. In these terms, it would be similar in kind to many earlier revisions that can be traced back to the university during the Renaissance, which added pagan and secular literary works to the medieval academy's list of religious and philosophical texts, or to the inclusion in the nineteenth-century of the writings of their great national authors alongside the classics in Latin and Greek. Like these predecessors, the revisions of multiculturalism call for the expansion of the texts read in the curriculum, both in elective and prescribed studies. Seen solely in this light, the distinctive feature of the current revision would then be the inclusion of works written by women, by designated minorities, and by non-Western writers.

There are three different arguments in support of this curricular ex-

pansion. The first is that there are great works, great by universally recognized standards, which because of cultural parochialism, ideological
myopia, or other unwarranted grounds for neglect have not received the
appreciation they deserve, so that they have been unjustly excluded.

The second argument is the educational goal of replacing inherited
works that do not reflect the changed contemporary values or consciousness with works which are more expressive of the People that we
have become. Just as Latin and Greek texts in periods of romantic nationalism were to be supplemented or replaced by the developing national literatures, so the once-dominant tradition of Anglo-American or
Euro-American culture is to be supplemented or replaced by works that
explore the new cultural self-consciousness. These are the works, which
may range from high culture to midcult, pop, or the various countercul-
tures, of the emergent groups in American society. Just as the champions
of nationalism, like Herder, had once advocated that the university open
its classrooms to the new European cultures, the American university
should now participate in the revolutionary explorations of the diverse
and multicultural American people of the new age. These works need
not meet some neoclassic test of aesthetic greatness since they meet the
more relevant test, which is of equal or greater educational validity, of
expressing our authentic collective selves in the here and now.

The third reason is derived from the need, which is presumed to be
present in every responsible system of higher education, to cultivate the
sensitivities of the students. On this ground, some exposure to works that
reflect the experience and assert the values of cultures and communities
that are alien or that may have been neglected by the majoritarian culture is required. This includes the work of political and cultural dissidents
across the unconventional political spectrum such as anarchists or terrorists and, *a fortiori,* victimized groups within the society. This cultivation
of sensitivity also is another reason for the introduction of courses in
non-Western cultural traditions, both of large religious or national societies in Africa or Asia and of small ethnic groups. Just as Michael
Oakeshott had argued that education was learning how to participate in
a conversation with the cultural tradition, so multicultural education has
been justified as an initiation into sensitivity to the cultural traditions of
diverse communities, some of which have become or ought to become
participants in our own cultural space.

When the issue is set in terms of curricular expansion, without the
corollary implications of changes in methods of teaching, the decision
depends only on empirical and pragmatic considerations. It is primarily
an empirical question, for example, whether there are works of great

merit which have been overlooked because their authors were women or members of racial minorities. If so, then their inclusion should be universally welcomed, particularly since rotation among works on the list is a necessary aspect of course design.

Yet there is a pragmatic difficulty related to the ability to teach works of a different tradition within the time constraints. To be appreciated, such works may require the knowledge of context or the initiation into the genre which is not feasible within a prescribed curriculum. The texts of Kabbalah and the Talmud are clear examples of major literary works in a different religious tradition, which would be opaque, misunderstood, or negatively evaluated if taught in the framework of a course in non-Western classics. The list of great works from other cultures which require appropriate initiation for meaningful study is a long one.

The exclusion of many works, particularly those that reflect contemporary cultural self-consciousness like movies or popular music, does not raise a principled objection to their study as cultural products of the age. Such exclusion can be based upon a higher priority to teach the students the complex elements that are present in a masterpiece. The neglect of this priority by a faculty member choosing, for example, pop ular novels and movies as the texts of a course, whatever their multicultural breadth, may demonstrate a pandering avoidance of the challenge of teaching the masterworks of any cultural tradition, singular or plural.

In the multicultural controversy one major issue which Arthur Schlesinger, Jr. has emphasized, the neglect of the values of cultural commonality for the sake of cultural pluralism, involves both the empirical question of the nature of the American people as well as questions of value, of the kind of nation that America ought to become. Yet this aspect of the controversy primarily applies to the school curriculum in the formative years before college. Even if the justified decision were to go against multiculturalism, with a need to stress cultural assimilation into traditional American values, for example, this would not be a strong argument against the inclusion of works drawn from other cultural traditions in college study.

Thus, if the focus could be limited to the educational arguments and counterarguments for curricular inclusion, the differences of opinion might be reconciled. But the intensity and depth of the disagreement suggest that another agenda is present in the debate. The works introduced to cultivate sensitivity to cultures outside the conven tional mainstream are seldom defended or refuted by any empirical evidence of how an understanding of alternative or dissident culture is attained. Rather, the position taken on the issue seems to hinge on different grounds.

One ground is the attitude toward the legitimacy of the "raising of consciousness" as part of university teaching. On this issue, the critics of "consciousness-raising" courses in the curriculum have argued that such courses cultivate or presuppose a set of views shared by the instructor and all of the students. Hence, underlying a decision on curricular expansion is an attitude toward instruction in which the class is a community of faith or belief rather than a forum of critical inquiry. In the study of a literary work that is chosen as a representative expression of the values of a deprived group, the cultivation of sensitivity is transposed into politicization. For in the examination of the work, a spectrum of beliefs that are not considered sufficiently sensitive or sympathetic to the deprived is beyond the pale. This tacit adoption of unchallengeable assumptions about deprived groups has been legitimized, for example, in workshop courses that focus on human rights violations in selected areas of the world or in social work classes that concern such issues as homelessness. With the adoption of representative multicultural texts, views which are not politically correct become proscribed in the study of literature.

Thus, as noted at the outset, the question of curricular inclusion shifts from what new works are to be taught to how any text is to be taught. Two special aspects of the multicultural debate confirm that the issues go beyond the apparent question of adding new works to the curriculum. One of these is the stress on canon formation; the other is the stress on the new texts as those of a deprived or victimized community.

Legitimation: The Sacred and the Demonic Texts

Advocates of multiculturalism argue that the prescribed curriculum is comprised of a canon of texts written by members of the privileged elite groups of the society, and accordingly reflecting the values and methodologies (the *episteme,* in the phrase of Michel Foucault) of the historically dominant culture. The metaphor of a "canon" magnifies the significance of curriculum construction. The adoption of a text written by a member of an outsider group (perhaps not in point of current fact and fashion by Jane Austen or Ibn Rushd but by Virginia Woolf or Zora Neale Hurston) is a blow against the imperial rule of the cultural canon and, consequently, an act tinged with the aura of resistance and liberation.

It is instructive to recall what a debate on canon formation in its literal and historical sense, as in the determination of what works are to be included in the Bible or in the New Testament, is about. The main assumption of that debate is that there are sacred texts and profane texts. The sacred texts are the reflection of a divine revelation; that is, they are either the actual product of such revelation or an authentic witness to it, and profane works are not. To study the sacred texts is to be initiated into a valid covenant which provides a way of redemption or salvation for the individual or group. When an authentic sacred text is denied due recognition as part of the canon or when a profane text falsely receives canonic status, then the instruments of human redemption have been placed in jeopardy.

Admittedly, the concept of the canon is being applied in a metaphorical way in a secular context. Yet the multiculturalist is using the metaphor in order to argue that removing some texts from the curriculum, those which embody attitudes that are tacitly racist, sexist, or exploitative, is to delegitimize these expressions of the dominance of race, gender, and class. To include the works which are the voices of minorities, women, and other exploited groups is analogous to a revelation or bearing witness to a true revelation. It is a process of legitimizing the new egalitarian values, through sacralization of the texts that reflect opposition to discrimination based on race, class, gender, or sexual orientation. In the sense of secular faith, then, the establishment of the new canon is part of the process of redemption for the community.

Along such lines, it follows that to mandate the reading of the speeches of Martin Luther King on equality or civil disobedience, rather than Shakespeare's *Tempest*, is to purge the intellectual community of its historically accepted, that is, "institutional" racism, and begin to replace it by the new self-consciousness of equality. Similarly, to replace Aristotle's *Politics*, which has equivocal comments on the equality of women, with a feminist account by, say, Betty Friedan, of the struggle for equal rights, is appropriate in light of the requirement that a cultural canon reflect the values of a liberal and evolving society. George Bernard Shaw expressed this view when he spoke of the way in which future theater audiences, who would grow up in a socialist society, would have overcome the cult of Shakespeare's greatness, embedded as that is in the exploitative society of colonial England, and have replaced it by the heightened appreciation of the superiority of Shaw's or other socialist authors' works. Shaw concluded *An Unsocial Socialist* with the comment:

> The first literary result of the foundations of our industrial system upon the profits of piracy and slave-trading was Shakspeare [sic]. It is our misfortune that the sordid misery and hopeless horror of his view of man's destiny is still so appropriate to English society that we even today regard him as not for an age, but for all time.

The Significance of "Victimology"

The second confirmation of the deeper agenda of the debate is the stress on the setting up of interdisciplinary programs of studies on deprived or victimized groups. The early models of these programs were the postwar departments of religion. In the early fifties, the argument had been advanced by supporters of religion that the secular university and secular educational system had deprived students of knowledge of even the rudiments of any historic religious culture. As a result, departments of religious studies were widely introduced. The curriculum in these areas reached beyond the disciplinary approaches set by history, literature or linguistic study to provide an interdisciplinary approach to topics like Christianity, Buddhist studies, or Jewish studies. The challenges involved in these curricular innovations were recognized and debated at that time.

One such challenge was to guarantee that courses in religious studies were not exercises in consciousness-raising but involved a critical scholarly approach to even the most sacred aspect of the religion. This also meant that, unlike extracurricular group activities which could appropriately be restricted to members of the same religious community, the courses in Islam, Judaism, Buddhism, and so on would be conducted as academic studies for believer and nonbeliever alike. Instructors in such courses in principle, whatever the practical empirical exigencies, would not have to be recruited from sympathetic or committed practitioners of the historical religion that formed the curricular subject matter. In many instances the instruction in these areas, sensitive to the potential charge that it had been transferred from its traditional domicile in the theological seminary or other religious academy, reacted with vigorous pursuit of scholarly standards and aggressive expression of critical inquiry.

The pace of neglected studies leading to interdisciplinary "victimologies" has since been accelerated. The model of religious studies could readily be applied to various programs in ethnic studies. The curriculum, especially where the ethnic group has a history of deprivation, involves an element of sensitivity to the group's historical experience, a kind of consciousness-raising. In such an interdisciplinary program, the literature of the group is freed from some of the disciplinary constraints that require a forum on literary form and aesthetic value, in order to celebrate group identity. Similarly, whatever the constraint of historical objectivity, the history of group deprivation and suffering presupposes, in this context, an element of affirmative solidarity with the situation of the group.

This approach is virtually built into the demarcation of the curriculum in areas like "ethnic studies" or "Holocaust studies." The path of interdisciplinary studies has moved beyond religious studies or ethnic studies through such a transitional period piece as Holocaust studies. The hierarchy of ascent, with each rung marking greater legitimation as victims, can be charted as continuing from Hispanic Studies to Black Studies to African Studies and other Third World Regional Studies, particularly Palestinian Studies, to Native American Studies, culminating in Women's Studies, surpassed only by Gay and Lesbian Studies.

From the perspective of the competition in victimology, the considerations that entered into canon formation gain force. On pain of violating the rule of never blaming the victim, the study of the culture of the victimized group will tend to the identification and indictment of the social forces that led to victimization. Thus, the inclusion of the area in the curriculum becomes a kind of legitimation of claims of political and social deprivation.

Further, the texts of the legitimated authentic spokesmen of the victims emerge as sacred texts, immune from standards of criticism. They may be debated, in the spirit in which scholastic debate on sacred texts was carried out in the medieval university, but their fundamental premises are not to be questioned. Those who do not share these premises or do not wish to be sensitized by immersion in the literature are not part of the community of political faith. In effect, they are invited to withdraw from elective classes in these areas, which become *de facto* segregated.

Thus, the effort at formation of the new canon and the justification of interdisciplinary departments organized around perceived victimized communities generate an approach to texts which rejects traditional methods of scholarly research and criticism. Historically, in the academic tradition, admission to the prescribed curriculum or "canon" effectively guaranteed a targeted stream of critical analysis. In contrast, the introduction of a work into the contemporary prescribed curriculum virtually guarantees immunity from criticism. Hence, the intensity of the struggle for inclusion.

This intensity also derives from the previously mentioned thesis (usually advanced in the contemporary context in the neo-Marxist versions of Gramsci or Foucault) that the cultural product is part of the intellectual superstructure which reflects and rationalizes the social structure with its dominating ruling class. The current version, revising Marx, stresses that access to that class has been restricted on grounds of race, gender, and sexual orientation.

Although not always formulated in theoretical fashion, the conceptual framework of many groups involved in multicultural curricular revision is that the university curriculum represents traditional Western culture as an expression of the historical domination and therefore an instrument of the illegitimate hegemony of the West. University prescription of Western classics is a kind of intellectual "occupation," and curricular change is then revolutionary liberation. Such a framework also provides multiculturalism with its characteristic response to the charge that in the name of heightening sensitivity for victims, it is pursuing or condoning the politicization of inquiry. That response is that all the traditions of the university, including free inquiry and objective scholarship, are tacitly political, since they derive from the forces of political domination. Confronting and displacing these covert political traditions, including their canon of great works, are actions by which institutionalized political bias is to be overcome with a more correct perspective of the human condition.

The difference in the approach of multiculturalists and traditionalists to scholarship and critical inquiry can be clarified, therefore, not so much in the argument for the inclusion of the new works of cultural pluralism, as in their approach to the classics of Western civilization. For if the new works are to be sacralized as expressing the consciousness and the rights of victims, then by parallel logic, the old works are to be demonized, for they are inescapably reflective of the historic hegemony of exploitative male European aristocratic or capitalist culture.

The ways in which Aristotle and Shakespeare, to cite again these master targets, are taught can provide confirmation. At a leading-edge Southern university, the chairman of the English department stated that Shakespeare could today only be taught in terms of "race, class, and gender." At an Ivy League university's faculty seminar on the teaching of a course which is widely cited as sustaining the values of the tradition, every single one of the questions on Aristotle's *Politics* related to his comments on sexual equality. The inference was that this would be the focus of the few hours of classroom discussion.

Regardless of the actual meanings of any of the classic texts, the interpretive strategy of reading the text as an expression of its morally flawed social genesis guarantees its exhibition in the catalogue of Western intellectual oppression. Thus, the multicultural focus on curricular expansion shifts when it is projected through the prism of the legitimation of the canon for the study of the culture of the designated groups of victims. The character of the university which emerges after its adoption of multiculturalism is not that of the classical university augmented by an expanded curriculum but of an institution that has changed its approach to teaching, to the independent appreciation of the humanities, and to freedom of inquiry. So, as previously claimed, implicit in the multicultural program for expansion of what is to be taught is an argument about how works are to be taught. Instruction in the Western humanities should defer to a "genetic" reductionist interpretation of the classic texts while a politicized advocacy approach is to be adopted for the privileged new works.

The logic of the argument is confirmed, to a degree, by observation. The development of a large number of programs of interdisciplinary studies in which the preferred interpretations of privileged texts are sheltered by a cohesive faculty community can be documented at many campuses. There have also been some vigorous campaigns for the adoption of politically correct texts in the core curriculum. Such adoption is presented as legitimation of the point of view of the work, which then becomes safeguarded from dissenting criticism. The empirical investigation, presumably an anthropology of the classroom, which would demonstrate how strong or how weak these tendencies are in the country's universities, does not exist. For the protection of the tradition of free inquiry in the traditional university virtually excludes undertaking the kind of investigative research which could demonstrate the extent of abuses of free inquiry by classrooom politicization in the contemporary university.

Institutional Transformation

For the most part, the preceding account has developed an analytic portrait or line drawing of a complex moving picture of institutional change. The practical question, whatever the precise degree of truth or validity in the analysis or portrait, is whether the direction of the current movement can shift to restoration or reintegration of the historic university of objective scholarship and free inquiry, or whether it will continue its current trends to politicization. An evaluation of the factors that are usually cited as sources for restoration can clarify the present situation.

Apart from the continuing efforts by small groups within the academic community that have organized in protest of specific violations of academic freedom, there are major institutional groups whose interests would seem to support academic freedom and academic integrity. While the faculty has been presumed to be historically the primary supportive constituency, there is also an interested public which is closely involved with the governance of the university, particularly boards of trustees, as well as the hypothetically decisive "consumer" interests of students and their parents. Thus, although Aristotle may have overstated the case when he began his *Metaphysics* with the opening line, "All men by nature desire to know," there is, among a proportion of those persons who are attracted to the academy as scholars and teachers, a desire, even a commitment to defend academic freedom if only to defend the favorable features of the academic environment. So some elements of the faculty may represent a constant interested party against politicization.

Again, the American political community, whose support is necessary for the financial security of the university, has not been noted for its attachment to such cutting-edge academic tendencies as Marxism, radical feminism, and other ideologies of racial or sexual separatism or liberation. The historical record of that community contains several much-rehearsed instances of instrusion or assault on faculty rights when they were suspected of supporting much less pervasive varieties of perceived radical ideologies. Interestingly, and somewhat surprisingly, the elite media community, which since the late 1960s has found itself aligned with the social and political agenda of the radical faculty groups, has participated in a satirical campaign against "politically correct" conformism on campus. Ironically, even while circulating the anti-academic barb, these same media have maintained political correctness in their own domain.

Any review of the present situation would recognize the inertial force of the established tendencies for politicized instruction. There is no accepted moral position which demonstrates the illegitimacy of scholarship or criticism seeking to justify a political agenda. Since the great majority of the faculty share the liberal or radical political views and values identified as politically correct, there is no felt need to rise to the defense of the nonconformist on grounds of principle. All the more so if, as in the case of multiculturalism, the operation of a politically correct conformism can be defended as experimentalist in terms of curriculum and supportive of historically victimized minority groups within American society. Further, the result of past confrontations between the community and the university faculty has resulted in the general acceptance of the illegitimacy of intervention by the community or even university boards on academic issues. The university faculty, having won the battle for non-intervention against external pressures for political conformism, now is placed in a position where, with rare exceptions, it either ought not, cannot, or will not appeal to an external power for protection against pressures for ideological conformism or political correctness from within the university.

The well-known case of Professor Jeffries at the City College of New York provides an interesting confirmation of these trends. Informally, many faculty will cite chapter and verse of Professor Jeffries's violations of standards of academic freedom in class discussion or of academic integrity in scholarship. Yet there is no faculty support for any procedures which would be able to probe these assertions or to take action upon them. The action of the board of trustees in removing Professor Jeffries from his chairmanship but not denying him his professorship, tenure, or salary, was taken very reluctantly on what were judged to be adequate legal grounds. But the legal result was a reinstatement of Professor Jeffries with an award to him of monetary damages, on the ground that his rights to freedom of speech had been denied. The jury's verdict suggests that politicized scholarship, set in the framework of a minority studies program, can receive support from the related minority constituency. A perceived group interest in multiculturalism outweighs a less urgent abuse of academic standards. So while the discrepancy between radical faculty views and community sentiment may be a source of tension, it is not likely to generate a movement toward any external pressure for academic freedom or for protecting standards of scholarship.

A third interest group for depoliticization is the student body. It has been often noted that the current student generation demonstrates much greater conservatism in economic and political attitudes than its teachers, many of whom came of age in the period of student revolt on campus. Thus, there has been a widespread doctrine of conservative consolation and radical lament that what is taking place is the working-out of a transitory generational phenomenon. Just as the universities were radicalized as the age cohort of the sixties came to power, so the process will be reversed as the academic inheritors of the eighties come into their own.

Against any such assessment of the potential for change in current politicization, or in the balance in representing the political spectrum of American society, there is the understanding of the process of faculty formation. On faculty formation, Senator Daniel Patrick Moynihan once cited a comment he attributed to Professor von Hayek of the University of Chicago: his better students in economics became successful bankers if they were conservative, and recognized professors of economics if they were liberal. Among minority groups, this self-selection process would be intensified, with conservatives opting to enter the mainstream professions, and radicals or liberals choosing to devote themselves to the studies in the social sciences or in literature from which professors are recruited.

More generally, this kind of self-selection seems to be at work in faculty recruitment. In the case of the social sciences, there may even be an element of "professional deformation," since its explanatory structures for economic or social ills tend to relate them to institutional causes, a liberal mode, rather than to individual responsibility and social disincentives, a conservative mode. In addition, there is the pressure of selective reinforcement built into the peer promotional system. Without any resort to censorship or confrontation, the current groups in power within the university can send the appropriate signals of encouragement to the ideologically compatible and of exclusion to those who reject the current trend. Like the great historic universities that flourished on the rites of succession to professorial chairs, the politicized faculty can also achieve self-perpetuation if it attains sufficient consolidation of its institutional power.

In terms of community reaction to a process of academic politicization, there are two factors that constrain it, apart from its characteristic inability to match its policies to targeted goals without counterproductive fallout. One of these is the insularity of current ideological radicalism. The goals of the radical segment of the faculty in the thirties or the sixties were to effect political change in the greater society. Faculty activism, whether in teaching students or in more direct forms of expression, believed that the university or the faculty's position in it should be a base for political outreach. A political reaction to this activism resulted, and it included some appropriate and many harmful responses.

The current radical faculty community, the Marxists for example, do not propose to establish or resurrect their social model in the society. That world having been lost, their goal has been to pursue radical theorizing separated from the failures of radical practice. The cultural hegemony is achieved within the academic haven or its cultural allies, but it is not organized for direct social action.

Multiculturalism also provides a strong reason for the irreversibility of the present trends, for it enables politicized teaching to be sheltered in the university within groups which are generally perceived as having suffered deprivation or discrimination on grounds of race, sex, or sexual orientation. Some forms of Marxism gain immunity from criticism because they are part of a feminist movement which represents the point of view of an historically deprived group. If such constraints function in the general community, they are even stronger among the foundation boards, university trustees, and other leaders in educational policy, who, for reasons of conviction or image, tend to avoid confrontation with groups or individuals who can be perceived as victims.

Further, there is little empirical evidence to demonstrate the interest or the commitment of parents and students, as, so to speak, consumers of university education, to foster a university which has greater freedom of inquiry. The primary concern of students or parents is the university's function as an institution for socialization and for economic mobility. As long as the university, whether or not politicized in its humanities or social sciences, provides these functions, including the necessary credential-ization for admisson to professional schools, it is not perceived as being in violation of its implicit contractual obligation to these constituents. For the majority, a college education has been viewed as a rite of pas-sage, with a limited role for humanistic scholarship.

From such a perspective, governed by short-term results, the "serious" part of the university or, more appropriately, the multiversity, is not placed in jeopardy by politicized departments in the humanities and in the social sciences. These can coexist with prestigious professional schools and with excellent scientific faculties and research institutes. The transformation of the university into an institution which will continue its traditional functions, whether in research in the natural sciences or in the socialization of the younger generation after secondary school, while at the same time serving as a forum for politicized scholarship and teaching, marks a new phase in the long history of the university. The novel features of the change should be appreciated, for they are ominous for its future.

The Western university during the centuries of its evolution became the recognized seat of intellectual authority in the culture. As such it was a magnet for gifted minds to achieve peer recognition in the intellectual disciplines, participate in a centuries-old conversation, and share in that authority. The conditions of free inquiry that served as a guarantee for intellectual authority were reasonably explicit, though not constitution-ally fixed. In order that the intellectual authority would be recognized and preserved, the university scholar would not let his scholarship be per-verted by religious, political, ideological, or commercial purposes. In re-turn, so to speak, the society recognized the rights of the scholar and the illegitimacy of imposing upon his discipline any tests of conformity to religious, ideological, political, or commercial dogma. This arrangement was particularly true of the humanities.

The existence of a seat of intellectual authority has had significant social and cultural influences. The partisan political culture, which re-solves issues by exercise of political power has, in many contexts, recog-nized the university as an arbiter of questions that require scientific re-search. Even the media of communication, which assert their role as the interpreters of current events, have appealed to the university as the ar-biter of the historical record.

To some degree, the growth of the social sciences within the uni-versity has raised the question of politicized scholarship in earlier periods.

For while maintaining the authority of the sciences, it was evident in many areas that the inquiry was determined by political and social attitudes. Yet the characteristic university resolution was to aim to ensure that the social scientific results would meet the standards of an apolitical science.

In the present situation, a politicized faculty abdicates the role, or at least reneges on some of the historical terms of the understanding of the university as the seat within the culture of its highest intellectual authority. This change of role is most explicit in those literary and philosophical approaches that currently have academic popularity, which combine extreme relativism on matters of truth or knowledge in any area with a high degree of commitment to political purposes. Nietzschean-Marxism, for example, is one of a number of ways in which the claim that any intellectual authority is arbitrary is combined with political expression in education.

This transformation of the university is not complete. As with any institutional change, relics and survivals of the older way coexist alongside the new trends and dominant style. Accordingly, the implications of the politicized university for the educational system, for the other cultural institutions, and for the society are not fully apparent. Yet it seems evident that such an historical change in one of the most conserving institutions of Western culture does have important social consequences.

Multiculturalism has not, of course, been the only movement which has contributed to the politicization of the university. Many of the motivations for the movement, and much of its aspiration, are independent of the tendencies to politicization. Yet in the current condition of the universities, it is a powerful instrument, precisely because of its intrinsic and irresistible attractiveness, in the advance of the politicized university.

FRED SIEGEL

Anti-rationalism

Who now reads R. D. Laing? Who for that matter remembers that earlier movement for diversity, anti-psychiatry? In the name of intellectual equality for the mad, Laing and other anti-psychiatrists convinced themselves and others that schizophrenia was a social and not a medical disorder, the product of a capitalist conspiracy. Much as minorities are now said to be kept in their place by "white male" rationality, mental illness, it was argued by the likes of Laing, was designed by bourgeois psychiatrists to keep society's natural rebels in their place. The upshot has been disastrous, as anti-psychiatry managed to move the mentally ill from the back wards to the back alleys of our cities. I bring up this ancient history because political correctness is so often dated from some point in the mid-1980s. But in fact almost all of its basic stances were well-established a quarter of a century ago.

It was Stokely Carmichael who denounced integration as a "subterfuge for the maintenance of white supremacy"; it was Susan Sontag who pronounced the white race a "cancer"; it was the student strikers at Columbia who disparaged science as "white," and the student strikers at San Francisco State who called for "black science." And there is little in the way of curriculum revisionism that goes beyond Justice Douglas's pronouncement, "The guarantees expressed in the Bill of Rights are no monopoly of the West. . . . their roots are deep in Eastern philosophy."

Today's passion for political correctness is the pale bureaucratic offspring of the passions produced by the antiwar, black power, and feminist movements. The "enthusiasms," to use Locke's phrase for religious passions, produced both a total rejection of the liberal regime and a search for a new faith to live by. For deep-dyed '68-ers, the little Luthers of the New Left, people whose parataxic moment came at the Chicago Convention, America's evil was none less than revealed truth. Out of that revealed truth was born what might be called leftist fundamentalism, the assumption that the '68-ers, having achieved veridical truth, were then required to impose that truth on the unbelievers. Enter Marcuse and his 1969 left-wing attack on free speech:

> Liberating tolerance would then mean intolerance against movements
> from the right and tolerance of movements from the left. As to the
> scope of this tolerance and intolerance . . . it would extend to the
> stage of action as well as of discussion and propaganda, of deed as
> well as word.

None of this necessarily seemed indefensible at the time.

Richard Hofstadter, who once described the sixties as "the age of
rubbish," saw where all this might lead for the life of the mind. Writing
after the end of McCarthyism but before the sixties took off, he saw that
"if anti-intellectualism" has so often gained wide currency, it is "because
it has often been linked to at least defensible causes," our "humane and
democratic sentiments" and our "passion for equality." He was so right.

How, it was asked, given the horrors of Vietnam abroad and racism
at home, could reactionaries be allowed to speak? It's easy enough to
view these matters dispassionately now. But at the time it was a close call
for even the level-headed of my generation. Leave the matter of power
aside; it didn't seem too much to ask that we sacrifice some of our freedoms on behalf of the oppressed.

The beginning of the end of debate on the campuses came with the
fight over the 1965 Moynihan report on the condition of the black
family. Initially it had been well-received by Martin Luther King, but it
soon became an exercise in line-drawing. To even discuss a degree of
black accountability was, in the words of William Ryan, to "blame the
victim."

By 1972 when Vietnam was deescalating and the rioting had for the
most part calmed down, James Q. Wilson wrote that "the list of subjects
that cannot be publicly discussed . . . in a free and open forum has
grown steadily, and now includes the war in Vietnam, public policy towards urban ghettos, the relationship between intelligence and heredity,
and the role of corporations in certain overseas regimes." In effect the
substantive commitments to supporting the "victims" overwhelmed the
form of university life organized around debate.

Shortly thereafter William Ryan, of "blaming the victim" fame and
one of the "founding fathers" of PC issued an ideological call to arms.
He asked for an army of intellectuals to join ranks to "get back into
uniform" as "ideological shock troops" in order to fight off the emerging array of critics skeptical of what was described as "the equality revolution." But if the attitudes associated with PC were already firmly in
place, the institutional enforcement mechanisms were not. The primary
problem with PC, after all, is not the opinions held by those with plu-
perfectly-raised consciousness per se, but their power at some schools to

make their dogmas into the equivalent of a religious test for institutional membership.

The early to mid-1970s were the heydays of Naderism and an almost revolutionary expansion of federal regulatory powers. From the era of Progressive reform through the New Deal and up until 1964 "only one regulatory agency (the Food and Drug Administration) had been established at the Federal level whose primary responsibility was to protect either consumers, employees, or the public from institutional malfeasance." But, writes David Vogel, "between 1964 and 1977 ten regulatory agencies were created with this as their mandate."

As the federal government sprayed itself into every nook and cranny of American life, the once largely autonomous universities were caught up in the new regulatory web. J. Stanley Pottinger of HEW's Office for Civil Rights explained in 1972, "We have a whale of a lot of power [over academia], and we're prepared to use it" to rectify what was then described as the "underutilization of minorities." "When representatives of HEW were told that there were no women or minority students in the department of religious studies at one university, in part, because, a reading of Greek and Hebrew was required, representatives of HEW advised orally that such requirements had to be revised so that, in the name of relevance, there could be more minority participation." HEW's affirmative-action oversight produced a tremendous demand for paperwork like racial identification surveys which in turn produced the need for more administrators, and so on.

The growth of affirmative action administrators would over time be an important element for yet more affirmative action. But their original source of power was the threat to federal funding of EEO lawsuits. Writing his memoirs in 1990 an anonymous dean described the advice given by his university's attorney: "I think we should give them whatever they ask for. . . . We certainly don't want the EEO people to think we are not cooperative."

Business responded to the new wave of regulation with a counter-offensive that in part produced Reaganism, which in turn eased the regulatory burden. By contrast, academia – and here I generalize broadly – internalized the new regulatory regime. It responded to Reaganism with new forms of regulation designed to make the universities over, the sciences partly excepted, into kinder and gentler and even therapeutic congregations.

But I'm jumping ahead of myself. To go back, the late 1970s saw two related developments of considerable importance, the decline of social science and the rise of what Ernest Gellner has described as "epistemological hypochondria."

For three centuries, beginning with Newton's rise to control of the

Royal Academy of Science, rational inquiry had progressively triumphed over all other forms of explanation. Science and freedom had become, it seemed, permanently linked. Walter Lippman in *Drift and Mastery* expressed the general understanding. "Democracy in politics," he wrote, "is the twin-brother of scientific thinking. . . . As absolutism falls, science arises. It is self-government." "The discipline of democracy, the escape from drift," he concluded, is "the outlook of a free man."

Social science, starting even before the 1944 publication of Gunnar Myrdal's *An American Dilemma,* had been given the task of extending a full measure of freedom to racial minorities. Writing about the 1950s, Robert Nisbet noted that "except for the footnotes there really wasn't much difference . . . between the meeting of a social science association and of the Americans for Democratic Action." But by the mid-1970s the utopian hopes for racial harmony aroused by the civil rights movement and its social science literature crashed into the dystopian reality of what would shortly come to be known as the underclass.

"We want to eliminate poverty, crime and drug addiction," said the prestigious Social Science Research Council in 1975, "but we don't know how." For years the cry of the academy had been "give us more time, we're only beginning, more research will give us the solid underpinning needed for scientific understanding." But tens of thousands of Ph.D.'s later the traditional image of scientific research as a ladder, with each study building on, amplifying, or qualifying earlier research, was replaced, in part, with the more fitting image of a widening puddle. Daniel Patrick Moynihan, then of Harvard, was speaking for other former liberals termed neoconservatives when he was asked what had gone wrong. He replied that the real disaster was the overextension of social science. It was time, he said, for the social scientists to acknowledge their lack of "knowledge with respect to many of the urgent issues. . . ." Moynihan called for the disestablishment of the predestinarian Church of Social Science, but he did so without challenging the value of technical evaluations of social experiments in particular and reason more generally. But others didn't stop there, and in a radical replay of the concept of the end of ideology, they mounted an assault on the Western tradition of rationality itself.

The spirit of '68, the spirit of unrestrained subjectivity, redefined not only science but rationality itself and majoritarian democracy as authoritarian restraints on individual desire. Theodore Roszak, whose 1969 book, *The Making of Counter Culture,* was an enormously influential assault on the "arrogance" of science, looked back a decade later with some satisfaction. Writing in the January 1981 *Harper's* Magazine, he argued, "If we can agree that Western society's most distinctive cultural project over the past three centuries has been to win the world over to an exclusively science-based reality principle, then we have good reason to believe . . . the campaign has stalled and may even be losing ground in the urban-industrial heartland."

The Enlightenment idea of progress, the growth of usable common knowledge, and the liberal politics built on it had by the mid-1970s lost what had once been its birthright of self-evident superiority to all other forms of perception. Where radicalism was once defined by its commitment to debunking "ruling class myths," the new dispensation embraced mythmaking as a path to personal and political transcendence. "There are," wrote George Steiner, summarizing the change, "three times as many registered astrologers in Europe and the United States as there are chemists and physicists. . . . Narcotics and horoscopes, little men with pointed ears and margarine-gurus, the pitiful bullying of encounter groups and the trek to Katmandu, the orgone box and the nauseous, million-dollar industry of Satanism in the movies, on television and in magazines – all breathe and feed the same hunger, the same solitude, the same bewilderments."

The triumph of "the reenchantment industry" went increasingly upscale in the 1970s, winning numerous adherents even in academia. Mysticism was holding its own, Roszak noted, even in the universities, where numerous Zen and Tibetan "spiritual masters" had found their most fertile recruiting ground. In the more high-flown renderings, the late writings of the enigmatic Austrian philosopher Ludwig Wittgenstein and the theories of the historian-philosopher of science Thomas Kuhn were invoked to explain why knowledge is inevitably subjective and group-bound.

In Wittgenstein's version of linguistic romanticism, it is community, "togetherness, not intellectual penetration of the nature of things that constitutes the life of the mind – truth neither individual nor universal is at the mercy of contingent, unpredictable communal custom." Intellectual consensus was said to be a matter of social compulsion. And a new consensus, it was argued, in a misappropriation of Kuhn's concept of paradigmatic leaps, became a matter of new groups seizing academic power. In effect, the new epistemology held out "hope" for a new revolutionary seizure of the means of producing meaning.

What does this all have to do with PC? The norm of objectivity had until the mid-70s served as a regulatory ideal for academic life. Difficult though it was to obtain, it served as a kind of guiding principle. But, concludes Ernest Gellner, "because all knowledge is dubious, being theory-saturated/ethnocentric/paradigm-dominated/interest-linked (please choose your own preferred variant. . .), the anguish-ridden author . . . can put forward whatever he pleases." In practical terms, the upshot on the campus was that a mixture of a bullying moralism and interest-group politics organized as competing claims to victimization came to dominate campus life. Reality was to be rewritten and reinforced by a new form of coerced consensus.

This all involved a fundamental misunderstanding of both Kuhn and the history of science. All judgement is theory-saturated. But if science dogma but in channeling it by pitting dogma against dogma."

This brings us up to the 1980s, when the contest of competing dogmas was largely turned inward. The victory of Reaganism and home and the decline of third-world revolution abroad made campus politics into a compensatory prize. "Today the streets may be quiet," read a 1981 article in the short-lived periodical *democracy,* "but journals, university presses, and lectures bristle with defiance. Especially in literary criticism . . . at great risk to the participants."

Self-dramatization aside, the article's author, Michael Fischer, unintentionally drew the connections between sixties radicalism and eighties irrationalism:

> The radicalism of the 60s prepared us for Derrida's association of freedom with mobility or endless possibility, as well as his attack on hierarchies and on arbitrary, invidious distinctions between right and wrong, sane and insane. His program of releasing interpretation from the constraints of logic, authorial intent, the text, and the dictates of authorities meshes with ideas we have all heard before: that students have a right to their own language; that expertise is a dangerous undemocratic charade; that standards are elitist; that correcting someone smacks of ridicule, arrogance, even tyranny; that claiming truth for one's values means imposing them. The political appeal of Derrida's work lies in its familiarity, not its novelty. He keeps alive themes that no longer animate political movements. . . . he offers . . . hope. . . . The power we have lost in Congress we can recapture in our prose.

Perhaps, though, the power of the prose he refers to seems to come from the assumption on the part of some undergraduates that its very indecipherability suggests hidden/forbidden knowledge. And there is nothing teenagers like better than to be let in on adult "secrets."

For all its rhetorical swagger and bureaucratic muscle on campus, PC is, in part, a counsel of despair. It says that objectivity and rationality have to be ceded to the right because it is no longer possible in classic leftist fashion to speak truth to power. The attempt to contain debate by arguing for a new "right not to be offended" is likewise an admission of failure. It's an admission that the left-liberal policies of the past quarter century, particularly on the racial quotas to which the universities are so deeply committed, can't stand up to critical scrutiny.

In the long run PC will fail not only the universities but the "victims" over whose interests it promises to stand guard as well. If the earlier "diversity" movement on behalf of the mentally ill is any guide, there is little reason to expect a promising future for the new "beneficiaries" of radical mythmaking.

Say what you will about R. D. Laing, before his death he acknowledged the biochemical basis of schizophrenia, effectively repudiating the writing that made him famous. The same can't be said of other '68-ers, many of whom cling to their outmoded glory days like ex-jocks hanging on to their high school championship jackets. The ideas of '68 have for them been replaced by newer variations but never repudiated. For those struck blind by "the singular evil of America," political correctness was and is to campus politics what water is to fish.

HELEN VENDLER

Anxiety of Innocence

Of all the handsome volumes of The Library of America, *American Poetry: The Nineteenth Century* is the most useful. There is simply nothing else like it in print. John Hollander, a poet and a professor of poetry at Yale, has collected "poetry" in the broadest sense, housing American Indian ritual chants, anonymous folk songs, and black spirituals under the same roof with Emerson, Dickinson, and Whitman. Between the nameless folk poets and the well-known authors lie the many lesser verse-writers, some of them remembered for only a single poem, such as "The Night Before Christmas" or "We Three Kings of Orient Are," "The Old Oaken Bucket" or "Home Sweet Home." (I give the familiar titles rather than the formal ones.) And this grand and fascinating collection prompts thoughts about the poetry of the New World, and about what has recently been called "canon-formation," or the recommending of some authors above others.

Hollander's eye as a prospector is expert, and it generates trust in the reader. He pans for flashes of gold and he finds them. The gold, in the minor poets, appears as theme rather than as manner; but even in the more faded poems the themes are interesting enough, and the conventions of verse well-enough observed, that the pieces are not formally painful to read. The informative notes on the writers fill out the impression left by any unknown poem that catches the reader's eye. I had never heard of Josiah Canning (1816-1892), but Hollander, who rightly picks out poems of continuing cultural interest from those of his poets who are relatively unoriginal, prints a poem of his called "The Indian Gone!" which tracks the guilt of a New England farmer finding Indian relics turned up by his plough:

> Beneath me in the furrow lay
> A relic of the chase, full low;
> I brushed the crumbling soil away -
> The Indian fashioned it, I know,
> But where is he?

When I turned to the notes, I found that Canning, who was an educated farmer in Gill, Massachusetts, adopted the pseudonym "The Peasant Bard"; and that one of his books was called *The Harp and Plow*

(1852) and another *Connecticut River Reeds* (1892). From such small facts, a whole world arises: a world of emulation of England and its eighteenth-century ploughman- and thresher-poets, but also a world that knows about Pan and Syrinx and the birth of verse. A few years later in Ireland, Yeats would call an early volume of his own poems *The Wind Among the Reeds,* claiming the same classical ancestry for Irish poetry as Canning claimed for American work.

The classical poets and the English poets haunt the new colonies; and in the Unites States, as in Ireland (and later in Canada and Australia), the question for the local poet is how, since the colonized are only "peasant bards" in European eyes, he is to make a literature. The reeds are not lacking and the breath is here. But what will be the words, and what the tune? The best poem on this perplexity postdates Hollander's volumes. It is "Pan with Us" by Robert Frost, and it shows that Canning's anxieties about American reed flutes were still very much alive in the early twentieth century. Frost's Pan (derived from Elizabeth Barrett Browning's) throws away his reed pipes, and wonders what instrument, and what tune, will suit the American poet:

> They were pipes of pagan mirth,
> And the world had found new terms of worth.
> He had laid him down on the sunburned earth
> And raveled a flower and looked away.
> Play? Play? - What should he play?

One could read Hollander's comprehensive anthology as our re-sponse, as Americans, to European tradition. And although the story of our uncertainty, our imitativeness, our abjectness and our bumptiousness is in outline well known, I found that Hollander's unfamiliar poets, such as Canning, put new glosses on the familiar narrative. Even "The Night Before Christmas" (that domestication of Santa Claus) and the "Three Kings of Orient" are important to the young country; Yeats saw the Magi in Ireland, and later Eliot re-domesticated them in American poetry. In songs such as "Home Sweet Home" and "Carry Me Back to Old Virginny," the nostalgia felt by early American settlers for "home," meaning England, is transformed into an indigenous longing for American scenes. Even scenes from the outer limits of American poetry - Poe's dismal tarns in a "dream land" haunted by ghouls - form part, now, of America's legendary landscape, populated by the poets with the shades of Hiawatha and Evangeline, Annabel Lee, and Little Orphan Annie.

Almost any random page of this collection will yield yet another set of tangled feelings about America and Europe: the "nature" of the one compared with the "art" of the other, the cultural inferiority felt by the colony combined with its asserted moral superiority to the corrupt "Old World" (an assertion sardonically countered by Ella Wheeler Wilcox, who in "No Classes!" jeers at the idea that America had abolished the class system). These nineteenth-century anxieties were not laid to rest until after the Second World War.

The tailoring of evidence in poems that set Europe against America is always, needless to say, of cultural interest. William Cullen Bryant, addressing the painter Thomas Cole as Cole departs for Europe, describes an America offering a set of wide and unpopulated vistas:

> Lone lakes - savannas where the bison roves -
> Rocks rich with summer garlands − solemn streams −
> Skies, where the desert eagle wheels and screams -
> Spring bloom and autumn blaze of boundless groves.

Not only are there no Indians visible in these nineteenth-century savannas, there are no Americans visible either. In Europe, by contrast, Cole will see "every where the trace of men,/ Paths, homes, graves, ruins . . . ." Cultural historians have repeatedly pointed out how necessary to the idea of "manifest destiny" was the obliteration from the consciousness of the long possession of America by indigenous tribes of (erroneously named) "Indians" (now erroneously renamed "Native Americans," as if they had not immigrated here too). It is from such documents as Bryant's poem, with its erasure of human habitation in the "boundless groves," that cultural historians draw their damning evidence of the silent literary obliteration of the Indians.

Turn a page in the anthology, however, and here is Bryant fully conscious, in "The Prairies," of the mound builders and "the roaming hunter tribes" who preceded the European arrival. And yet manifest destiny here, too, smooths out the scene, as races "arise . . . and perish" according to God's will:

> . . . . The red man too -
> Has left the blooming wilds he ranged so long,
> And, nearer to the Rocky Mountains, sought
> A wider hunting ground . . .

No explanation for the departure of the "red man" is offered, but an analogy is immediately given: "The beaver builds/ No longer by these streams but far away . . . ."

One is ashamed, today, of the analogy between Indian and beaver, not out of "political correctness" but out of the conviction that in

Bryant's day one would oneself have found this analogy unexceptional. Bryant accepts the given order of his world; when he thinks of the future, his imagination can go no further than to imagine "the sweet and solemn hymn/ Of Sabbath worshipers." It will take Wallace Stevens, in "Sunday Morning," to imagine, with imperfect conviction, an American religion that has dispensed with Christianity. To dispense with Christianity is to emancipate oneself at last from Europe.

In making his selection from the minor poets, Hollander has decided, as I have said, to print verse of topical or thematic interest to us today, so that we can perceive how our predecessors thought about the New World - its patriotism, religion, art, Indians, war, and landscape. Conflicting voices — whites often complacent, blacks righteously indignant, Indians elegiac — create here a fiercely dissonant chorus. On facing pages, for instance, we can find James Gates Perceval (1795-1856) and George Moses Horton (1798?-1880?). Perceval, a learned physician and geologist, is performing one of the duties of a poet in the new world, describing a phenomenon (a coral reef) unknown to England and to English poetry. Yet the only vocabulary available to him is the English pastoral lexicon of groves and boughs, of "corn on the upland lea":

> Deep in the wave is a coral grove,
> Where the purple mullet, and gold-fish rove . . .
> From coral rocks the sea-plants lift
> Their boughs, where the tides and billows flow . . .
> There with a light and easy motion,
> The fan-coral sweeps through the clear deep sea;
> And the yellow and scarlet tufts of ocean,
> Are bending like corn on the upland lea . . .

George Moses Horton, across the page, was known as "the Colored Bard of North Carolina." The question marks after the dates of his birth and death suggest the unimportance of blacks to nineteenth-century white record-keeping. Horton did not have the luxury of wondering at varieties of coral. His outburst "On Liberty and Slavery" is a cry to heaven:

> Alas! and am I born for this,
>   To wear this slavish chain?
> Deprived of all created bliss,
>   Through hardship, toil and pain!

The taste of today finds the slave's despair moving and the scientist's praise of coral pallid. But neither a sympathy for the slave nor an indifference to the coral-lover is a properly aesthetic response. Both poems are equally uninteresting as accomplishments of art. The physician writes conventional pastoral; his palate has none of the sharp "colors of rhetoric" that would fit the menacing brilliance of the tropics (for that, American poetry would have to await Hart Crane). And Horton's ritual invocation of "the grief/ And anguish of a slave" merely recycles well-worn words. It was in the prose of slave narratives that these clichés were surpassed, and that the reality of slavery found more adequate expressive language. Still, Perceval on the one hand and Horton on the other – and many other minor poets in this collection - contribute to the gradual work of cultural synthesis by which, very slowly, Europe became less threatening and America is given a verbal equivalent, its coral reefs and its slaves both part of its emerging literary identity.

Insofar as verse engages in providing representations of America in language, it performs that primary work not very differently from other verbal means: novels, essays, journalism, sermons, advertisements, drama, vaudeville, school texts and so on. Perceval's admiration of the flora and fauna of the New World is as old as the conquistadors, and is a frequent feature of American self-description in prose as well as in poetry; Horton's indignation is an inevitable feature of all slave literature, prose as well as verse. That these authors cast their sentiments into rhyme means that they honored "poetry" as a repository of cherished and intense moments. We learn from them what their culture thought suitable for verse, and what sort of writing might find publication: descriptions of nature's harmless beauties and expressions of religious hope.

But when we pass from Hollander's minor poets to his major figures, we learn what it is that makes a poet earn a place in the esteem of fellow writers and eventually in the esteem of fellow citizens – a place that poets like Perceval and Horton, however sincere their thoughts and feelings, will never attain. There has been so much tendentious writing about canon-formation that it is useful to see, in Hollander's generous-spirited anthology, just what his "canon" is, and why he does not allot, to Perceval or to Horton or to dozens of others, the fifty or more pages he gives to his "canonical" authors. These latter are – these names will surprise no one - Bryant, Emerson, Longfellow, Whittier, Whitman, Melville, and Dickinson. The poet Poe is rightly demoted below this group. (His true talents, which were in fiction and criticism, are amply represented elsewhere in the Library of America.)

The canonical writers, then, are all white and all male, except for Dickinson. And this, according to current cant, can lead to only one conclusion: that white males such as Hollander have "constructed" the canon after their own image, admitting Dickinson as a sort of token pet or mascot. Many recent critics, expressing this opinion, willfully refuse to see that most of the writers "excluded" from "the canon" are also white males; but this is only the most egregious suppression of fact by those convinced that canon-formation is wholly political and "hegemonic." White male writers are in fact "excluded" in greater numbers than any other group, since there are proportionally more of them in our publishing history. The first question of those interested in canon-formation ought to be: Which white males have made it into the canon, and which have not, and why? This would eliminate all the dishonesty and tedium about the "exclusion" of women and blacks, and would focus on the real question, which is not about politics, but about the degree of talent in verbal expression.

It is true that many verbally and rhythmically talented people were, in the nineteenth century as now, denied training in their talent because they lacked money, education, and opportunity. This is a properly political fact. It is as applicable to poor white males as to women and blacks, and it should be addressed - it has been addressed, if insufficiently - in political terms, by the establishment of public schools and public libraries, by scholarships for the poor, by giving women and blacks the vote, by desegregating schools and so on. But canon-formation is a process that takes place long after writing and publication. It deals only with the *faits accomplis*. Faced with all the poetry written in the United States during the nineteenth century, and published then (or, in the case of Dickinson, later), how is Hollander to allocate his pages?

Two principles of allocation come to mind: representativeness and talent. Hollander has honored both. With respect to representativeness, he leaves out nobody with any reputation at the time, so far as I can see; and he chooses poems with interestingly representative themes and forms. The usual genres (the elegy, the love poem, the patriotic poem, the war poem, the nature poem, the religious poem, the historical poem, the sonnet, the blank-verse meditation, the ballad, and so on) are all on lavish display. The wide representativeness of the anthology is one of its great claims on our attention. It was clever of Hollander to have found Mark Twain's "Ode to Stephen Dowling Bots, Dec'd," and Edith Wharton's "Mona Lisa." It was more than clever to have included almost seventy pages of much-loved anonymous folk songs and spirituals (besides the many familiar songs by named authors scattered through the volumes). And it was both responsible and creative to have unearthed and reproduced almost one hundred pages of nineteenth-century versions of American Indian poetry.

These Indian materials will provoke first a pain that so much should have been lost, and second a regret that so much of what was preserved should have been transcribed into saccharine English verse, such as this

"Medicine Song of an Indian Lover":

> Who, maiden, makes this river flow?
> The Spirit – he makes its ripples glow –
> But I have a charm that can make thee, dear,
> Steal o'er the wave to thy lover here.

The more suggestive renditions of Indian verse do without rhyme. The beautiful and elliptical transcriptions of Southern Paiute poems, songs and chants made by John Wesley Powell between 1868 and 1880 read like American haiku. Here is one:

> The crest of the mountain
>   Forever remains,
>   Forever remains,
> Though rocks continually fall.

And here, another:

> The edge of the sky
> Is the home of the river

There are grimmer moments. A Kwakiutl song of a cannibal spirit, recorded by Franz Boas, runs:

> I went all around the world to find food.
> I went all around the world to find human flesh.
> I went all around the world to find human heads.
> I went all around the world to find corpses.

Like the folk songs and spirituals, the Indian chants come to us from Hollander's pages lacking their music, their improvisational changes, and their social context. Still they belong here as a part of the historical poetic deposit of this terrain that we loosely call "American" (for want of an adjective derived from "the United States"). The Indian poetic legacy did not much affect our poetry in English in the nineteenth century, when Longfellow attempted to render its spirit in "Hiawatha," but it has increasingly been mined by contemporary poets, those of Indian descent and others.

Almost unwillingly, I withdrew my gaze from the great variety of the representative poetic scenery, much of it unfamiliar, set before me by Hollander, to turn to the writers of significant talent here recanonized. These poets would be less important, of course, in an anthology called

"Nineteenth-Century Poetry in English": Bryant and Whittier and Emerson would shrink in importance next to Wordsworth and Byron, not to mention Keats and Tennyson. The local relativity of importance in "canon-formation" is often forgotten by political critics; and even though Hollander, for the purpose of this American collection, elevates American poets, he would be the first to class some of them lower in another, broader kind of anthology.

Here, of course, they have pride of place. And since more than one hundred of Hollander's one hundred and forty-one poets are white males, the real question about canon-formation is why, out of one hundred white males, only six are allotted fifty or more pages. After one had answered that question in a reasonable way, one might, as I have said, be allowed to proceed to questions about women and blacks. The loose expression by which certain people are said to have been "excluded" from "the canon" has been used, confusingly, to cover several social facts. The first is that of exclusion, in life, from privileges such as education or access to publication. A decent level of education is necessary for distinguished literary production, and the rise in the number of well-written works by women and blacks is directly proportional to the accessibility of higher education for those groups. In this sense, the possibility of authorship is indeed linked to class privilege.

But "the canon" is not made from possibilities; it is made from publications. And for this reason, class privilege in itself gets you nowhere as an author. Not all the class privilege in the world can get you into the canon. The Percevals of the world, in spite of their Yale degrees and their social positions and their publications, are "excluded" from the canon even by their fellow white males from Yale like Hollander. And no tears are shed on their behalf. Their minor talents have decreed for them a minor place.

Canonical status may come more swiftly, of course, for those of the talented who are well-placed by birth, sex or education to have their talents recognized; but it comes more lastingly to the talented who must master and renew their medium. In life, Longfellow had it easier than Whitman, Whittier than Dickinson; but in the long run Whitman's two hundred and twenty pages here and Dickinson's ninety pages proclaim them the poets by whom others are measured.

What, one can ask, is Hollander seeing in them when he gives them the lion's share of his pages? "Transgression," it would be tempting to answer fashionably. Whitman's unrhymed lines and Dickinson's erratic syntax proclaim some wish for formal deviation; and the notable blasphemies of each are arresting enough, and frequent enough, to make us certain of their often transgressive thematic intent. It is even true that, after the bland "beauty" and the pious clichés of the minor poets, we welcome the "hankering, gross, mystical, nude" Whitman, or Dickinson's scornful repudiation of the "Dimity Convictions" of her fellow Amherst "Gentlewomen." But the defiance of convention in both Whitman and Dickinson is a sign of something much larger than mere contempt for bourgeois tractability.

It is the sign of a soul extending itself as far as it can, and occasionally (but only tangentially) confronting – with indignation, irritation or asperity - a set of social limits that it encounters in its path. The social limits are not the point; it is the awe-inspiring extension of consciousness in both poets that defines them. That a reclusive New England small-town virgin should work herself up into becoming the authorial presence we call "Emily Dickinson" is only slightly less terrifying than the inborn talent that drove her to such fierce attainment.

Dickinson's own account of the poet's work, of her own work, is not at all a transgressive one:

> This was a Poet – It is That
> Distills amazing sense
> From ordinary Meanings
> And Attar so immense
>
> From the familiar species
> That perished by the Door –
> We wonder it was not Ourselves
> Arrested it – before –

The ordinary "selves" who appear in this poem do not find the poet "transgressive" or "blasphemous"; they find, rather, that the poet "makes sense" ("amazing sense," to be sure), a sense that is so immediately convincing that it seems they ought to have been able to grasp it by themselves. It is this uncovering of what is, this arresting of the moment when, as Stevens said, "the bright obvious stands forth in cold," that distinguishes genius from talent.

Genius is transgressive more by accident - as it strives valiantly toward its intuitions of reality, stumbling along the way over the hurdles of convention - than by intent. The plainest effort of realism – say, Dickinson's Fly, buzzing in the death chamber – almost unconsciously overturns, in that poem, the conventional invoking of the King descending to claim the Christian soul:

> The Eyes around - had wrung them dry –
> And Breaths were gathering firm
> For that last Onset - when the King
> Be witnessed – in the Room –

> I willed my Keepsakes – Signed away
> What portion of me be
> Assignable - and then it was
> There interposed a Fly –
>
> With Blue - uncertain stumbling Buzz –
> Between the light - and me –
> And then the Windows failed – and then
> I could not see to see –

Dickinson's narrative soberly foregoes the atheist's crow of triumph, and it is respectful toward the Eyes and the Breaths gathering in vigil for the King. It is almost as though, if the Fly had not "interposed" itself, the Vision might have arrived. But if you are, as Dickinson was, a skeptic, then you are bound to report that it was the Fly, and not the King, that you saw with your failing sight. Transgression, even blasphemy, is incurred as a by-product of accuracy, not as an end in itself.

What makes the great poets "great" is that they are always of two minds. Unlike the ordinary and practical skeptic, Dickinson is fully aware of the compulsions of belief:

> This World is not Conclusion.
> A Species stands beyond -
> Invisible, as Music –
> But positive, as Sound -
> It beckons, and it baffles –
> Philosophy - don't know—
> And through a Riddle, at the last -
> Sagacity, must go –

At times, reading the great poets as they discover the "bright obvious," one thinks that greatness is simply a matter of refusing prejudices, abhorring singlemindedness and exerting an acute and many-sided intelligence. Though Dickinson knows the truth of all that she has said about faith in the first stanza of "This World is not Conclusion," she ends the poem with one of her most corrosive epigrams:

> Narcotics cannot still the Tooth
> That nibbles at the Soul -

Yet revealing the obvious alone, being of two minds alone, will not suffice for great poetry. As soon as one wants to define poetic genius by Dickinson's sharp and allegorical moral insight, she reminds us of the indispensability to all poetry of that music which is the sensual support of imaginative intelligence:

> Nor would I be a Poet –
> It's finer – own the Ear –
> Enamored – impotent - content -
> The license to revere,
> A privilege so awful
> What would the Dower be,
> Had I the Art to stun myself
> With Bolts of Melody!

We notice that Dickinson is not afraid, in her conclusion here, to imagine herself as Jove, unleasher of thunderbolts. Genius is not modest in its musical ambitions.

It would be a mistake to read Dickinson's metaphor of Jovian bolts ideologically, as a "transgressive" gender-image. Dickinson, as she said of herself, speaks as a "representative" person: as a soul, rather than as a self, one might say. Her poems are often not gendered. Her "passive" position in this poem as listener (to poetry) and beholder (of painting) is a position occupied by males, too, when they are confronted by a work of aesthetic power. Recall Keats before the Elgin marbles, apologizing to them, "My spirit is too weak," or Stevens before Botticelli's *Birth of Venus,* defensive about his own "paltry nude."

Often, what Dickinson says of herself is by no means "transgressive." It is what any Christian in Amherst could have said, had she the strength of her Christian convictions. Dickinson's self-descriptions could be affirmed by any Christian soul who had come to inhabit those cosmic vistas in which Dickinson faced the chaos of the physical and moral world. Here is Dickinson as a Crescent soul - the New Moon poised in heaven, reflected in the sea:

> Behind Me – dips Eternity -
> Before me – Immortality –
> Myself – the Term between . . .
>
> 'Tis Miracle before Me – then –
> 'Tis Miracle behind – between -
> A Crescent in the Sea -
> With Midnight to the North of Her –
> And Midnight to the South of Her -
> And Maelstrom – in the Sky -

Class privilege (which Dickinson had) and education (which she received) can only confirm, it cannot confer, this sort of blazing way with language.

How does the canon-maker decide that a poet is less than extraordinary? Dickinson's friend Helen Hunt Jackson appears in this anthology as a good example of what an educated writer of limited talent can turn out. Her best-known poem, "September," gives a list of autumn characteristics beginning

> The golden-rod is yellow;
>   The corn is turning brown;
> The trees in apple orchards
>   With fruit are bending down.

It then concludes, somewhat coyly,

> But none of all this beauty
>   Which floods the earth and air
> Is unto me the secret
>   Which makes September fair.
>
> 'Tis a thing which I remember;
>   To name it thrills me yet:
> One day of one September
>   I never can forget.

The passion and the imagination visible in Dickinson are entirely lacking here; the verse is pleasant, and no more.

Canon-formation relies on a set of informed comparative judgments, not on a conspiracy of "exclusions," as political criticism would have us believe. Since there is no single criterion for inclusion in the canon, inexperienced readers, who are often content with unmediated passion (like that found in Horton's outburst against slavery) see no visible reason why one passion is not as good as another. The criteria for canonizing Longfellow and Whitman, for instance, might seem troublingly antithetical: Longfellow, the college professor writing smoothly about Chaucer and Dante, appears to embrace an aesthetic that contradicts the one we associate with "Walt Whitman, one of the roughs." Yet both writers fulfill several of the indispensable criteria for the considerable poet: an ambitious set of experiments in various lyric genres; an acquaintance with the tradition of poetry known to the culture; a critical interest in conflict and contradiction; an attachment to musicality for its own sake; human sympathy; responsiveness to sense-experience; and originality in personal gesture and style.

We all know the populist Longfellow of "Hiawatha" and "Paul Revere's Ride," but in Hollander's wonderful and wide-ranging selection we meet the Longfellow who foretells America's ruin through slavery:

> There is a poor, blind Samson in this land,
>   Shorn of his strength, and bound in bands of steel,
> Who may, in some grim revel, raise his hand,
>   And shake the pillars of this Commonweal,
> Till the vast Temple of our liberties
> A shapeless mass of wreck and rubbish lies.

This Miltonic echo must have sent a shiver of apprehension through Longfellow's contemporaries. There is also the Longfellow from whom Frost learned so much, the exquisite poet of "Snow-Flakes" and "Aftermath," those desolate poems that remark the drearier beauties of New England:

> When the summer fields are mown,
> When the birds are fledged and flown,
>   And the dry leaves strew the path;
> With the falling of the snow,
> With the cawing of the crow,
> Once again the fields we mow
>   And gather in the aftermath.
>
> Not the sweet, new grass with flowers
> Is this harvesting of ours;
>   Not the upland clover bloom;
> But the rowen mixed with weeds,
> Tangled tufts from marsh and meads,
> Where the poppy drops its seeds
>   In the silence and the gloom.

Longfellow's poem of a second, thinner harvest conveys, in its lingering music, all the temptations of nostalgia for youth; but it also takes a stoical and raw pleasure in the sadder poetry of crow, weeds, and tangled tufts. This piece, too, like Keats's autumn ode from which it derives, springs from an "obvious"" seasonal observation, neither "transgressive" nor "revolutionary."

So Whittier, too – almost as lyric as Longfellow, equally moved by historical incident, similarly conscious of poetic precedent – knows that American reality requires a keen search for authentic non-English surfaces.

He admits,

> I love the old melodious lays
> Which softly melt the ages through,
> The songs of Spenser's golden days,
> Arcadian Sidney's silvery phrase,
> Sprinkling our noon of time with freshest
> morning dew . . .

yet he realizes that American verse requires something different, more effortful:

> The rigor of a frozen clime;
> The harshness of an untaught ear,
> The jarring words of one whose
> rhyme
> Beat often Labor's hurried time . . .

It was Whitman whose "untaught ear" and rhyme beating to Labor's time fulfilled Whittier's prophecy. Whitman's unexampled and cinematic eye animated his words, words he had learned by touch as he set them letter by letter in his printing press. When Whitman appears to us in his poems, he is almost always looking, appetitively and voyeuristically, at the world:

> Looking in at the shop-windows in Broad-
> way the whole forenoon . . . pressing the
> flesh of my nose to the thick plate-glass,
> Wandering the same afternoon with my
> face turned up to the clouds; . . .
> Far from the settlements studying the print
> of animals' feet, or the moccasin-
> print . . .
> By the coffined corpse when all is still,
> examining with a candle . . .

"I fly the flight of the fluid and swallowing soul," Whitman tells us, making us notice, by contrast, how few among the minor poets have fluid souls, how few among them swallow as well as taste.

Reading any major poet is an experience in how description may be renewed. "I have a soul," any contemporary of Whitman might think. But only Whitman, hunting through the columns of his internal the-saurus, will come up with "fluid" as the first adjective for his soul, and

"swallowing" as the second – the first transferred from descriptions of
the physical universe ("fluid" versus "solid"), the second deriving from
the actions of the body. Of all the receptive actions of the body,
"swallowing" is chosen because the poet is speaking of flight. He delights
in the pun on the bird-meaning of "swallow." "I fly by the flight of the
aerial, lighter-than-solid, swallow-like soul," goes the undersong to the
printed line.

Unimaginative writers – the Helen Hunt Jacksons and the James
Gate Percevals and the George Moses Hortons – do not write this way;
and that, not their gender or their color or their social inferiority, is
why they are not in the canon. It is a slander against writers and critics
to suggest that they can admire only people of their own gender or
class. Poets (like the young male Robert Browning writing in
admiration to the older unseen female Elizabeth Barrett) admire other
writers who are bold and intelligent and experimental and musical and
original. Just as Hopkins admired Whitman, though he thought him "a
very great scoundrel," or as Bridges admired Hopkins, writers often
revere authors with whom they profoundly disagree on moral questions.
Over time, writers and critics have historically "excluded" from the
canon those who publish feeble, conventional, unmusical, and
unimaginative verse, no matter how intelligent or morally worthy or
passionate its sentiments.

Comparison of the selection in Hollander's anthology with the
nineteenth-century selections of another excellent (but much shorter)
collection, Richard Ellmann's *Oxford Book of American Verse,* which
appeared in 1976, shows Hollander's comparative upgrading (among his
six chief poets) of Bryant, and more importantly, of Melville. It is
Melville who most comes into his own in Hollander's book (he gets
eighty-six pages, close to Dickinson's ninety). Through the labors of
three generations of poets, scholars and critics, Melville's significance as a
poet of epic and lyric power has gradually been established.

Melville, like Whitman, feared ruin for America, given the paradoxical and unstable compound of constitutional liberty and legal slavery:

> I muse upon my country's ills –
> The tempest bursting from the waste
> of Time
> On the world's fairest hope linked with
> man's foulest crime.

And he is vivid about the Civil War:

> With shouts the torrent down the
>   gorges go,
> And storms are formed behind the
>   storm we feel:
> The hemlock shakes in the rafter, the oak
>   in the driving keel.

The shouts, the torrents, the storms, the shaking hemlock, the driving keel: these are all emblems of Melville's own tumultuous nature as it infiltrates his every thought. His wide and unacademic embrace of life as a young sailor remained eager and ardent until time broke it with literary failure, an unsuccessful marriage, unrewarding work, and a son's suicide. But a grim strength of mind and will in Melville held on against breakdown, and his poetry is full of wild despair checked, of abysses gaping but withstood, of an affirmation of life's forces (even if they are such as "tawny tigers feel in matted shades") against "death's silent negative." I envy those readers discovering "The Berg" and "To Ned" and "The Maldive Shark" and "After the Pleasure Party" for the first time.

Melville's short poem "Art" will do as well as anything in these powerful volumes to define what makes a piece of verse something we are willing to call by the canonical and honorific name of "poetry." Melville struggles to describe what must happen for form to be bestowed on thought, for "pulsed life" to be created:

> . . . form to lend, pulsed life create,
> What unlike things must meet and mate:
> A flame to melt – a wind to freeze;
> Humility – yet pride and scorn;
> Instinct and study; love and hate;
> Audacity – reverence. These must mate,
> And fuse with Jacob's mystic heart,
> To wrestle with the angel – Art.

Minor poetry wrestles with nothing inside itself; it blandly or contentiously asserts. Whether it is verse of the left or verse of the right, it is all audacity or all reverence. It may flame with indignation, but it does not remember to freeze its flame into patient and coldly considered form. It may scorn a mote of baseness, yet it lacks humility about the beam in its own eye. It forgets to study its predecessors in its rush to give its own instincts their unmediated expression. For Melville, passion's "mystic heart" must always, in the artist, wrestle with the austere severity of aesthetic demand – itself "angelic" in that it seems, by comparison to easy passion, almost inhuman.

Critics who would idly promote any politically correct or sociologically representative text to canonical status have contempt for the taxing work entailed in the writing of a genuinely powerful poem. They scant the painful and exhilarating work of dispassionate observation, the intricate work of melodic construction, the amused work of lexical invention, and, most of all, the stoical and informed work of disciplining feeling into original form. To those indifferent to art, Melville's contending energies, Dickinson's metaphysical leaps, Whitman's deeply felt adjectives, will have no special appeal.

"Taste," political critics tell us, is "historically constructed," a matter of class and its ideology. To be sure, there are powerful constraints of period and class and gender on the reach of taste (as every literary historian has always recognized); but society has never been able to "set" taste, as the entire failure to indoctrinate writers in Socialist Realism bears witness. It is the sheer dreariness of single-minded and uninventive writing – no matter how worthy its subject matter or how passionate its beliefs – that ensures the continual process of canon-formation, which, after all, only says (as Hollander implicitly does by his allocation of space) that some writers are more rewarding than others.

The Western literary canon from Homer until now – by which I mean, to use Hugh Kenner's definition, writers long admired by other writers – is enormously large and capacious and inclusive and multi-generic. It is not to be confused with the tiny pedagogical canon, which we may define as various lists of books that an average class of under-prepared American college students can be asked to read in one semester. No university teacher thinks that one need read only "the canon" in the sense in which it it is puerilely defined in the popular press. We have all had to go beyond "the canon" to understand any literary work that we have written about, and we all have enjoyed reading reams of highly un-canonical work (in my own case, Matthew Arnold's reports as a school inspector, or the entire run of Harriet Monroe's *Poetry,* or minor metaphysical verse, or contemporary poetry as yet unsifted by time).

Pedagogically speaking, what can be learned from reading any sample of writers from the Western canon is the unique power of the word-as-form, the word when it is deployed to aesthetic, as well as philosophical or moral or descriptive, effect. Lesser writers, though they may be philo-sophically or morally or descriptively representative, do not exemplify or teach the power, discipline, and enacted insight of aesthetic form. We ought to be clear about the desirable educational value of a student's being exposed to representativeness, and the very different and more desirable educational value of a student's encounter with supreme artistic achievement. Democratic education is bound to value representativeness, but that is no reason not to value aesthetic singularity, strength, and beauty as well. An anthology such as John Hollander's is satisfying because it values both sorts of verbal work, and sensible because it distinguishes between them. Hollander has allotted space on the basis of genuine aesthetic brilliance. He honors many things in making his choices, but most of all he honors depth of feeling, struggle with internal contradiction, seductive musicality, and intelligence of heart.

ALAN WOLFE

The New Class Comes Home

The emergence of political correctness in the late 1980s reveals a university bearing little resemblance to an earlier image of academic life. Far from cloistered, this university is politically engaged. Its humanities professors are more preoccupied with Madonna than Milton. Rather than academic freedom and skepticism, the emerging university pursues certainty (in the name of radical doubt), while contemplating restrictions on free speech. Its scholars, anything but absent-minded, are vigorously professional and career-minded. What was once a milieu of gentlemanly conservatism has become the home of assertive women and minorities. For an institution that, because of tenure and tradition, is supposed to change slowly when it changes at all, the academy in the course of twenty years turned upside down.

One change in particular has been noticed by many of the commentators on political correctness, but its significance has not been fully appreciated. I refer to the role played in these transformations by academic leaders: presidents, provosts, and deans. If the political correctness movement of the late 1980s is the outcome of the politics of the late 1960s, then one of the more puzzling of its aspects is how those who once tried to lock college presidents out of their offices came to depend on presidents to support their demands. Just as today's activists campaign to let homosexuals into the same military from which yesterday's radicals were trying to escape, academic leftists cannot obtain their objectives without the support of the college leadership they once denounced.

Some of the more notorious of the stories recounted in the political correctness debates have involved academic administrators more than English professors. At Hampshire College, an institution widely known for the radical political commitments of its faculty, professors acted quite responsibly in recommending two humanists for reappointment. But the president of the college, determined to appease a vociferous group of multicultural radicals, went out of his way to find a committee that would dismiss them. Proposals to diversify faculties or, as at Clark University, to include more materials in classes dealing with multicultural themes, come from above, not from below. Administrators led the fight for speech codes at institutions like the University of Wisconsin, a fight that did not interfere with the climb of one of them to the position of Secretary of Health and Human Services in the Clinton Administration. Administrators at the University of Pennsylvania seemed determined to monitor the speech and conduct of white students, while excusing the questionable tactics of minority students. At most private four-year liberal arts colleges, the office of the dean of students has become a partisan of feminist and minority complaints. By now, most of the dissenters from the political correctness trend know that they will have little sympathy if they appeal to those who lead their institutions.

It would be natural to conclude that the role played by academic administrators in these controversies is a product of a long march through the institutions, planned well in advance by 1960s radicals. But this is too simple an explanation for too interesting a phenomenon. It was once not uncommon to find an occasional intellectual as a college president, someone with deeply held ideas about how the world in general, and the university within it, should be organized. Nowadays college presidents tend to be professionals who hop from one position to another. They are not leftist ideologues determined to transform their universities through five-year plans into bastions of radical thought and action, for they tend to have no particular visions at all, not even radical ones. If anything, today's college presidents are far more managerial than the same breed was a couple of decades ago.

In theory, pragmatic managers should try to find compromise positions between competing factions in the hope of keeping peace. But while universities are contentious places, a significant number of college presidents go out of their way *not* to find a balance between the race-class-gender faction and the traditionalists. The reason for this, I believe, lies in the theory, not the fact. The nature of what it means to lead a university has undergone a significant transformation since the days when college presidents were simultaneously more authoritarian and more interesting. And that change, in turn, is related to new ways in which all of America's major organizations, including corporations and government, think of managerial style and substance.

Academic social scientists from both the right and left began to notice the emergence of a new leadership style more than twenty years ago. The term that came to symbolize this transformation was "the new class." There were as many variations of new class theories as there were proponents of the concept, but most of them agreed that leadership roles were passing to a younger generation whose power lay more in command over communication than it did in command over substance. There was once a time when large corporations were dominated by production people, such as engineers, who were intimate with the products made by the company. They were slowly replaced by specialists in organization itself, people who were trained to achieve objectives, no matter what the particular objective may have been.

The success of the new class was to some degree related to the success of the new left, for both were the product of the same chronology. As Peter Berger and his colleagues have shown, new–class leadership styles came to embody the look and language of the therapeutic side of new left politics. Managers were facilitators, helping all the members of their organization reach their full potential. They sponsored weekend retreats in which notions of participation and sharing were exchanged. Authoritarian styles of leadership were replaced by committee decision-making that required consensus whenever possible. Inclusion became the objective of the organization, as minorities and women were made to feel at home. The new class of managers were trained at business schools whose faculties were far more attracted to leftist ideas than, say, academic departments of ecomonics. They were comfortable talking to their counterparts in other organizations, such as governments, foundations, churches, and unions, for there, as well, a new class of facilitators had emerged. The old class may have managed things; the new class managed people.

In the 1980s, the new class came home to the universities that first formulated the concept. Just as General Motors was once led by men who, in their personalities, seemed to reek of General Motors, university presidents had at one time been closely identified with the universities over which they presided. They were chosen in secret by small groups of trustees who generally restricted themselves to alumni or faculty from the institution in question. Once chosen, they remained in office for long periods of time, usually around two decades. They were not paragons of intellectual virtuosity; according to Thorstein Veblen they were little different from the captains of industry with whom they liked to hobnob. But although they usually had given up on scholarship, they also tried at least to be familiar with the academic work that characterized their institution. From time to time, one of them might even write a book or contribute an interesting article to a symposium on the future of the academy.

Almost overnight, the process changed. New college presidencies were filled through search committees that included faculty and, from time to time, students. Women and minorities were given far greater consideration; they were even, on occasion, chosen for prestigious positions. Fundraising became the primary job of the president. There were so many committees and so much activity that there was no time left for reading, let alone writing. No wonder the average length of time served by a sitting college president decreased. The job demanded unlimited energy, unusually thick skin, and, most importantly of all, the ability not to offend any constituency while presiding over an institution whose product, ideas, usually offend someone.

While all this was taking place, the university itself underwent those changes that David Riesman and Christopher Jencks labeled "the academic revolution." The sheer number of faculty and students increased dramatically in the 1960s and 1970s. New branches of new universities opened as fast as anyone could count. As the old professoriate retired, or as brand-new academic positions were created, jobs went to children of the 1960s, including an unprecedented number of women and minorities. This new generation was suspicious of power. Academic self-governance became its watchword. The university was a place in which others would take responsibility for fund-raising while they would take responsibility for choosing their colleagues, shaping their curriculum, and hiring their administrators. The changes were so dramatic that they extended also to boards of trustees (or state legislative committees), which themselves became more diverse and open to the currents of the time.

The coming of the "new class" to the university preceded the controversies over political correctness, but the latter cannot be understood without appreciating the significance of the former. When demands for multiculturalism, speech codes, and diversity hit the campus, a structure was already in place to receive them. In some cases, a new breed of college leadership, uncomfortable with academic traditionalism, was prepared to jump out ahead of any demands for inclusion that might appear, anticipating them, even encouraging them. It sometimes seemed as if those who led educational institutions and those who claimed they were excluded from them formed a natural alliance with each other. And well they might, for there were at least three things that held them together.

First, demands for inclusion, despite occasional militant rhetoric, were conservative demands; they accepted the university as it had become. In the particular environment of the 1990s, it is actually the traditionalists who have the radical platform. To satisfy them, college administrators would have to revise every single aspect of contemporary educational experience: ending grade inflation, restoring a common curriculum, requiring the study of foreign languages, imposing standards, eliminating frivolous majors, expelling the unqualified, pruning courses, rewarding merit. Any one of these reforms could absorb the full-time energy of a college president for years; think of what would be required just to eliminate grade inflation in higher education. From the perspective of a new class administrator, the traditionalist agenda is utopian, and, even where possible, expensive. And if that were not enough to damn them, the advocates of traditionalism, like utopians everywhere, appear to the new class administrators as unlikeable people: obsessive, impractical, old-fashioned. They constitute a hindrance to the new president's plans, irrespective of whatever those plans happen to be.

By contrast, administrators may find some of those arguing for inclusion shrill in demeanor or exotic in language, but they recognize that their demands leave in place those features of the modern university with which they are familiar. Generally speaking, the reformers want three things: programs, power, and money. None of these are all that difficult to give, especially when compared to what the traditionalists want.

No college president makes a reputation by strengthening and improving old programs; the new class craves new initiatives. Presented with a demand for a new major or institute, the president's mind wanders to the Rolodex. There is always a foundation executive, potential donor, or new recruit who would be interested to hear of plans for a new program, especially one so resonant with the contemporary Zeitgeist. It may even be possible to find hard money for the program; after all, the classics department is losing majors, its faculty are overtenured, and there are a couple of retirements coming up. The president may have no particular intellectual sympathy with the proposed program, but the faculty member urging its creation is getting nibbles from other institutions; it would be a blemish on the president's record to lose a person who contributes to the university's diversity. There is everything to be gained, and very little to be lost, by accepting a demand – no matter how militantly made – for a more inclusive cuurriculum.

Of course adding new programs means adding new members to the governance structure of the university. In the old days, this would have been a stumbling block, for presidents, believing themselves to be the embodiment of their institution's tradition, were jealous of their power. Power in the contemporary university, by contrast, is diffuse; already divided into innumerable committees, the addition of one more level in the structure – say, a committee to pass on whether any particular course satisifies a concern with multicultural issues – would hardly be noticed.

Administrators expect to sit on committees; that is the nature of their profession these days. But so, surprisingly, do a significant number of faculty. The traditionalist faculty tend to shun committee work as a waste of time, but many of those pushing for radical changes in the university actually like to fill their days with meetings. (Of course they never admit this, telling everyone in sight that they would rather be in the laboratory or the library.) Beneath the bombast, the president discovers, there is a bureaucrat trying to escape. Political militancy is a form of institutional conservatism; to see their new programs through to completion, the reformers must preserve the structure that will house them.

Finally, demands for inclusion are usually accompanied by demands for money: higher salaries for the faculty, financial aid for targeted students, and administrative underwriting of new programs and institutes. At a time of financial retrenchment, college presidents can hardly be expected to look favorably upon expensive new initiatives. Such initiatives, however, may not be that expensive after all. Faculty in the humanities and social sciences, particularly those attracted to academia as a political cause, tend to make very little money in the first place; it is far cheaper to support a Marxist economics department than a neoclassical one. Moreover, even though there are academic superstars making reportedly large sums of money, they are cheap compared to scientists; whatever the costs of building the Duke University English Department, the recognition came cheaply compared to what it costs to build a physics department. The money needed to be spent to respond to demands for inclusion is, from the new-class point of view, money well spent.

Besides the relative conservatism of the race-class-gender agenda, there is a second reason why university administrators tend to be receptive to it. The clash between multiculturalists and their opponents is not necessarily a clash over ideas. It is also a battle between those who claim that the university should be about ideas versus those who believe that the university should be about suffering and redemption. As Henry Louis Gates, Jr. has pointed out, some of the more exotic forms of Afrocentrism resemble twelve-step recovery programs. They do not so much search for new ideas about race and ethnicity as they affirm the pain of racism and the exhilaration involved in recognizing that pain. The demands of those who want the university to acknowledge the contributions of once-excluded groups take on the character of psychodramas; it is not what you say but how you "really feel" that matters. The period when political correctness achieved its high point was a period of emotion, not one of reason.

If this psychological propensity is true of issues of curriculum, it is far more the case when universities deal with policies involving racial and sexual harassment. Here again one notes an odd reversal; 1960s radicals sought to abolish *in loco parentis;* 1990s radicals, often the same people, seek to reimpose it. This is not necessarily an inconsistency, however. Those who wanted colleges and universities to stop regulating sex were basing their positions on a tradition of thought; students are autonomous individuals conducting their own lives, the reasoning ran, and if they were treated paternalistically, how could we expect them to learn to think for themselves? By contrast, the arguments in favor of sexual regulation are psychological more than they are intellectual. Although there is a good deal of talk about power – we need to regulate sexual harassment because women have so little power – what is really at issue is a question of recognition and identity. The passage of a sexual harassment policy is a sign that the institution is willing to listen to the demands of its female members. At the University of Virginia, all sides agree that a proposed policy banning sex between students and teachers would have been ineffective, but many supported it nonetheless because its passage would have constituted a step toward female self-assertion.

Cries for recognition would have been impossible for academic administrators of the old school to heed; both corporate autocrats and veterans of the Stalinist wars are equally ill at ease with terms like "empowerment." But the college presidents picked under the new rules find demands for redemption more comfortable than demands to take ideas seriously. The management style they understand best is one that speaks in psychological jargon. The position of university president is no longer, in Max Weber's sense of the term, a calling demanding the sacrifice of self-interest for some higher purpose. It does not require character and rectitude, but the ability to get along with diverse groups and find compromise formulae that make everyone feel wanted. When they call for sensitivity workshops, new class college presidents are applying the principles of Management 101. They are trying to create an environment responsive to personal growth and institutional cooperation. Their job is not to make distinctions between good ideas and bad ones, let alone right ideas and wrong ones. To pass judgement is to condemn, while leadership is about acceptance. Those pressing for a more intellectual curriculum tend to be abrasive types who hurt the feelings of others. If they, in their zeal for argument, sometimes step on the toes of others, the least the president can do is make everyone feel welcome.

A third factor also enters into the elective affinity between new class university administrators and the demands for more inclusion. Both stand in opposition to those who entered academic life during a brief moment: the period after universities curtailed the practices which retained the privileges of white Anglo-Saxons but before they opened themselves up to those whose position in the university would be justified by the sufferings imposed on them by the larger society.

The cultural war in the universities is a generational war. The "traditionalists" are usually men and usually in their fifties. They seem disproportionately ethnic, as if still marked by the streets of Brooklyn. Hard-nosed realism and cynicism color their outlook on the world, despite their success and academic acheivement. They tend to share an "old left" disposition; they long ago gave up their radical politics, but they retain a preference for strong organization, discipline, and the standards they believe they have mastered. Otherwise suspicious of idealism, they do believe passionately in merit, a principle, they feel, only recently acheived, but now increasingly threatened. Convinced that they may be the one and only generational cohort to benefit from a relatively open system, they approach university debates in a tone verging from hysteria to resignation. They find the class of professional grievance managers – those who speak for the excluded – loathsome, for, from their point of view, they are standing in the way of all those aspiring minority children who ought to be able to test themselves out in the marketplace of ideas without hand-holding.

New-class college presidents find such people difficult to work with, not only because of their intellectual intensity, but also because they are so focused on meritocratic principles. If college presidents were chosen for the depth and reputation of their scholarship, they might not mind an emphasis on merit, but the criteria that go into their selection are far murkier than this. Indeed fundraising often involves having the right connections and traveling in the right circles, criteria that emphasize conditions of birth rather than achievement. Nearly all college presidents these days govern a faculty far more accomplished than themselves with respect to the business of the university, not a situation conducive to an emphasis on the rewards of merit.

But merit is also suspect among those who advocate the incorporation of a race-class-gender perspective. From their perspective, advancement within the university involves the representation of groups, not as the accomplishment of individuals. Merit, like so many other concepts brought under the scrutiny of a postmodern consciousness, is understood to be an artificial construct imposed by those who have power upon those who lack it. A liberal college president of impeccable WASP background and a black militant advocating Afrocentrism have this much in common: both, having gotten to where they are in some part due to circumstances of their birth, think that merit is not necessarily the most important criterion in making academic judgements. They are more likely to understand each other than either can understand the insistence of the traditionalists on standards and the importance of objectivity.

For all these reasons – the institutional conservatism of political radicals, the triumph of therapy over intellectuality, and the impact of different historical experiences on different academic cohorts – university administrators, trained to find compromises and to soothe hurt feelings, tend instead to become partisans in the academic wars over which they preside. As newsworthy as some of the stories involving political correctness may have been, the real story was not the incidents themselves, but the transformation of the university, that made them possible. American institutions of higher learning had been preparing themselves for something like the political correctness phenomenon for decades. Many of those forms of preparation have not been discussed here, such as the rise of scientism in the humanities and social sciences or the lingering effects of notions, such as that of "repressive tolerance," which represented the less attractive side of the 1960s. But one in particular does stand out: the missionary zeal of university administrators to make the world a better place. What we now know as political correctness will last as long as the universities find so many things to do other than discover new knowledge and pass it on to new generations.

C. VANN WOODWARD

Political Fallacies in the Academy

The received opinion is that if democracy is so good for everybody and everything else, surely it is good for universities as well. Before we leap to unqualified endorsement of that idea of mutual welfare and compatibility, and embrace all the numerous (and sometimes contradictory) notions of democracy as good for the academy, I think we had best pause for reflection, think twice, and draw a few distinctions and qualifications. This might spare us the embarrassments of having to teach things we do not believe – like East Europeans have had to do until recently. A democracy can be as much of a menace to the academy as a tyranny.

In speaking of the history of academic freedoms and rights, I cannot avoid the use of such expressions as *privileges, immunities, indulgences,* and *exemptions*. These terms have more of an aristocratic than a democratic ring about them. They do not go down well with ardent democrats, and their linkage with freedoms for universities is not easy to explain and justify in a democratic age. Good democrats stress equality and denounce privilege. They say equal rights for all and no immunities or exemptions for anybody, however learned. They sincerely question the right of anybody to publish or teach truths that are offensive to any citizens, and reject authority based on superior knowledge.

Given the very nature and purpose of the academy, however, all members cannot be equal in all things. If all members were equal in learning, for example, there would be no point in scholars teaching or students attending. If all were equal in authority, then grades, honors, and degrees would be meaningless. So it is that distinctions like grades are drawn, rank prevails, and authority is acknowledged. Some students are better than others, some more advanced than their fellows, some are *summa cum laude,* and some flunk. It is the business of the faculty to make such distinctions or, to use a more unpopular term, "discriminations." The faculty itself is divided in ranks from junior to senior, characterized by a degree of hierarchical order that in age of democracy has taken on a quaint, old-fashioned sound.

For a few years in the late 1960s and early 1970s many universities, with radical students leading the way and some faculty joining in, experimented with running universities without resort to these quaint institutions of rank, authority, and distinction. All distinctions were abhorred, including those of merit and learning, faculty and students. Equally abhorrent were all claims of authority, whether those of tradition, teachers, classics, arts, or sciences – not to mention the authority of administrators and presidents. If his secretary replied by phone that the president was tied up at the moment, one did not know whether to call back or call the police. Classes met to "rap," not to learn. Those members held forth who felt so inspired, whether teacher, student, or visiting revolutionary. Intellectual discourse was conducted in the language of the street, "jive talk," so-called, and everyone received an *A* who would not settle for a *B*. Equality, for the time being, reigned supreme, or appeared to.

But it did not last long and it did not work as a way to run a university. And so, with many compromises and concessions, and still bearing the scars of the sixties, we returned as quickly and completely as we dared to the old standards and ways. After such an experience, we can only wonder how universities will make out with democracies in the long run. Since they somehow managed to survive under popes, princes, emperors, and dictators, universities surely have reason to hope that they can reach some understanding with democracies that will not demean their standards and trivialize their curriculums. We can *hope,* but we cannot be sure. Evidence continues to mount that it will not be easy.

Only recently the U. S. Supreme Court in a unanimous decision deprived universities of the ancient privilege of privacy of peer review in appointment and promotion of faculty. One consequence is that instead of qualified scholars, government agents will have the final say on who is the best molecular biologist or quantum physicist among those considered for a university chair if an appointment is contested. I wonder how that decision will read in the universities of Prague, Budapest, and Warsaw now emerging from government domination in all their affairs. In writing the decision, the learned justice who spoke for the court adopted a tone bordering at times on sarcasm and levity when dismissing university claims to the privileges of privacy in peer review. At one point he went so far as to compare these claims with those for tax exemptions.

Does this imply that tax exemption is another right that may be placed in jeopardy? To touch the right of tax exemption is to threaten the very lifeline of private universities. If such privileges and immunities as peer review and tax exemption are withdrawn or threatened, what then of the other privileges, for example the right to determine our own curriculum, police our own campus, teach our own classes unsupervised or spied upon, and set criteria for admission of students and award of degrees?

A moment's reflection will recall instances in which all of these privileges and exemptions have already been challenged, either in court or in practice. These challenges and threats of government intervention have been justified in the name of justice and righteous causes, as they have been in pre-democratic times. One trouble about the righteous causes and purposes offered to justify democratic intervention in university government and affairs is that we in the academy so often share belief in the good causes ourselves. Typical of them is the desire to prevent discrimination against minorities in appointments to faculties or in admission to student bodies. Scarcely any academician would now approve discrimination because of race, sex, or religion, and most of them would welcome and legitimate means of preventing such discrimination. That is one thing that makes it so difficult to defend the walls of the academy against democratic assault: the defenders within are so often disarmed by sympathy with the slogans and professed purposes of the assaulters without.

What is urgently needed is that we in the universities make clear what kind of discrimination and distinctions we are for and what kind we are against. Those we insist on making are distinctions between the true and the false, between things we hold high and those we hold low, between the immortal and the ephemeral, between excellence and what falls short of it. There is no need to permit confusion between the kind of discrimination we deem vital to our calling and the kind of discrimination we deplore as undemocratic and immoral. We must discriminate without being discriminatory. We must use authority without being authoritarian. Those are distinctions not easy to explain, but we must insist upon them.

I took heart in reading that university officials all across the country spoke out in opposition to the Supreme Court decision denying universities privacy of correspondence in peer review. An official of the American Council of Education, representing some fifteen hundred colleges and universities, joined in to deplore the decision. I wish more had done so. I strongly hope that universities will continue a vigilant opposition against the current assault upon academic freedoms, rights, privileges, and immunities. Universities have much to lose and had best defend what they still have. If they take care to explain what they are doing and why, they may be able to restore peace between the universities and the democracies and end by defending both with good conscience.

If they are wise, however, defenders of the university and its values and missions must strive to understand the wild confusions that rage among their opponents. In their zeal to promote equality, minority rights, and amicable race relations – values which we often share with them – they are quite willing to seize and use the university, its curriculum, its faculty and administration to promote their ends. And a strong element among them is quite prepared to attack or abandon academic freedom, freedom of speech, and freedom of the press in their protests and crusades for good causes. And furthermore anyone who seeks to defend these freedoms may expect to be denounced as a conservative or a reactionary. And those who so characterize the defenders are likely to claim the designation "radicals."

It is obviously something of a paradox to find freedom of speech, freedom of expression, freedom of the press, and academic freedom – classic liberal values, all of them – used to identify as conservatives or re-actionaries any who undertake to defend those values. The paradox is sharpened into irony by the reflection that threats to those freedoms in American history are popularly assumed and believed to have come most often from the right. And the ironies are multiplied by presumably liberal critics denying academic freedom by acting to control and police aca-demic appointments, admissions, curriculum, teaching, and thought in order to promote their political programs. And yet these same critics ac-cuse their opponents of politicizing the academy. Thus they attempt to turn the tables on the defenders of freedom by bringing the same charges against them that are leveled against the assault on freedom.

One explanation for this confusion (though not the only one) is that both sides sometimes share sympathy for the cause, the ideal or the minority about which the conflict over the principle arises. The issue is not about the need for justice and civil rights, but over the means of attaining these ends. Few would deny the existence of injustices and deprivations in American society, or the need for correcting such evils. But we *are* divided over where and how they are to be corrected. Is the university the right place to conduct these political struggles, and are teaching and reading and classes and curriculum and admissions and appointments the right means to use?

Attempts to use such means in American universities of late have pro-duced conditions that should be cause for concern among all responsible academics, whatever their political persuasion. For one thing, efforts to overcome neglect, disadvantage, and injustice to radical, ethnic, and cultural minorities have sometimes promoted fragmentation, separation, and re-segregation of these groups in their dormitory, dining, social, and recreation facilities. Instead of holding with Chief Justice Earl Warren's opinion of 1954 that segregation "generates a feeling of inferiority," the ethnic separatists, multiculturalists, and their mentors now hold that *integration* generates such a feeling and that segregation is the cure instead of the cause.

The drive toward separatism has also penetrated teaching, as well as what subjects are taught, and by whom. Separate classes, even separate departments, have appeared with teachers and administrators of matching race, sex, culture, or creed. By such means students are supplied with so-called "role models" befitting their groups. They are instructed in group pride, group heroes, group identity. Naturally they come to think, act, and study as groups rather than as individuals.

When we object that the individual pursuit of truth and excellence in any field of learning and that the capacity for appreciating the greatest achievements of intelligence and genius are the very purposes of higher education, that group indoctrination and propaganda have no place in universities, these objections are brushed aside. Extremists are ready with the contemptuous response that there really is no truth to peruse, no standard to meet, and no achievement of excellence that commands universal respect. Indeed, all canons and curriculums, they contend, are instruments of cultural propaganda and all pedagogy is, consciously or not, engaged in the indoctrination of students for political ends.

I do not for a moment concede that the alignment of opinion on such doctrines, the line between their supporters and their opponents, can rationally be accepted as a line that divides liberals from conservatives or radicals from reactionaries or makes any sensible definition of either. I, for one, am certainly not willing to permit a long career of liberal convictions and support of causes often to the left of center to be defined in any such manner. And I very much doubt that there are many who are more aligned to the political center or to the right of it than I who would willing accept such a definition. Rather, I believe, there exists among majorities on both sides agreement that the essential division over the issues here addressed lies between responsible and intelligent members of the academy on the one hand and intruders and their converts within its walls who are too often swayed by enthusiasms and fashions of the moment. Surely that leaves ample ground of rationality on which both left and right can gain footing to resist inroads of irrationality.

Given that opportunity, that margin of common ground, they should try to advance together from a defensive to a more positive and assertive position. They should be able at least to agree on things that the university is *not*. I would hope and believe that these things would include agreement, first that the university is not a political institution and must not be misused as such. Secondly it is not philanthropic in its mission, nor is it paternalistic or therapeutic in its responsibilities to its students. Furthermore, it is not a club seeking to promote good fellowship and amicability. As important as those functions are and as needful as the values they strive to achieve, they are *not* primarily the responsibilities of the university but of other institutions in society.

In words I have used elsewhere, and which are now endorsed as official policy at my own institution, the university is a place where the unthinkable can be taught, the unmentionable can be discussed, and the unchallengeable can be challenged. Such a place must encourage and protect to the fullest the rights of dissent and complete freedom to express views that some will find offensive, even painful. The university may and should urge civility in such discourse, but given the range of freedom of expression granted under the First Amendment, it cannot guarantee civility, much less enforcement of good fellowship and amicability.

It may be that I have exaggerated the extent of common ground between liberals and conservatives, or between left and right in academic and non-political matters. I hope not. But I am bound to admit that fundamentalists and extremists on the left as well as on the right are never likely to find common grounds of rationality or common sense. Both must realistically be assumed to be poised to seize the posture of obstructionists. And depend on it, they will always be with us, squared away for combat.

The hopeful thing about them is that they normally constitute a minority on the left as on the right, usually a small, if noisy minority. As long as they remain so they are a serious problem only for defenders of speech who are rightly determined that they shall have their say, no matter what. But there are times, some of them within quite recent memory, when fundamentalist and fanatical minorities, left or right or both, appear to loom larger in influence if not in numbers. Extremists on the one side grow in response to the growth of extremists on the other. They feed upon each other.

In the university populations with which I am best acquainted the majority, faculty as well as students, presently lean to the center or to the left of it. I do not believe the threat comes from "tenured radicals," but rather from tenured and untenured conformists. Any organization suspected or accused, even falsely, of rightward inclinations is in trouble. I would urge that we resist influences of extremists and stake out common ground of academic freedom on which we unite in fighting for the integrity of the academy, for the future of the university, and for what a university should be.

ABOUT THE CONTRIBUTORS

ROBERT ALTER is Class of 1937 Professor of Comparative Literature at the University of California, Berkeley. His most recent books are *Necessary Angels* (Harvard University Press) and *The World of Biblical Literature.*

BRIGITTE BERGER is Professor of Sociology at Boston University and the author of *The War over the Family: Capturing the Middle Ground* (Anchor Press/Doubleday), among other books.

ROBERT BRUSTEIN is Artistic Director of the American Repertory Theatre and Professor of English at Harvard University. His newest book is *Dumbocracy in America: Studies in the Theatre of Guilt,* published by Ivan R. Dee.

ANDREW DELBANCO is Professor of English at Columbia University. *The Death of Satan: How Americans Lost Their Sense of Evil,* his most recent book, is available from Farrar, Straus and Giroux.

MORRIS DICKSTEIN is Director of the Center for the Humanities at the City University of New York Graduate School. His books include *Double Agent: The Critic and Society* (Oxford University Press).

EUGENE GOODHEART is Professor of English at Brandeis University and the author of, among other books, *The Skeptic Disposition* (Princeton University Press) and *Desire and Its Discontents.* (Columbia University Press).

SUSAN HAACK is Professor of Philosophy at the University of Miami. Her books include *Deviant Logic* and *Philosophy of Logics* (both available from Cambridge University Press) and *Evidence and Inquiry: Towards Reconstruction in Epistemology* (Blackwell Publishers).

ROGER KIMBALL is Managing Editor of *The New Criterion* and author of *Tenured Radicals: How Politics Has Corrupted Our Higher Education* (HarperCollins).

HILTON KRAMER is the art critic for *The New York Observer* and Editor of *The New Criterion*. His books include *Abstract Art: A Cultural History,* available from the Free Press.

CHARLES KRAUTHAMMER is a syndicated columnist for *The New Republic.*

LEONARD KRIEGEL's newest book is a collection of essays, *Falling into Life,* published by North Point Press.

EDITH KURZWEIL is University Professor of Social Thought and Director of the Center for the Humanities at Adelphi University, and Editor of *Partisan Review.* Among her books are *The Age of Structuralism* (Columbia University Press), *Italian Entrepreneurs* (Praeger) *The Freudians* (Yale University Press), and the just-published *Freudians and Feminists* (Westview Press).

MARY LEFKOWITZ is Andrew W. Mellon Professor in the Humanities at Wellesley College. She is the author of *Women in Greek Myth* and *Women's Lives in Greece and Rome* (with Maureen B. Fant), both published by Johns Hopkins University Press, and *Mythistory: The Deconstruction of Greece* (Basic Books).

DAVID LEHMAN is the author of *Signs of the Times: Deconstruction and the Fall of Paul de Man* (Poseidon Press) and *The Line Forms Here* (University of Michigan Press), and Series Editor of the annual anthology, *Best American Poetry* (Scribners/Touchstone). His new book of poems is entitled, *Valentine Place.*

DORIS LESSING is the author of many novels and books. HarperCollins has just brought out her memoir, *Under My Skin. Volume One of My Autobiography, to 1949.*

MARK LILLA teaches political theory and French theory at New York University. He is the author of *G. B. Vico: The Making of an Anti-Modern* (Harvard University Press) and is the editor of *New French Thought. Political Philosophy*, published by Princeton University Press.

GLENN C. LOURY is Professor of Economics at Boston University. His new book, *One by One from the Inside Out: Race and Responsibility,* is available from The Free Press.

HEATHER MAC DONALD is a Contributing Editor of The Manhattan Institute's *City Journal*.

STEVEN MARCUS is Vice President for Arts and Sciences and Dean of the College at Columbia University. His books include *The Other Victorians* (Basic Books).

JERRY L. MARTIN has served as Assistant Chairman for Programs and Policy at the National Endowment for the Humanities. He teaches in the Department of Politics at Catholic University of America.

DAPHNE MERKIN is the author of the novel *Enchantment* (Harcourt Brace Jovanovich) and is at work on a new novel. She is a critic for *The New Yorker*, and her essays are included in the anthologies *Out of the Garden. Women Writers on the Bible* (Ballantine)and *Testimony. Contemporary Writers Making the Holocaust Personal* (Times Books).

MARK MIRSKY is Editor of *Fiction* magazine and author of three books of fiction, *Blue Hill Avenue* and *Proceedings of the Rabble* (both from Bobbs-Merrill), and *The Secret Table* (Fiction Collective).

WILLIAM PHILLIPS is Editor-in-Chief of *Partisan Review* and Professor of English at Boston University. His books include the anthologies *Writers and Politics* and *Literature and Psychoanalysis* (coedited with Edith Kurzweil) and *A Partisan View. Five Decades of the Literary Life*.

RONALD RADOSH is Senior Olin Professor of History at Adelphi Universiy and coauthor (with Joyce Milton) of *The Rosenberg File* (Holt, Rinehart and Winston)

DIANE RAVITCH is a former Assistant Secretary of the U. S. Department of Education, she is also the author of *The Troubled Crusade: American Education, 1948-1980* (Basic Books). Her new book, *National Standards in Education*, is available from The Brookings Institution Press.

JOHN R. SEARLE is the Mills Professor of Philosophy of Mind and Language at the University of California, Berkeley; his most recent book is *The Rediscovery of the Mind* (MIT Press).

DAVID SIDORSKY is Professor of Philosophy at Columbia University. He served for a number of years as Chairman of the University Seminar on General Education.

ARTHUR SCHLESINGER, JR., historian and writer, has held the Albert Schweitzer Chair in the Humanities at the Graduate School and University Center of the City University of New York. His most recent book, *The Disuniting of America,* is available from W. W. Norton.

FRED SIEGEL is Professor of History at The Cooper Union for the Advancement of Science and Art.

HELEN VENDLER is A. Kingsley Porter University Professor at Harvard University and Poetry Critic for *The New Yorker.* Her essays have been collected in two volumes, *Part of Nature, Part of Us,* and *The Music of What Happens,* with a third volume – *Soul Says* – forthcoming in 1995 from Harvard University Press, which will also publish *The Given and the Made,* her T. S. Eliot Memorial Lectures, and *The Breaking of Style,* her Richard Ellmann Memorial Lectures.

ALAN WOLFE is University Professor and Professor of Sociology and Political Science at Boston University. His books include the recently published *The Human Difference: Animals, Computers, and the Necessity of Social Science* (University of California Press).

C. VANN WOODWARD is Sterling Professor of History Emeritus at Yale University. Author of ten books of history, he is the editor of numerous others, including *The Oxford History of the United States* in eleven volumes, now in progress.

Acknowledgments

Grateful acknowledgment is made to all of the contributors to this volume for permission to include their essays.

"Knowledge and Propaganda: Reflections of an Old Feminist" by Susan Haack is a modifield version of a paper delivered at the American Philosophical Association in December 1992 and published in *Reason Papers,* 18, Fall 1993, as part of a symposium on the present state of feminism. The reader is referred to that publication for full footnotes and references.

"Defining Deviancy Up" by Charles Krauthammer first appeared in *The New Republic,* November 22, 1993.

"Self-censorship" by Glenn C. Loury is excerpted from a longer and more complete analysis, "Self-censorship and Public Discourse: A Theory of Political Correctness and Related Phenomena."

"The Postmodern Argument Considered" by Jerry L. Martin is adapted from an essay in *The Imperiled Academy,* edited by Howard Dickman (Transaction Publishers, 1993). Citations for all quotations may be found in the original essay.

"Multiculturalism v. The Bill of Rights" by Arthur Schlesinger, Jr. was first presented as the Frank M. Coffin Lecture given at the University of Maine Law School in October 1993.

"Anxiety of Innocence" by Helen Vendler first appeared in *The New Republic,* November 22, 1993

This book was composed by Partisan Review at Boston University, Boston, Massachusetts. It was printed and bound by Town Printing Inc., North Andover, Massachusetts.